What Makes Life Meaningful?

Can human life be meaningful? What does talk about life's meaning even *mean*? What is God's role, if any, in a meaningful life? These three questions frame this one-of-a-kind debate between two philosophers who have spent most of their professional lives thinking and writing about the topic of life's meaning.

In this wide-ranging scholarly conversation, Professors Thaddeus Metz and Joshua W. Seachris develop and defend their own unique answers to these questions, while responding to each other's objections in a lively dialog format. Seachris argues that the concept of life's meaning largely revolves around three interconnected ideas—mattering, purpose, and sense-making; that a meaningful human life involves sufficiently manifesting all three; and that God would importantly enhance the meaningfulness of life on each of these three fronts. Metz instead holds that talk of life's meaning is about a variety of properties such as meriting pride, transcending one's animal self, making a contribution, and authoring a life-story. For him, many lives are meaningful insofar as they exercise intelligence in positive, robust, and developmental ways. Finally, Metz argues that God is unnecessary for an objective meaning that suits human nature.

Metz and Seachris develop and defend their own unique answers to these three questions, while responding to each other's objections in a dialog format that is accessible to students though—given their new contributions—will be of great interest to scholars as well.

Key Features

Offers an up-to-date scholarly conversation on life's meaning by two researchers at the forefront of research on the topic.

Provides a wide-ranging, yet orderly discussion of the most important issues.

Accessible for the student investigating the topic for the first time yet also valuable to the scholar working on life's meaning.

Includes helpful pedagogical features, like:

- Chapter outlines and introductions;
- Annotated reading lists for both students and research-level readers;
- A glossary; and
- Clear examples, thought experiments, narratives, and cultural references, which enhance the book's role in thinking about life's meaning and related topics.

Thaddeus Metz is Professor of Philosophy at the University of Pretoria in South Africa, and is often credited for having helped develop life's meaning as a distinct field in Anglo-American philosophy over the past 20 years. Metz has published more than 300 professional works, including the books *Meaning in Life: An Analytic Study* (2013) and *God, Soul and the Meaning of Life* (2019).

Joshua W. Seachris is Assistant Teaching Professor of Philosophy at the University of Notre Dame, and managing editor of the *Journal of Analytic Theology*. From 2012–2023, he was Program Director for the Center for Philosophy of Religion at Notre Dame. In addition to his published journal articles, he is the editor of *Exploring the Meaning of Life: An Anthology and Guide* (2012); co-editor (with Stewart Goetz) of *God and Meaning: New Essays* (2016); and co-author (with Stewart Goetz) of *What Is This Thing Called the Meaning of Life?* (2020).

Little Debates About Big Questions
Tyron Goldschmidt
Fellow of the Rutgers Center for Philosophy of Religion, USA
Dustin Crummett
University of Washington, Tacoma, USA

About the series:

Philosophy asks questions about the fundamental nature of reality, our place in the world, and what we should do. Some of these questions are perennial: for example, *Do we have free will? What is morality?* Some are much newer: for example, *How far should free speech on campus extend? Are race, sex and gender social constructs?* But all of these are among the big questions in philosophy and they remain controversial.

Each book in the *Little Debates About Big Questions* series features two professors on opposite sides of a big question. Each author presents their own side, and the authors then exchange objections and replies. Short, lively, and accessible, these debates showcase diverse and deep answers. Pedagogical features include standard form arguments, section summaries, bolded key terms and principles, glossaries, and annotated reading lists.

The debate format is an ideal way to learn about controversial topics. Whereas the usual essay or book risks overlooking objections against its own proposition or misrepresenting the opposite side, in a debate each side can make their case at equal length, and then present objections the other side must consider. Debates have a more conversational and fun style too, and we selected particularly talented philosophers—in substance and style—for these kinds of encounters.

Debates can be combative—sometimes even descending into anger and animosity. But debates can also be cooperative. While our authors disagree strongly, they work together to help each other and the reader get clearer on the ideas, arguments, and objections. This is intellectual progress, and a much-needed model for civil and constructive disagreement.

The substance and style of the debates will captivate interested readers new to the questions. But there's enough to interest experts too. The debates will be especially useful for courses in philosophy and related subjects—whether as primary or secondary readings—and a few debates can be combined to make up the reading for an entire course.

We thank the authors for their help in constructing this series. We are honored to showcase their work. They are all preeminent scholars or rising-stars in their fields, and through these debates they share what's been discovered with a wider audience. This is a paradigm for public philosophy, and will impress upon students, scholars, and other interested readers the enduring importance of debating the big questions.

Published Titles:

Do We Have Free Will?
A Debate
By Robert Kane and Carolina Sartorio

Is There a God?
A Debate
by Kenneth L. Pearce and Graham Oppy

Is Political Authority an Illusion?
A Debate
By Michael Huemer and Daniel Layman

Selected Forthcoming Titles:

Should We Want to Live Forever?
A Debate
by Stephen Cave and John Martin Fischer

Consequentialism or Virtue Ethics?
A Debate
By Jorge L.A. Garcia and Alastair Norcross

For more information about this series, please visit: https://www.routledge.com/Little-Debates-about-Big-Questions/book-series/LDABQ

What Makes Life Meaningful?

A Debate

Thaddeus Metz and
Joshua W. Seachris

Routledge
Taylor & Francis Group
NEW YORK AND LONDON

Designed cover image: © Roydee / Getty Images

First published 2024
by Routledge
605 Third Avenue, New York, NY 10158

and by Routledge
4 Park Square, Milton Park, Abingdon, Oxon, OX14 4RN

Routledge is an imprint of the Taylor & Francis Group, an informa business

© 2024 Taylor & Francis

The right of Thaddeus Metz and Joshua W. Seachris to be identified as authors of this work has been asserted in accordance with sections 77 and 78 of the Copyright, Designs and Patents Act 1988.

All rights reserved. No part of this book may be reprinted or reproduced or utilised in any form or by any electronic, mechanical, or other means, now known or hereafter invented, including photocopying and recording, or in any information storage or retrieval system, without permission in writing from the publishers.

Trademark notice: Product or corporate names may be trademarks or registered trademarks, and are used only for identification and explanation without intent to infringe.

ISBN: 978-1-032-56606-1 (hbk)
ISBN: 978-1-032-56615-3 (pbk)
ISBN: 978-1-003-43638-6 (ebk)

DOI: 10.4324/9781003436386

Typeset in Sabon
by KnowledgeWorks Global Ltd.

To my mother, Ellen,
and the memory of my father, Michael
Thaddeus Metz

To my parents,
Lonnie and Loma
Joshua W. Seachris

Contents

Acknowledgments xii
Foreword xiii
BY JOHN MARTIN FISCHER

Opening Statements 1

1 Triadic Meaning and the Benefits of God 3
   JOSHUA W. SEACHRIS

   1.1 Introduction: The Human Need for Meaning 3
   1.2 What Is Meaning? The Meaning Triad 8
   1.3 Meanings Small and Big; Narrow and Wide 29
   1.4 Parts in Wholes: Meaning's Tilt Toward the Cosmic 32
   1.5 The "Loss" of Meaning: Meaning's Tilt Toward Transcendence 35
   1.6 Absurdity: Meaning's Tilt Toward Existential Coherence 37
   1.7 Death: Meaning's Tilt Toward the End 42
   1.8 Why Theism Is Better News: Meaning's Tilt Toward God 53
   1.9 Summary 68

2 Making Life Meaningful Without God or a Soul 70
   THADDEUS METZ

   2.1 Introducing an Earthly Approach to Meaning 70
   2.2 What We Are Talking About 75

2.3 What Is Central to Life's Meaning 87
2.4 Moderate Supernaturalism 120
2.5 Rebutting Nihilism; Or, Yes, Your Life Has Meaning in It 130

First Round of Replies 137

3 "Some" Meaning Without God or a Soul: Reply to Metz 139
JOSHUA W. SEACHRIS

3.1 Introduction 140
3.2 Points of Agreement 141
3.3 God and Objective Value 143
3.4 Meaning Pluralism 2.0: Reconsidering Extreme and Moderate Supernaturalism 155
3.5 Meaning Pluralism 2.1: Passively Conditioned Meaning vs. Actively Conditioned Meaning 160
3.6 Making Meaning too Difficult? 162

4 Considering the Benefits of God: Reply to Seachris 167
THADDEUS METZ

4.1 Introduction 167
4.2 What Does "Life's Meaning" Mean? 168
4.3 What Would Make Life Meaningful? 170
4.4 Is Life Meaningful? 180

Second Round of Replies 183

5 God Is Still Better News for Meaning: Response to Metz's Reply 185
JOSHUA W. SEACHRIS

5.1 Introduction 185
5.2 The Meaning Triad and the Meaning of Life's Meaning 186
5.3 God Is Still Better News for Meaning 188

    5.4 On the Supposed Immodesty of Moderate Supernaturalism: The Inescapability of the Cosmic Frame 199
    5.5 Existential Desires: Deep and Universal vs. Shallow and Parochial 203
    5.6 Is Life Meaningful? 206

6 **Types of Meaning and the Natural as Their Source: Response to Seachris' Reply** 210
THADDEUS METZ

    6.1 Introduction 210
    6.2 Whose Lives Have Meaning and How Much? 211
    6.3 The Sources of Objective Value 214
    6.4 Which Source Would Be Better? 219
    6.5 Which Source Exists? 221
    6.6 Concluding Remarks 223

Further Readings	225
Glossary	232
References	239
Index	247

Acknowledgments

Thad composed most of his contribution to this book during periods of turmoil, including the Covid-19 pandemic; large-scale rioting and looting in South Africa; transitions to a new workplace and residence; and ill health on the part of loved ones. It was some welcome respite to spend time in front of a fireplace thinking about life's meaning—and moreover in conversation with a colleague who has also spent more than 15 years reflecting carefully on the topic.

Josh extends his deep appreciation to the following individuals who read and commented on various parts of his contributions to this debate: Brian Ballard, Stewart Goetz, Jonathan Gregory, Grace Hibshman, Samuel Newlands, Gary Osmundsen, and Corey Seachris. The quality of my work in this book is enhanced because of your thoughtful input. And thank you, Thad, for your professional encouragement to me over the years.

We both take this opportunity to thank the editors of the Routledge Little Debates about Big Questions book series, Tyron Goldschmidt and Dustin Crummett, for their support of this project, as well as an anonymous reviewer for valuable suggestions. Each of our contributions is informed and influenced by other voices, extending to our family, friends, colleagues, students, and many more—both near and far, past and present. Finally, we thank our home universities, the University of Notre Dame and the University of Pretoria, for positions that allow us to research and write.

Foreword

Sometimes—more often perhaps than I'd like—when I meet someone new and tell them I'm a philosophy professor, they laugh and let me know that it was their very favorite (or least favorite) course in college. Then they might chuckle again and ask, "So, what is the meaning of life?" There follows an awkward pause, after which I do my best to avoid the question or say how hard it is and leave it at that. The question indicates a stereotype of philosophy, and pokes fun at what is taken to be our self-importance (or maybe presumptuousness) in divulging our thoughts on these matters. Who are we to pontificate on this profound question; and isn't it, in any case, futile? Perhaps the apparent profundity masks a deep obscurity, or even silliness.

Some of these themes are present in this passage from the American philosopher Robert Nozick:

> A person travels for many days to the Himalayas to seek the word of an Indian holy man meditating in an isolated cave. Tired from his journey, but eager and expectant that his quest is about to reach fulfillment, he asks the sage, "What is the meaning of life?" After a long pause, the sage opens his eyes and says, "Life is a fountain." "What do you mean, life is a fountain?" barks the questioner. "I have just traveled thousands of miles to hear your words, and all you have to tell me is that? That's ridiculous." The sage then looks up from the floor of the cave and says, "You mean, it's not a fountain?" In a variant of the story, he replies, "So it's not a fountain."
> (Nozick 1981).

Maybe there is no "meaning of life"; and, in any case, it seems pointless to seek it from a guru or "sage." Even so, human beings are "meaning-seeking creatures": we strive to understand the point of our lives—life's meaning, so to speak. This passage from Leo Tolstoy's *My Confession*, captures this arguably universal human drive:

> In my writings I advocated, what to me was the only truth, that it was necessary to live in such a way as to derive the greatest comfort for oneself and one's family.
>
> Thus I proceeded to live, but five years ago something very strange began to happen with me: I was overcome by minutes at first of perplexity and then of an arrest of life, as though I did not know how to live or what to do, and I lost myself and was dejected. But time passed and I continued to live as before. Then those minutes of perplexity were repeated oftener and oftener ... These arrests of life found their expression in ever the same questions: "Why? Well, and then?"
>
> (Tolstoy 1884/2005).

The desire to make sense of our lives—to find its meaning—is indeed important to almost all of us, even if it is not universal. Joshua Seachris and Thaddeus Metz come to grips with the set of issues surrounding life's meaning in this fascinating debate. It is striking that they do not simply appeal to "authority," especially a guru or even the teachings of a church or other institution. Rather, they explore the issues via the distinctive resources of philosophical analysis—calm, respectful employment of reason and argumentation—not taking anything as settled and beyond doubt. As in the "tagline" of the radio program *Philosophy Talk*, in philosophy we question *everything*, except your intelligence.

It is interesting to see how far we can get in wrestling with these issues about meaning, despite the skepticism of the jokes and stories referred to above. Seachris and Metz make noteworthy progress in clarifying the questions (half the battle, it seems) and answering them. The answers are not meant to be "final" or irresistible. They are invitations to the reader to think further, given the analytic framework and ideas on offer in this book: no trace of self-importance or presumption here!

Contemporary philosophers typically distinguish "the meaning of life" from "life's meaning" or "meaningfulness in life." Many are skeptical that there is a "meaning of life," where this implies a meaning of human life in general—the same meaning for all of us. They do not thereby doubt the coherence of the idea that various factors add to the meaningfulness of a human life (and others detract from it). Meaningfulness in life is a "scalar" notion: it admits of degrees—some lives are more meaningful than others. That a life is meaningful at all is not scalar, but all-or-nothing.

What is this notion of "meaning" or "meaningfulness"? It is a bit of a challenge to get a firm grasp on it. (I once taught a seminar with a colleague on the meaning of life. We spent most of the quarter trying to figure out the meaning of "the meaning of life," barely getting to the proposals for activities that make a life meaningful. Well, that's (analytic) philosophy for you ...!) First observe that the meaningfulness of an activity gives a person a *pro tanto* reason for engaging in it (i.e., a reason with some, but not necessarily decisive, weight). Meaningfulness—like morality and happiness—is a "normative" notion, in that it generates *pro tanto* reasons for action. Most philosophers think of meaningfulness as separate in the sense that one can live a moral and/or happy life without its being meaningful, and a meaningful but not moral or happy life. There is, however, disagreement about the precise relationships between the three categories. Some hold that an immoral (or even monstrously evil) life could nevertheless be meaningful in certain respects (Metz); others come close to denying this, building some sort of "positive normativity" into their account of meaningfulness (Seachris).

The three sorts of reasons—morality, meaningfulness, and happiness—can conflict; and there is disagreement about how such conflicts are to be resolved. Some follow Kant (and other ethical theorists) in contending that moral reasons are the hegemonic ones, outweighing the others. Other philosophers do not accept this Kantian thesis and hold that there is no algorithmic way of deciding in a case of conflict; in this sort of case, one has to exercise discretion in coming to an "all-things-considered" judgment about what to do.

So far, we know what meaningfulness is *not*—it is not identical to morality or happiness, even if there might be some overlap. It is fair to add that it is a necessary condition of an individual's having a meaningful life (and thus a meaningfulness "score") that she be conscious and free. I would add that she must not be significantly and intractably wrong about the nature of reality—deluded, as in psychosis; but this is at least somewhat contentious.

Susan Wolf has written that meaningfulness is located at the intersection of subjective and objective value. That is, the individual must have at least some affective engagement with or even passion for the activity; and it must be objectively valuable (in some suitable sense of "objective") (Wolf). On this view, an individual who doesn't care at all about activities which are objectively valuable does not live a meaningful life; nor does a person who is passionate about something of no objective value. Others have challenged Wolf's claim, imagining, for instance, a scientist who does important work in analyzing and solving scientific challenges, but has no passion for what she is doing; perhaps she finds the work tedious and doesn't really care about it, but she does it nevertheless. On Wolf's view, this would not be a meaningful life; but I would guess that many disagree.

Although we are close to hitting our target of meaningfulness, we don't yet have a "positive characterization." Often theorists decline to offer one, but simply present examples and invite us to consult our intuitions. Examples of meaningfulness-enhancing activities are fulfilling God's purposes for us; creating art of lasting significance; being creative in general; pursuing science and making an important discovery; achieving excellence in athletics; loving another; raising a family; participating in relationships of friendship and teamwork of all sorts; making a lasting "mark" on the world, and so forth. This list just scratches the surface, but it helps to specify the notion of meaningfulness in a positive way.

Metz gives the following list of activities (some due to other authors) that do not add to the meaningfulness of a life: a person who spends her life in Nozick's Experience Machine or involuntarily hooked into a virtual reality device; Sisyphus rolling his rock up and down the hill forever; or a human being who strives to maintain exactly 3,732 hairs on his head, lines up balls of torn newspaper in neat rows, or has perfected her prowess at long-distance spitting. In general, activities that are simple and involve mere counting—such as counting the blades of grass in one's front lawn, the grains of sand in a certain area of a beach, or the lightbulbs on a billboard— are not meaningfulness-enhancing. Tic-tac-toe is fundamentally different from chess, or even crossword puzzles (especially those in the *New York Times* on weekends). Making balloon animals is perhaps in between; it involves *some* creativity, but can this be sustained over time? Don't the species of balloon animals eventually become extinct?

How do we characterize meaningfulness in a more "basic" way? That is, what general principles underlie the intuitive distinction between the two kinds of cases? Seachris and Metz present some interesting proposals. Seachris offers the "Triad of Meaning": mattering, sense-making, and purpose. Simplifying, he holds that a life is meaningful insofar as it is oriented around what matters, thereby motivating purposive activity that gives the life direction and allows it to make sense, all of which would be enormously enhanced by God. This is indeed an oversimplification, but there is a fuller development of these ideas in Seachris' chapters in this volume.

Metz offers a different principled way of distinguishing the meaningfulness-increasing activities from those that are not. He holds that the exercise of intelligence (broadly construed) is central to meaningfulness. He writes:

> The rich life at the core involves the use of a person's rational nature in effortful, complex, and progressive ways, whereas the poor lives do not. There might be more to meaning in life than that, but that constitutes a lot of it (Metz).

As the debate proceeds, Seachris and Metz fill in, develop, and defend their ways of systematizing our intuitive judgments about meaningfulness (and lack of it). They also leap into the deep waters of the role of religion. More specifically, they address the issue of whether God's existence (conceptualized in the Western, monotheistic "perfect being" tradition) is necessary for meaningfulness in life.

In their thoughtful debate about this difficult set of issues, Seachris and Metz helpfully distinguish two doctrines: "extreme supernaturalism" and "moderate supernaturalism." The extreme view claims that God's existence is necessary for *any* meaning in life. The moderate view holds that, whereas certain activities could endow a life with meaning, even in the absence of God, God's existence would *enhance* the meaningfulness of these activities. Both authors reject the extreme view; and whereas Seachris adopts the moderate view, Metz also rejects this attempt to get God into the picture (so to speak). Metz offers a thoroughly "naturalistic" view of meaning in life. Their debate is lively, penetrating, and enlightening. It will, of course, not resolve the disagreement, which has been around (and aroused passionate disagreement) for millennia; but it identifies and clarifies the issues in a fruitful way, opening possibilities for productive inquiry in the future.

It is interesting to consider why one might think the existence of God (a perfect being) would increase the value of meaningful human activities. Perhaps we yearn for "approval" or "validation" from an objective perspective, and a perfect being occupies just this sort of point of view. Seachris points to this human yearning in various dimensions, which he calls meaning's "tilt toward the cosmic," toward good endings, and toward God. Metz questions this tilt, wondering whether it is universally (or even generally) held. Further, he contends not only that it is not necessary to have any sort of "cosmic" or divine validation to have meaning in one's life, but that this sort of validation would not *add anything* to the meaningfulness of a rich human life.

Suppose it is indeed a general human desire for a perfect God who orders and directs the universe in a beneficent way. Imagine, further, that we yearn for approval or validation of our life's activities by this God. We could concede these psychological facts, but still wonder whether, upon reflection, such validation would really endow the activities with meaning (or greater meaning). Perhaps, as Metz's view suggests, God's blessing would simply make us feel better about our efforts, or more confident in their value. But this would be a psychological fact, not (arguably, at least), a fact about meaning.

How might God's existence enhance meaningfulness of human activities? Consider the phrase, "God's-eye view." The standard interpretation is an "objective" or all-encompassing view "from above"—something like Nagel's "view from nowhere" (Nagel). There is, however, another possible interpretation: a view through God's eyes—that is, through the eyes of a wise and beneficent being. Such a being would know what is genuinely meaningful in human life.

Consider this passage from a paper by Howard Wettstein:

> There is another possible dimension to God's role ... God's blessing, as it were, would indicate that our values matter to the universe, that there is some significance that is not just a function of what matters to us ... Life's meaning would then be a matter of our values connecting deeply with the universe.

On this sort of view, we would not *just* receive a psychological benefit, akin to satisfying the deep human desire for "parental approval." We would receive that, but also something more: a realization that what matters to us is not *merely* what matters to us, but has a greater, more resonant significance. Here taking the

God's-eye-perspective is not simply to see the world from "above," but to see it through the eyes of a perfect being. This is just a suggestion of mine (based on work of Howard Wettstein), and I do not wish to attribute it to Seachris or Metz.

To wrap up, this is a compelling and illuminating debate, conducted with a collegial spirit, into some of the most fundamental of human concerns. I found myself agreeing with Seachris, then Metz, then Seachris, then Metz, and so forth. That's a sign of a good debate. In the end, I was sure that I had learned a lot, and enjoyed the ride!

John Martin Fischer

References

Nagel, Thomas. 1989. *The View from Nowhere*, revised ed. Oxford: Oxford University Press.
Nozick, Robert. 1974. *Anarchy, State, and Utopia*. New York: Basic Books.
Nozick, Robert. 1981. *Philosophical Explorations*. Cambridge, MA: Harvard University Press.
Tolstoy, Leo. 1884/2005. *My Confession*. Mineola, NY: Dover.
Wolf, Susan. 2010. *Meaning in Life and Why It Matters*. Princeton, NJ: Princeton University Press.
Wettstein, Howard. "Ungrounded." unpublished ms. Department of Philosophy, University of California, Riverside.

Opening Statements

Chapter 1

Triadic Meaning and the Benefits of God

Joshua W. Seachris

Contents

1.1 Introduction: The Human Need for Meaning 3
1.2 What Is Meaning? The Meaning Triad 8
1.3 Meanings Small and Big; Narrow and Wide 29
1.4 Parts in Wholes: Meaning's Tilt Toward the Cosmic 32
1.5 The "Loss" of Meaning: Meaning's Tilt Toward Transcendence 35
1.6 Absurdity: Meaning's Tilt Toward Existential Coherence 37
1.7 Death: Meaning's Tilt Toward the End 42
1.8 Why Theism Is Better News: Meaning's Tilt Toward God 53
1.9 Summary 68

> My father would say that a sparrow isn't just a sparrow.
> Because its fall means something, cosmically speaking.
> (Marilynne Robinson, *Jack*, 35).

> "Everyone's story matters," said Morris.
> (William Joyce, *The Fantastic Flying Books of Mr. Morris Lessmore*).

1.1 Introduction: The Human Need for Meaning

I suspect you want your life to exhibit a wide range of **value**: physical and emotional wellbeing; knowledge and understanding; hard-won achievement; moral integrity; justice; loving relationships with other human and non-human animals, and, for many, with God. Some values are **instrumental:** we want them in order to get something else—for example, money to buy that vacation which we hope will bring us happiness. Others are **intrinsic**: we want them for their own sake—for example, happiness itself, about which it makes little sense to ask what further sort of value it brings us. All else being equal, a life in which a broad range of such values is present is a better life.

Not unconnected from some of the above values is our desire for *meaning*. There are those who think that meaning is a kind of fundamental value—perhaps even preeminent to all other value: a value that we want more than any other in life. I am sympathetic to this view. According to twentieth-century Freudian psychoanalyst Bruno Bettelheim (1903–1990), "our greatest need and most difficult achievement is to find meaning in our lives" (Bettelheim 1978: 3). Quite aside from the daunting juxtaposition of our "greatest need" also being our "most difficult achievement," Bettelheim captures a popular idea: that one of the many values that we seek in our lives as humans—perhaps the most prized—is a *meaningful* life. Fellow psychoanalyst, Holocaust survivor, and father of the psychoanalytic approach of **logotherapy**, Viktor Frankl (1905–1997), said that the human "will to meaning" motivates human activity in deeper ways than even our will to pleasure or our will to power (Frankl 2006: 99).

Our desire for meaning finds vivid expression in the stories we tell, the diaries we keep, the hobbies we pursue, the relationships we build, the hopes we cherish, and the fears we dread. We express our concerns about meaning in varied contexts. When struggling to make important decisions in college about what to do with our lives. When trapped in a job we hate, wondering if there is more to life than the often-monotonous cycles of daily existence. When diagnosed with a terminal illness. When experiencing the loss of a loved one. When feeling exceedingly insignificant while pondering the staggering size of the universe. When wondering if this universe is all there is and why it is even here in the first place. When questioning whether life and love will have a *lasting* place, or whether the whole show will end in utter and everlasting silence. With differences in framing, focus, and scope, one finds the human preoccupation with meaning in philosophy, theology, science, and literature; in the ancient world, and then increasingly in the modern and contemporary worlds; in the East and the West, in unique forms; in college advisors' offices; during midlife crises; on deathbeds; and even in animated films.

Disney Pixar's *Soul* (2020) may be its most **existentially** arresting movie to date. *Soul* is a film about Joe Gardner (voiced by Jamie

Foxx), a middle-school band teacher whose dream of becoming a professional jazz pianist remains unfulfilled at midlife. On the day he finally gets his opportunity to realize his dream—and presumably truly experience a meaningful life—Mr. Gardner falls from the street into a sewer and ... dies. Well, almost. He finds himself in a disembodied state, which provides the setting for his discovery of what makes life meaningful. The story is filled with memorable twists and turns, all of which attempt to illumine the shape of meaningful human life. What Joe discovers—much like the main character of another film, George Bailey from the classic *It's a Wonderful Life* (1946)—is that much of what we take to be ordinary about our lives is precisely where we should look to discover meaning, especially in our day-to-day interactions *with others*. At the end of the film, Gardner recommits to living mindfully and being fully present for all the moments of his remaining life—"big" and "small" moments in community with others; and in so doing, he believes he has found what makes life meaningful.

Along with the creators of *Soul*'s animated jazz pianist Joe Gardner, a great number of us are concerned with meaning—enough so that this concern is often and earnestly voiced in our intellectual, vocational, and cultural enterprises. Our preoccupation with meaning significantly defines and depicts the **human condition**. We are meaning-seeking, meaning-making creatures. The obvious next question is: *what is meaning?* Or, put slightly differently: *what makes life meaningful?* The latter version is the title and topic of this extended "conversation" (a noun I prefer to "debate") between my friend and colleague Professor Thaddeus Metz and myself. Professor Metz, more than anyone else in the field, has put the philosophical study of life's meaning on the map in contemporary **analytic philosophy** with his publication of dozens upon dozens of articles and books on the topic over the last few decades. His work figured prominently in the story of my own entry into this area of research.

A Note on Terminological Conventions

Following Professor Metz, I will adopt the conventions below in my use of four key terms. An important rule for discussions like this is to ensure that participants mean the same thing by the words they choose. That way, we can eliminate unnecessary disagreement, since there will be enough real disagreement to keep us busy.

- **Theism:** The view that an omnicompetent, personal God—all-powerful, all-knowing, all-loving—exists and is responsible for the universe's existence.
- **Atheism:** The view that denies theism. More broadly, it denies that a spiritual realm exists, and claims that the physical space-time universe as understood by science is all that there is.
- **Supernaturalism:** The view that spiritual conditions (e.g., a proper relationship with God) are necessary for meaningful life.
- **Naturalism:** The view that neither God nor spiritual conditions more broadly are necessary for meaningful life.

Readers will see that one could be, for example, an atheist-supernaturalist, given these conventions. Put simply, one could believe that the theistic God does not exist, but that the existence of such a God is necessary for meaningful life.

Professionally, I have thought about meaning extensively for roughly the past two decades. Personally, I have worried about it since about fourth grade. My views about what constitutes meaningful life have evolved since then, and I suspect this process will continue. The dust has sufficiently settled, though; and I now feel comfortable framing my thinking, research, and earlier writing in a fresh, more focused effort in order to answer the question: *what makes life meaningful*?

That is a difficult question! My own answer claims that meaning:

- Is a unique kind of value that our lives can possess to a greater or lesser degree;
- Is best understood in terms of the triad of mattering, purpose, and sense-making;
- Requires minds with sufficient capacities (e.g., human minds as opposed to insect minds); and
- Would be substantially enhanced in non-trivial ways in a **theistic** universe, where a necessarily existent, essentially good, infinite Mind is causally responsible for the universe.

Though I will return to the following definition in more detail in Section 1.2 (hereinafter, this format will be shorthand for chapter and section references from the text of this debate), it is worth introducing the answer I give in response to the question posed in the title of this book: *what makes life meaningful?*

> **Meaningful Life:** One's life is meaningful to the degree that it is oriented around that which matters (mattering that is of positive rather than negative value), which in turn fuels the purposive activity one pursues to give one's life direction, and, therefore allows one's life to make sense and exhibit proper fit with reality—a fitting place within the whole of what is true, good, and beautiful. Someone who lives such a life will tend to be happier, more fulfilled, satisfied, and engaged.

No doubt there is a lot packed into this brief but dense account of what meaningful life is. In the remainder of my opening statement, I will provide a longer account of meaning, from which this definition emerges. This account ventures into broad territory, including history, philosophy, theology, psychology, and literature.

Not too long ago, widespread suspicion accompanied talk of life's meaning. Intellectual luminaries of the last few centuries voiced suspicion of questions about life's meaning. Here are some brief examples:

- "No Why. Just here." John Cage (1912–1992)
- "Has the question itself any meaning?" George Bernard Shaw (1856–1950)
- "The moment a man questions the meaning and value of life, he is sick ... By asking this question one is merely admitting to a store of unsatisfied libido to which something else must have happened, a kind of fermentation leading to sadness and depression." Sigmund Freud (1856–1939)

Such suspicion is understandable. Getting to the bottom of the meaning of *meaning*—and thereafter *life's* meaning—is like trying to assemble a big, complex jigsaw puzzle, some of whose pieces appear stubbornly resistant to unified assembly. Numerous pieces require assembly: pieces with labels such as *mattering, significance, purpose, sense-making, transcendence, absurdity, futility, death, immortality* … and so on. These and related ideas are central for understanding the questions, concerns, and indeed hungers that define and depict human preoccupation with life's meaning. In the remainder of this opening statement, I investigate these ideas and important connections between them in order to bring into relief what our concerns over meaning involve; what a meaningful life is; and why theism is better news than atheism for the prospects of leading a robustly meaningful life. That, of course, makes me a supernaturalist, given the terminological conventions of this debate.

> **Summary**
>
> Our desire for meaning is one of the more basic, unique, and interesting features of human existence. In this opening section, I have set the stage for my overall argument to come, which is built around the following claims:
>
> - Concerns about meaning:
>   - Cluster around the following triad of ideas: *mattering*, *purpose*, and *sense-making*;
>   - Have both personal and cosmic foci;
>   - Are often connected with the perceived "loss" of transcendence; and
>   - Are closely connected to the end of life (in terms of both **teleology** and termination).
> - Theism allows for deeper forms of meaning than atheism, making theism, on balance, much better news for the human condition.

1.2 What Is Meaning? The Meaning Triad[1]

Before answering the question: *what makes life meaningful?* we should answer a more basic one: *what is meaning?* Meaning is a value that most of us want our lives to possess; though it appears relevantly distinct from other values we want in our lives, like

---

1 Section 1.2 borrows substantially from Seachris 2019.

moral goodness and happiness, even if it overlaps with them. For example, if meaning is primarily about fulfillment, as some argue, one could be fulfilled engaging in a wide variety of morally suspect activities, like bullying or worse. Alternatively, if meaning is primarily about making objectively good impacts on the world, as others argue, a person could substantially increase the amount of good in the world through her efforts, even if she was deeply dissatisfied with her life while doing so. On influential theories of meaning, then, meaning can come apart in relevant ways from happiness and morality. Why do so many use the concept of *meaning* to pick out a unique kind of value that we want in life?

Meaning-talk is all around us. Ordinary discourse abounds with uses of "meaning." Such uses provide important clues for understanding the kind of request(s) we make when inquiring into life's meaning. Most ordinary uses of "meaning" can be grouped into the following triad: *mattering, purpose,* and *sense-making.* I call this the *Meaning Triad.* Whatever sort of value *meaningfulness* is when attributed to the cosmos, life in general, an individual person's life, or parts of a person's life, it is similar to the sort of thing *meaning* is when used in everyday discourse. Let us take a closer look at the Meaning Triad.

Meaning as Mattering

- "That was such a *meaningful* conversation."
- "That shirt *means* so much to me."
- "That is a highly *meaningful* event in the life of that city."
- "What do his first six months in office *mean* for the country?" (Overlaps with sense-making.)
- "That is a *meaningful* finding."
- "You *mean* nothing to me."
- "What does it *mean* to be a Midwesterner?" (Overlaps with sense-making.)

Meaning as Purpose

- "What did you *mean* by that face?" (Overlaps with sense-making.)
- "The tantrum is *meant* to catch his parents' attention."
- "I really *mean* it!"
- "I didn't *mean* to do it, I promise!"

Meaning as Sense-Making
- "I have no idea what you *mean*."
- "What did you *mean* by that statement?"
- "What did you *mean* by that face?" (Overlaps with purpose.)
- "What is the *meaning* of that book?" (*What* is it about?)
- "What is the *meaning* of this?" (E.g., when encountering a situation about which you want to know more.)

It is worth looking at each of these three broad categories of meaning in more detail in order to get a better sense of what meaning is; and also to draw some initial conclusions about how the meaning of *meaning* sheds light on what life's meaning is all about.

1.2.1 *Meaning as Mattering*

Meaning often conveys the idea of mattering; and mattering tracks a related cluster of notions like significance, importance, impact, salience, being the object of care and concern, and value. We contrast a cherished family heirloom with a piece of junk. The heirloom matters—it is meaningful; the piece of junk has no meaning—it is of no significance to us. Conversations about trivialities mean very little to us; whereas those about important topics are particularly meaningful. Actions and events with great impact and far-reaching consequences are significant, and—at least in cases where that significance is of positive value—are meaningful (whether a person can lead a meaningful life in virtue of making large *negative* impacts is controversial and worth discussing further; more about that later in this section). Designing a vaccine to stop a global pandemic is meaningful, partly because of its significant positive impact relative to our concerns about human health and flourishing. Meaning as mattering is also in focus in cases where information is salient and illuminating relative to some claim or question. All else being equal, that such a large percentage of the population living under certain conditions is suffering from a particular disease relative to the rest of the population likely would statistically matter— it would be *meaningful*.

Alternatively, when something does not matter to us, we might say, "That means nothing to me. Throw it away; it is junk. I do not care about it." That game did not matter because the playoff field is already set. The outside does not matter; it is what is on the inside that counts. That piece of information is not meaningful—it does not matter—relevant to the aims and questions guiding one's inquiry. Spending most of your life sitting on the couch and binging sitcom reruns on Netflix is meaningless; it is of negligible importance or value.

Something's mattering is often assessed via a perspective or point of reference, which is frequently dynamic. Something that matters from one vantage point may cease to matter when viewed from a broader horizon. Losing your favorite toy at age four matters—at least from a four-year old's perspective. It might even feel disastrous. When looking back four decades later, however, its significance likely wanes. Most events important enough to make it into the local annals of a tiny town like my hometown of Buhler, Kansas, will not matter enough to be included in a state history, let alone national, world and, especially, cosmic history.

In addition to being perspectival in the ways noted above, mattering also is **normative** and personal. When we say that something is meaningful in the sense of mattering, being significant, or being important, we make an evaluative claim about what is noteworthy, choice-worthy, good, or valuable. This moves beyond mere description to a kind of evaluation that something is more *deserving* of our focus and attention, of our care and concern. Also, things, most naturally, matter *to someone*. In this way, minds with sufficient capacities are preconditions for meaning (see Section 1.2.5). Of course, things can matter *for* something (rather than someone) without mattering *to* it. There need not always be someone around, as it were, in order to speak of mattering—for example, sunlight matters for trees even if it does not matter to them: it is important for their growth even though trees presumably are not conscious of this fact. It does not matter to them in the same way that graduating from college might matter to you as a person.

The idea of mattering is helpful for understanding, in part, what meaningful life involves. We seek to position our lives in proper relation to importance or significance. We might do so at two related but distinct levels: meaning *in* life (personally oriented) and meaning *of* life (cosmically oriented) (for more on this important distinction, see Section 1.3). To the extent that we want our lives to be meaningful, we will choose, for example, to devote more energy to making good impacts on those around us rather than, say, to binge watching reruns of *Frasier* or whatever it is that you binge watch. This, of course, is not to say that a meaningful life has no place for leisure and even some trivialities. Such things have a kind of value in balance, and are important for meaningful life. They matter. Meaningful life is not all work and no play.

Meaning in this way is about a life having an appropriate kind of existential and normative *depth*. Put simply, it is about a life properly attuned to the relevant range of value; generally, the deeper the value, the better. Such a life is the opposite of a shallow life—one merely attuned to trivialities or, in general, the wrong sort of stuff. The shallow end of the pool can be plumbed with great ease. It takes little effort and likely brings little reward. A shallow treatment of an issue barely scratches the surface; whereas deeper treatments dig below the surface into the complexity of a matter. They illumine, providing deep insight. Shallow treatments are ubiquitous on social media, for example, but they provide no insight. As such, they are worth comparatively little to in-depth analyses. Shallow people focus on trivialities: for example, they are preoccupied with the latest celebrity gossip and neglect issues of import. The meaningful tends toward depth rather than shallowness. In moments of existential clarity, most of us desire a life sufficiently connected to that which matters over a life focused primarily on the trivial.

Interestingly, mattering is neutral with respect to value. One thing can matter negatively; another can matter positively. Destroying someone's life because you made a quick, incorrect inference via social media about something they said matters. It is impactful. It has consequences—negative ones. Really getting to know those who, through no fault of their own, find themselves in disadvantaged situations, and really trying to understand the complex problems and work with others to find sustainable solutions, matters. It is impactful. It has consequences—positive ones. In both examples, someone is doing something that matters. But only in the latter example are we inclined to assess what they are doing as meaningful, as something praise- or esteem-worthy. A life whose negatively impactful elements outweigh its positive ones—though there is no simple value calculus one can apply here—will resist being described as a meaningful life, at least on this metric.

Complications ensue, however. There is a sense in which, say, Hitler's life was quite meaningful. For example, his life is key to understanding large swaths of twentieth-century history. You cannot tell the story of twentieth-century history without saying something about him. This complicates matters for meaning; but it does not undercut the basic plausibility of my triadic account. Generally, when we aspire to a meaningful life, we aspire to a choice-worthy life—a life that we and those relevantly similar to us *want* to live. Hitler's life, all things considered, is not choice-worthy in this way. Ultimately, his life lacked a kind of *fittingness* with reality—the true, good, and beautiful—that is also a condition on meaning (see Section 1.2.3).

As much as we want the energy we expend in our lives to be devoted sufficiently to that which matters, we also want our very lives themselves to matter—to ourselves; to those whom we love and respect; and, for many of us, within the cosmic scheme of things. This last desire, of course, generates worries, depending on what is true about the nature of the universe in which we live. Atheists and theists generally disagree on whether our lives can matter within the grand scheme of things—that is, from the perspective of the ancient, vast cosmos: what philosophers sometimes call the *sub specie aeternitatis* perspective (literally, "from the perspective of eternity"). If the cosmos is all there is, was, and will be (to quote the late Carl Sagan), and there is no God, no souls, and no afterlife (as atheism claims), it is doubtful whether our lives are cosmically significant in any important sense (though, for an alternative view, see Kahane 2013). However, if there is a God who is responsible for the cosmos and for human life therein, there is good reason to think that, even in an ancient, vast, silent universe, human life matters cosmically in crucial ways because it was intended by God. Both the universe and human life within that universe would be intended by the same infinite, creative Mind. In such a universe, our deepest ethical and existential impulses would, in the words of neuroscientist Bill Newsome, be part of:

> the central reality of the universe and the reason the universe was built from the beginning ... rather than a kind of downstream accident that has nothing to do with what the universe is about at the deepest level.
> (Newsome 2010).

Some people claim that it should not matter whether or not our lives matter *sub specie aeternitatis*. What matters, they say, is that our lives matter from a more localized perspective: the one associated with human cares and concerns—*sub specie humanitatis* (literally, "from the perspective of humanity"). Lives can still matter within this frame—and this one, so the argument goes, is the only one that really matters for assessments of human significance. Others, however, find it difficult to separate personal mattering concerns from cosmic ones. What is true at the cosmic level can be intensely personal. If the universe as a whole lacks significance—or if our lives from the perspective of the universe lack significance—some of us worry that our lives lack a crucial kind of meaning. The kind of meaning that would be missing requires that human life not be some accidental feature arriving on the cosmic scene—a scene that very easily could have been human-*less* given a shift this way or that in evolution. Stepping aside from the debate about how much one's life needs to matter, to whom it should matter, and from what perspective it needs to matter most, this much seems clear: meaningful life is closely connected with mattering and cognate ideas.

Finally, and apart from the relative sense of mattering within expanding frames of reference, most of us think that all human life matters in a distinct sense. Though humans, unfortunately, have not always treated other humans and specific human groups as if they mattered, most of us would say that human life matters *in virtue of the kind of life that it is*. Let us call this "intrinsic" mattering, where such mattering is explained in terms of one's consciousness, as a first-person subject of awareness who thinks and feels; or in terms of some inherent human dignity; or in more overtly theological terms of, say, being an image bearer of the Divine (*imago dei*). In this sense, Hitler's and every other human's life matters—it is meaningful. That said, I doubt that when we voice our desire to lead a meaningful life, we primarily have this sense of mattering in mind. Rather, we have in mind a kind of life sufficiently oriented around that which is of positive value, to include relationships, vocations, and other sought-after goods.

1.2.2 Meaning as Purpose

When we ask for the meaning of something, sometimes we seek its purpose. For example, if you ask me what the meaning of that face I just made is, you probably want to know *why* I made it. What was my reason for looking at you in that particular way? What message was I trying to convey? What was my purpose? The meaning of an action—in this case, a face—is our reason or purpose for doing it. We might also, for example, ask what the meaning of that little gear is in a machine. Here, again, we ask about its purpose—what it is *for*.

Inquiries into life's meaning are very often connected to the idea of purpose. We want to know whether we have a purpose(s), and if so, what that purpose is. Purposes motivate us to get out of bed and act. They energize the activities and rhythms of our day-to-day existence. They partly provide us with the drive to keep on living. They give us reasons to do the things we do. Ask yourself the question: "Why did I get out of bed this morning and why do I do much of what I do?" I suspect that many of your answers will revolve around aims and goals—*purposes*.

Purpose(s) in Life and Wellbeing

- People with a sense of purpose have a 15% lower risk of death compared with those who say they are more or less aimless (Hill & Turiano 2014).
- People with purpose are more likely to be confident in their abilities, feel optimistic and hopeful, and have more grit and diligence (Boyle, Buchman, Wilson, & Bennett 2010; Bronk, Hill, Lapsley, Talib & Finch 2009; Kass et al. 1991; Lyubomirsky, Tkach, & DiMatteo 2006; Steger & Frazier 2005).

These claims are, of course, subject to the caveat that sorting out correlation and causation are complex matters.

People experiencing some forms of depression speak in terms of having lost a sense of direction; of feeling aimless; of suffering from a lack of purpose (see "Purpose(s) in Life and Wellbeing" box). Many seek, or assume there is, a cosmic purpose as a blueprint around which to order their lives. Such a purpose likely would require transcendence or God. For the universe and our lives to have such a purpose requires that they be *intended by someone* (though see Aristotle, *Physics*, Book II, for a variation on this view appealing to an immanent though universal sort of purpose).

Of course, one might reject the idea of a cosmic purpose, and yet still acknowledge that meaning and purpose intersect. In this case, a meaningful life involves sufficiently structuring one's life around self-determined purposes—identifying, pursuing, and hopefully attaining goals. This goal pursuit will then structure many of the moments of one's day-to-day existence in a way that imbues them with meaning—much in the same way that the goal of making a sandcastle on the banks of Lake Michigan imbues the physical acts of moving and sculpting sand with meaning over and above merely grasping, releasing, and forming sand with one's fingers. There is directionality leading somewhere. It gives the activity a *point*. Most of us seek to lead lives of purpose—lives that are heading somewhere rather than nowhere in particular (though for an alternative—aptly named *episodic*—view, see Strawson 2004).

This is not the only sense in which meaning and purpose intersect. We also distinguish willful, purposeful actions from those done on accident, and use *meaning* to characterize the former. We say things like, "I really mean it" to indicate the deliberate use of our will. We want to do it; we intend to do it. Alternatively, our friend might say, "I didn't mean it, I promise!" to indicate that she did not purposely intend to drop your new iPhone in the swimming pool.

This sense of "meant" illumines something of perceived relevance to life's meaning. We want sufficient autonomy over the shape of our lives; and when personal control is absent or severely diminished, we worry about their meaningfulness (see Mawson 2016; Sartre 1973). Most of us do not want to walk through life haphazardly, or in a way that is largely determined apart from our own consent. We want to intend a sufficient range of what we do, unhindered by external coercion. We want to live our lives on purpose, where we choose our own goals, and have sufficient freedom to pursue them as we see fit. So, a meaningful life is one that is appropriately oriented around purposes that matter and that we choose—or at least *want*, upon reflection—to have. Your parents may want you to become an MD, but you do not. Perhaps you are much less excited about *their* purpose for your life than they are. Not only do we need purposes around which to orient our lives, we want those purposes to be ones that we choose, or at least recognize as being good *for us*. Imagine discovering that our purpose is to be food for aliens (e.g., see the disturbing original *Twilight Zone* episode "To Serve Man"). In this scenario, humans no doubt have a purpose—and, in a loose sense, a meaning; but it is a terrifying one. A more tragic scenario—one that I mention with the utmost of sensitivity, because it actually occurred (and still occurs to this day) rather often around the Earth—is when the purpose of one human being is as a mere instrument for the use of another human being, as in the tragedy of slavery. Here, one has a purpose, but has not had sufficient say in that purpose in a way consistent with human dignity.

The two shades of purpose are probably related. We want to really mean it as we select and align our lives with aims that will provide the rhythms of our day-to-day existence. In other words, we do not want to be alienated from the purposes that guide our lives. Walter White, the central character in AMC's hit drama *Breaking Bad*, voices this desire when he responds to his family during an intervention: "What I want, what I need, is a choice. Sometimes I feel like I never actually make any of my own. My entire life, it just seems I never, you know, had a real say about any of it." White wants more control over his life. He wants greater freedom to choose the kinds of purposes that will motivate him to get out of bed and act—and act in such a way that he will feel truly alive and invigorated, even if that happens to be by cooking crystal meth with a former student. One can begin to see how the existence of a cosmic meaning for human life might raise a potential concern here. If we have been given a purpose *from someone else*, what real say do we have in our lives? God might be too much like the parents above who have their child's life all planned out. We will explore this worry further in Section 1.8.2.

1.2.3 Meaning as Sense-Making

Many of our requests for meaning reveal our desire to render something intelligible. Perhaps you did not understand what someone said, so you ask what they meant. You want them to clarify what was at least partially obscure before. The same goes for non-verbal forms of communication: you might ask what that face your friend made means. It also applies to natural signs. For example, those leaves on the ground mean that fall has arrived; or those clouds mean that a thunderstorm is on the way. Meaning tracks the idea of intelligibility or sense-making. Something is meaningful if it is intelligible—if it makes sense. It lacks meaning if it makes no sense—if it is nonsensical.

The following arrangement of English letters—atgbovx—is meaningless unless an appropriate referent is fixed (i.e., "atgbovx" means the particular configuration of pine trees in my backyard). One way of thinking about sense-making—though not the only way—is through the idea of proper fit. Things—words, paragraphs, and musical notes; but also events and states of affairs, speaking more broadly—make sense and are meaningful if they fit together properly; if they lack fit, they make no sense (or at least not a relevant kind of sense), and are meaningless. This applies to logical and semantic constructions, but it has a broader application too. Making sense and not making sense each admit of at least two interpretations, narrow and broad—the latter of which is most relevant for life's meaning. Consider the narrow and broad versions of things not making sense (narrow and broad nonsense):

> **Narrow Nonsense:** Something makes no sense if it is logically or semantically incoherent, where incoherence can be understood as a kind of lack of fit.
> **Broad Nonsense:** Something makes no sense if it involves a lack of fit weaker than logical or semantic incoherence.

Asking the question, "What is smaller than the smallest thing?" fails to make sense narrowly in at least one important way: the concept of the smallest thing does not fit with asking what is smaller. There is a logical incoherence here—an incoherence partly understood as a *lack of fit*. But there are similar, though not explicitly logical, instances of lack of fit from which the charge of nonsense follows. We might say things like the following:

- It does not make sense to keep charging your phone after it is fully charged.
- The coach's decision to go for it on fourth down during the opening drive of the first quarter makes no sense.
- Asking students in a philosophy course to perform long division on their philosophy midterm makes no sense.

In each of these situations, we perceive a lack of fit—a lack of fit between what it means for a phone to be fully charged and the reason for charging a phone; between it being very early in the game and calling such a risky, unnecessary play and so on. None of these situations involves any sort of logical or semantic (or otherwise narrow) incoherence; but each fails to make sense in some other crucial way. Perceiving this broader lack of fit will be a product of beliefs, norms, and other details of the situation. As such, determining whether something involves a lack of fit (makes no sense or is nonsensical) in this broader sense often will be a messier affair than in cases of narrow sense-making.

Sense-Making and Meaning-Making

Social and cognitive scientists have long thought that sense-making and meaning-making go hand in hand. Some researchers argue that the human drive for sense-making is analogous to core biological drives like hunger, thirst, and sex; and that our sense-making proclivities are closely connected with our desire for meaning. In the words of social psychologist Thomas Gilovich, "We are predisposed to see order, pattern, and meaning in the world, and we find randomness, chaos, and meaninglessness unsatisfying. Human nature abhors a lack of predictability and the absence of meaning" (Gilovich 1991: 9).

- Do you think our meaning-making drive increases the likelihood of distorting the world?
- How much of meaning-making involves *imposing* or *inventing* rather than *discovering*?

Ascertaining meaning, then, is often about *fitting* something within a larger context or whole: words into sentences, paragraphs, and novels; musical notes into measures, movements, and symphonies (i.e., the movement from mere sound to music); parts of a photograph within the entire photograph. Meaning is about intelligibility within a wider frame; about "inserting small parts into a larger, integrated context" (Svendsen 2005: 29). Things partly (or largely) mean what they mean given their "location" within a larger whole.

Requests for life's meaning, at the cosmic level, are plausibly seen as inquiries into the overarching context through which we make sense of our lives in the universe. To borrow from an example above, our lives (or even human life) are like individual words or sentences, and we seek the novel in which to locate them. Our focus, in seeking *life's* meaning, is on existentially weighty matters that define and depict the human condition: questions and concerns surrounding origins, significance, value, purpose, suffering, and death and destiny. We want answers to our questions about these matters; and we want these answers to fit together in both an intellectually and existentially satisfying way. We want life to make sense. When it does not, we are haunted by the specter of meaninglessness. This worry can occur on both cosmic and personal levels.

Whereas meaning as mattering tracks the notion of existential *depth*, meaning as sense-making tracks the notion of existential *location*. Meaning is "geographical" in this sense. As indicated earlier, meaning is often a matter of locating something's place within a larger context—whether that be words, musical notes, or even parts of a picture. Wilhelm Dilthey (1833–1911), a nineteenth-century historian, psychologist, and sociologist, thought that meaning is a matter of belonging to a whole. A word's meaning is determined partly by its place in a larger semantic whole. A musical note's meaning is determined by its place in the larger musical composition. A portion's meaning in a picture is determined by its place in the entire picture. Life's meaning likewise is determined by its *place*—and not merely by the space it occupies—in the universe, given what is true about the universe in terms of origins, value, purpose, and destiny. Careful attention to existential location in addition to existential depth reveals another way in which a theistic view of the world is more hospitable to meaning—at least the kind of meaning that many seek. Life's *location* is strikingly different—it is existentially *centered*—in a theistic universe than it is in an atheistic one.

Sense-making is not unconnected from mattering and purpose. A life that matters and is heading somewhere will exhibit an important kind of fit with reality that allows us to say that such a life makes sense and, therefore, is meaningful. A life that fits together properly will be one in which all aspects are in their proper place—religion (or other ultimate devotions), family, friends, vocation, intellectual pursuits, leisure, mindful presence, and so on. When things are out of place, or out of balance, we begin to worry that such a life does not *make sense*, broadly speaking. For example, most of us, in our more reflective moments, would say that it does not make sense to spend the majority of life painting and repainting the walls of one's home, or spending hours upon hours on social media, even if one finds enjoyment in such activities. Why? Because preoccupation with such activities *does not fit* with what is generally thought to be most conducive to, and embodied in, human flourishing. Such lives lack a kind of intelligibility. They are not, of course, strictly unintelligible. They are not non-sensical, or obscure, or immune from description. They do not fail to have purposes, goals, and aims that motivate their activity. Rather, the *lack of fit* they exhibit is between their salient parts and what is of genuine importance. Readers will notice here that my emerging conception of meaningful life departs from a theory of meaningful life called **subjectivism**. According to subjectivism, if one enjoys painting and repainting walls 24/7, and binging social media to the exclusion of most else, one leads a meaningful life because a meaningful life just is what one *wants it to be*. I think this is misguided. What I think is true about the world at the level of value precludes such lives as ultimately *properly fitting* within such a world. Such lives fail to make sense in an important way.

> ### Meaning Questions
>
> Human preoccupation with meaning, and the sort of thing that meaning is, is partially revealed in a number of interconnected questions that many of us ask from time to time:
>
> - "Is this all there is?"
> - "Is there more to life?"
> - "Why am I here?"
> - "What should I do with my time?"
> - "What's it all about?"
> - "Do I matter in the grand scheme of things?"
> - "Will the ills of this world ever truly be redeemed?"
> - "How is it all going to end?"
>
> These questions are not obviously and at first about morality or happiness—two other values that most of us want to characterize our lives. Our focus here is on another, distinct sort of value to which we aspire. This value's contours are brought into relief through the Meaning Triad of mattering, purpose, and sense-making.
>
> - Have you asked one or more of these questions?

All three parts of the Meaning Triad—mattering, purpose, and sense-making—likely exist in organic relationship within a meaningful life. Mattering and purpose connect, given that we primarily select goals that matter *to us* (or that straight up *matter*, if one is a **realist** about value). Such goals motivate our activities, infusing them with significance, because they have both a point, and a point that matters. Pre-goal activity acquires some of its significance from the value of the goal in addition to the mere presence of the goal. This mattering-purpose dynamic, in turn, provides important sense-making structure to our life—structure through which our lives fit together properly. Lives that fit together are those that are sufficiently (though not exclusively) **teleological**. The presence of ends, goals, and aims provides important connections between discrete events in life, tying a life together properly, and giving it a measure of coherence. Lives lacking such elements in sufficient quantity are threatened by unintelligibility that results from being insufficiently structured by a telos. In the words of philosopher Alasdair MacIntyre:

> When someone complains ... that his or her life is meaningless, he or she is often and perhaps characteristically complaining that the narrative of their life has become unintelligible to them, that it lacks any point, any movement toward a climax or a telos.
>
> (MacIntyre 2007: 217).

Such a life is one that is adrift, untethered, and going nowhere of great value. We might think of it as *empty* and *aimless*. These are not what most people want to have as the most descriptive adjectives of their lives. These characteristics seem to be far from the target of meaning.

All three aspects of this triadic conception of meaning can be combined to form the following definition of "meaningful life":

> **Meaningful Life:** One's life is meaningful to the degree that it is oriented around that which matters (mattering that is of positive rather than negative value), which in turn fuels the purposive activity one pursues to give one's life direction, and therefore allows one's life to make sense and exhibit proper fit with reality—a fitting place within the whole of what is true, good, and beautiful. Someone who lives such a life will tend to be happier, more fulfilled, satisfied, and engaged.

Three immediate observations about this definition are in order. First, it is triadic in nature, incorporating each element of the

Meaning Triad. A meaningful life is one that is properly ordered around that which matters; which in turn fuels the right kind of purposes; which in turn allows for life to fit together properly.

The Meaning Triad: Relationships Between the Elements

Above, I claim that all three portions of the Meaning Triad—mattering, purpose, and sense-making—likely exist in organic relationship with one another, such that all three form a kind of unity. My definition of "meaningful life," on the other hand, seems to prioritize *mattering* over both purpose and sense-making. Here are some questions worth considering:

- Can the parts of the triad exist in organic relationship (e.g., all intrinsically relating to one another), while one is prioritized over the other?
- Is one element of the triad more *important* than the others in my definition of "meaningful life," in one sense or another?
- Can my definition of "meaningful life" be redefined to prioritize either purpose or sense-making while still being triadic in nature and maintaining the organic relationship between the three?

Second, in this way, meaning appears to be more normatively basic than, say, morality. There is a lot we want out of life: a lot of value (some, but not all of which is moral); a lot of what matters— either mattering full stop in some objective sense, or at least *to us*. Meaning may be more basic than other values, in that it is the meta-organizational principle that structures everything that we want in life and how we want it all to fit together. A fitting example of this comes from Dr. Louise Banks, the main character in Ted Chiang's award-winning novella *Story of Your Life*, which was adapted for screen in the acclaimed 2016 sci-fi film *Arrival*. Dr. Banks asks: "If you could see your whole life from start to finish, would you change things?"

Dr. Banks's question is one about meaning. She is reflecting on what she would keep the same, what she would change, and, in general, how she should prioritize the different parts of her life. The act of prioritization is connected with the triad. It is about arranging the distribution of that which matters in your life—adding some elements, removing others, reconfiguring, etc.—and in so doing, prioritizing the purposes to which you devote your life in order to get to a place where your life fits together properly. This is not unlike those who, on their deathbeds, take time to reflect back on their choices, devotions, regrets, laments, joys, and triumphs. What do they often tell us? As it turns out, they speak with a fairly unified voice about what they *now* see more clearly as truly important; what they take to be genuinely *meaningful*. Time and again, they say that what really matters is love, expressed through deep and abiding relationships (though for a skeptical view of what deathbed thoughts teach us about what is important, see Levy 2021).

The preceding also potentially illumines an interesting connection between meaning and morality. Most of us seek to lead moral lives because morality matters—it is significant—given the way the world is thought to be. Leading a moral life, then, would be an important part of leading a meaningful life; but it would not encapsulate and exhaust meaning. We also want to lead happy lives, given the kinds of creatures we are. These things matter, and a meaningful life will be a product of having them in their proper places. Having them "in their proper places" will in turn fuel our purposes, and ensure that our lives fit together properly, which covers the purpose and sense-making sides of the triad.

Third, and finally, readers will notice that my definition of "meaningful life" as currently stated is largely formal and general enough to be consistent with both supernaturalism and naturalism (and also largely consistent with subjectivism (mentioned above), **objectivism**, and **hybridism**). The theory is, first, about ordering one's life sufficiently around what matters, and leaves unaddressed what those things that matter actually are. By and large, though, I take our ordinary understanding of what matters to be on the right track: family; relationships more broadly, to include friends and community; morality; creativity; the accomplishment of worthwhile projects; kindness; love; happiness; and so on. Lives sufficiently ordered around these things are *meaningful* lives. These things can be present in both atheistic and theistic worlds. I will avoid discussion of the claim that this range of value could not be present in an atheistic world because God is necessary for *anything* to exist in the first place. For the sake of argument, I will set aside that view and assume that an atheistic world is at least a possible world. As such, I think that one can lead a meaningful life even if atheism is true. And yet I think the prospects for meaning ultimately are better if God exists. God brings a deep reason for why we exist at all, assurance of ultimate justice, and a lasting place for loving relationships. I will argue this in greater detail later (in Section 1.8 and in my replies to Professor Metz).

1.2.4 The Psychological Profile of Meaning

According to my theory of meaningful life, your life is meaningful in virtue of appropriately fitting within the nature of reality—with what is true, good, and beautiful—by being sufficiently attuned to that which matters, and where that which matters suitably grounds and guides the kinds of purposes you choose to pursue in life. *Feelings* are noticeably absent from my definition. And yet meaningful life generally and often feels a certain way. My theory makes room for affective states; though in a way that does not make emotions—or any subjective state, for that matter—*constitutive* of meaning. This account accords with the following widely shared, though not universal, intuition:

> **Non-Subjectivism:** A fulfilled life that is nonetheless devoted to trivialities or harming others is not meaningful.

On my theory of meaning, non-subjectivism is plausible because a life devoted to trivialities or harming others does not fit with what is true about reality at the level of value. Whereas fulfillment and related emotional states do not constitute meaning, my theory makes the following observation:

> **Emotional Correlates:** Leading a meaningful life is reliably correlated with positive affective states like fulfillment, satisfaction, contentment, and happiness.

On my view, a meaningful life is not—conceptually speaking—the same thing as, say, a happy life or one filled with all and only pleasure; though positive emotional states often accompany a life oriented around purposes that matter, and which allow for descriptions of that life as making sense. Lives that are meaningful are, in general and on balance, accompanied by a range of positive mental and emotional states. Engagement with perceived value, accomplishing important goals (though see Landau 1995; Schopenhauer

1970; and Setiya 2017 for cautionary tales on overemphasizing a certain kind of goal-directed activity), and concluding that the various aspects of one's life fit together properly will leave one generally feeling full as opposed to empty; engaged and passionate as opposed to apathetic; and satisfied as opposed to dissatisfied.

A summary of prominent mental and emotional states that correlate with meaning is set out in Table 1.

Table 1 Mental and Emotional Correlates of the Meaningful/Meaningless

Positive/Meaningful	Negative/Meaningless
Fulfilled	Unfulfilled
Satisfied	Dissatisfied
Full	Empty
Content	Discontent
Captivated	Aloof
Engaged	Disengaged
Invigorated	Lethargic
Passionate	Passionless
Enlivened	Apathetic

Notice that my claim here is rather modest: the positive emotional states set out in Table 1 generally *correlate* with the presence of meaning. They are not identical to, always causally produced by, or perfectly correlated with the meaningful. As such, I take it that under certain conditions, one could lead a meaningful life (at least on this Earth)—one filled with value that motivates one's purposes and therefore fits together properly with what is true, good, and beautiful in our world—but that nonetheless is fraught with deep and sustained negative emotions. The life of St. Theresa of Calcutta here comes to mind, who, by her own admission, suffered decades-long darkness of mind and spirit (see St. Theresa of Calcutta 2007).

It is worth noting that my theory of meaningful life closely tracks an emerging consensus in the psychological literature on meaning—or at least the *experience* of meaning. Below are some prominent examples:

- "Meaning is the web of connections, understandings, and interpretations that help us comprehend our experience [intelligibility/sense-making] and formulate plans directing our energies to the achievement of our desired future [purpose]. Meaning provides us with the sense that our lives matter [significance], that they

make sense, and that they are more than the sum of our seconds, days, and years" (Steger 2012: 165–184).
- "Meaningfulness is the basic trust that life is worth living. It is based on a (mostly unconscious) evaluation of one's life as coherent [intelligibility/sense-making], significant [significance/ mattering], oriented [purpose] and belonging [intelligibility/ sense-making]" (Schnell 2021: 7).

Indeed, psychologists increasingly see the experience of meaning in life in terms of a triadic conception of meaning, involving the following elements:

> **Coherence:** One has a coherent sense of one's life as fitting together properly with values, goals, and the way the world is thought to be—to include the notion of belonging, which often involves perceiving oneself to be part of a larger whole.
> **Mattering:** One perceives oneself to be engaged with that which matters, and that one's decisions or acts have beneficial impacts and consequences on our relationships and the world around us.
> **Purpose:** One views one's life as having direction and purpose.

The last portion of the first component above (coherence) is telling. We want to be part of something more than merely parochial. Some tell us that this desire is satisfied through family, community, and culture. Many others are hoping for some deeper kind of connection with and in the cosmic drama. A capital 'P' *Place*. A capital 'H' *Home*. Charges of megalomania aside, they want the cosmos, partly at least, to be *about them*: that they are, as it were, knit into the very fabric of the cosmic narrative from beginning to end; that they are more than accidental features of the cosmic story; and that at least some human purposes intersect with *the* Purpose for which the cosmos exists in the first place. A worldview like theism provides more hospitable conditions for the fulfillment of these desires.

1.2.5 The Meaning Triad and Minds

Given the kind of thing that meaning is—closely connected with the triad of mattering, purpose, and sense-making—it requires minds for its existence. Imagine a universe without minds: one with only inanimate matter—rocks, trees, planets, stars—and one having no personal, intelligent cause. In such a universe, meaning would not exist. There would be nothing of significance; no goals, aims, or purposes; and nothing with rationality out of which states of affairs are rendered intelligible.

Take mattering. Minds are required in order to evaluate something as significant; though, as I indicated earlier, there are loose ways of speaking where something can be significant—sunlight for trees, for example—without minds. An asteroid impact that destroys a planet would be significant *for* the planet but not *to* it. In general, things matter *to someone*. If there is no *one* around, nothing really matters. Minds also are required in order for there to be aims, goals, and purposes—at least in an important sense. There are, of course, biological purposes so that we can speak of the purpose of hearts—to pump blood; and the purpose of lungs—to respirate. We can naturally talk about the purpose of acorns—to become mature oak trees. But the narrower sense of purpose requires minds—minds that aim toward goals. And finally, sense-making requires minds. States of affairs can be inherently sensible in themselves such that *if* there were minds around, those minds could make sense of them. However, if there are no minds, such sense is not made. Meaning requires minds. Will *finite* minds do? Yes and no.

Under this triadic conception of meaning, where the generating conditions for meaning come into existence with certain kinds of minds, meaning is available in a Godless—atheistic—universe. As long as there are minds with a similar cognitive sophistication to human minds, there can be mattering, purpose, and sense-making. What seems unlikely is the possibility of meaning in a *mindless* universe. As long as one is not an **eliminitivist** about minds and their properties (e.g., see Rosenberg 2011, 2018), then why not think that finite minds to whom relationships and activities matter, who set and strive toward purposes, and who seek to make sense of their lives can ground and express meaning? Of course, even if eliminitivism about minds and mental properties is true, one can still retreat to the phenomenal point of view, or *how it appears to us from the inside*. From the inside—to us, regardless of what is true outside of our phenomenal interior life—life appears meaningful in cases where terrestrial versions of mattering, purpose, and sense-making are present within a life. Even if illusory, we can still talk of the appearance of mattering, purpose, and sense-making; and therefore, of the appearance of being meaningful. But back to the point: meaning requires minds in a way that it does not require God. For example, water is H_2O regardless of whether there is a God. Meaning is similar.

Meaning does not cease being about mattering, purpose, and sense-making if there is no God; and versions of each are available in a Godless universe—though not, I think, in a mindless universe.

And yet, as I will argue later, a universe without God precludes deeper versions of mattering, purpose, and sense-making. Accompanying an infinite Mind who is responsible for the universe would be a much more robust, lasting, and secure kind of Meaning Triad (see Section 1.8).

> **Summary**
>
> Questions and concerns about meaning generally focus on one or more of the following triad of ideas: mattering, purpose, and sense-making. We are in search of something's mattering: whether, or why, or how it is significant. We inquire into something's purpose: what it is for, or why it does what it does. We are interested in rendering something intelligible: what sort of sense we can make out of it, or how it fits together with our background information. Meaningful life largely revolves around this triad. My triadic theory of meaning harmonizes with an emerging consensus in psychological science. Finally, this triad requires minds at least as cognitively and affectively sophisticated as human minds. No minds = no meaning.

1.3 Meanings Small and Big; Narrow and Wide

This book focuses on the question: *what makes life meaningful?* This question's scope is personal, focusing on *your* life or *my* life. It is not immediately and directly concerned with the more cosmically oriented question: *what is the meaning of life?* This latter question is about the entire universe or all life in the universe; or at least all human life—which, of course, includes your life and mine. The two questions are, however, connected. In this section, and those to follow, I will show that our concerns about life's meaning often move beyond the personal and local. They are generated in and by conditions that often have a cosmically focused starting point. At one level, the definition of "meaningful life" that I propose is independent of these considerations. Yet we leave something important out of this discussion if we focus only on the personal. The questions and concerns of Sections 1.3–1.7 not only intersect with meaningful life, but also provide part of the foundation for why God is relevant for meaningful life—a claim I will consider in more detail in Section 1.8.

It is now commonplace to distinguish *the* meaning *of* life (MofL) from meaning *in* life (MinL). This distinction frames common claims like, "One can find meaning *in* her life, even if there is no grand, cosmic meaning *of* life." MofL is more global or cosmic in scope, and takes up the perspective of *the universe* in assessing the meaning of human life and existence. It is big and wide; and it has as its focus something like a kind of capital "M" Meaning. The existence of this sort of meaning is generally thought to be wrapped up with the plausibility of ideas like God, transcendence, religion, or a spiritual, sacred realm. In asking for life's meaning, one is often asking for some sort of cosmic meaning of it all—though one also may be asking for the meaning of one's individual life *from the perspective of the cosmos*, since many think the meaning of their individual lives is tied to whether there is a meaning of it all.

MinL is focused on personal meaning: the meaning of our individual lives as located in the web of human endeavors and relationships *sub specie humanitatis*—within the frame of human cares and concerns. Many think that we can legitimately talk about life having meaning in this sense regardless of what is true about the meaning of the universe as a whole, or about the meaning of our individual lives from the perspective of the universe as a whole. MinL is narrower than cosmic meaning. Some might be inclined to think of it as small "m" meaning, though this likely will be met with resistance from some atheists. For what it is worth, I, as a theist, do not consider it to be less real—even if somehow impoverished—in virtue of categorizing it as small "m" meaning.

Meaning *of* Life versus Meaning *in* Life and the Meaning Triad

In general, the phrase "meaning *of* life" is cosmically focused; whereas "meaning *in* life" is personally focused. The Meaning Triad relates to both levels. Cosmically, the triad results in the following questions:

- *Significance:* "Do our lives really matter in the grand scheme of things?"

- *Purpose:* "Why are we here? Were we created for a purpose?"
- *Intelligibility:* "What's it all about? How does it all fit together?"

Personally, the triad results in the following questions:

- *Significance:* "Does my life matter to me? To my family, friends, and community?"
- *Purpose:* "What should I do with my life?"
- *Intelligibility:* "What is my life about? How does it fit together? Is it coherent?"

Do you think most people have questions and concerns about meaning at the cosmic or personal level?

I will use this distinction between MofL and MinL at various points. While I think there can be meaning *in* life without there being a meaning *of* life, I nonetheless find the following claims to be plausible:

Cosmic Focus: Very often, asking questions about meaning—even about the meaningfulness of my personal life—is motivated by cosmic concerns and framed cosmically (MofL).

Comic[2] Theism: Religious views of the world, and theism in particular, provide greater depth to human mattering and a more "centralized" human locatedness (or fit) within ultimate reality, and are therefore more hospitable to a deeper sort of meaning given that they provide a MofL.

Tragic Atheism: Even though there can be real meaning in life (MinL) on atheism, such meaning is mitigated by a prominent undercurrent of tragedy, given that an atheistic universe lacks MofL, and especially given its ultimate ending.

---

2   I use "comic" here in contrast with "tragic" in the literary sense of tragedy, where a tragedy is a serious, sober story with a sad and depressing ending. Whereas, traditionally, a comic story is both lighter-hearted (even humorous) and has a happy ending, I focus on the narrative's movement toward a happy ending, rather than it being a humorous story. The theistic story is certainly consistent with lots of laughter, but it is no less serious and sober than an atheistic story; and for that reason, applying the label "comic" to it is a bit misleading.

I develop and defend Claims 2 and 3 in greater detail in Section 1.8. Let us first turn our attention to Claim 1 in the next few sections.

> **Summary**
>
> Inquiring into the meaning of life can be both personal ("What is the meaning of *my* life?" or "What makes *my* life meaningful?") and cosmic ("What is *the* meaning of life?" or "What's it *all* about?"). It is now standard for philosophers working on this topic to distinguish meaning *in* life (MinL) from the meaning of life (MofL). Many—especially **optimistic atheists**—think that the first question can be answered in a way that allows for an existentially satisfying life even if there is no answer to the second question; or even if the answer to the second question is simply, "There isn't one." I myself am skeptical that MinL and MofL can be so cleanly separated.

1.4 Parts in Wholes: Meaning's Tilt Toward the Cosmic

Questions about meaning are partly generated by our capacity to get outside of ourselves. In exercising this capacity, we are able to view our lives from a wider standpoint—a standpoint from which to existentially locate our lives, understand them, and secure answers to questions about who we are; why we are here; what we should be doing while we are here; where we are going after we are here; and, especially, where *here* even is in the first place. We want to know our *place*. We possess self-awareness and the ability to take self-reflective meta-perspectives on our lives. In this, we are able to shift from automatic engagement to observation and evaluation. We do more than simply respond to streams of stimuli. Sometimes we step back a few paces: is getting upset that my team lost the championship really worth it, given that I should be more concerned about my failing grades? Does a bad test score really matter against the backdrop of my entire life? Sometimes we step *all the way back*: does my life matter in the grand cosmic scheme of things? We can step back far enough to ponder what it all *means*.

We place our lives and the human drama as a whole within the widest frame and evaluate them from that frame (cf. Nagel 1971).

The discussion in Section 1.2.3 is relevant here. Securing meaning is often about fitting something within a larger context or whole. It works this way with words, musical notes, and parts of a picture. It is not a stretch to think the situation is similar with the parts of our lives and our lives themselves. As I noted earlier: things partly (or largely) mean what they mean given their "location" within a larger whole. This is why Dilthey said that meaning is primarily a matter of something belonging to a whole, and why he emphasized the role of **worldviews** as vehicles of meaning. To put it succinctly, a worldview is an account of the existentially relevant aspects *of the whole* within which to situate our lives. It is akin to an existential map that "constitutes an overall perspective on life that sums up what we know about the world, how we evaluate it emotionally, and how we respond to it volitionally" (Makkreel 2001: 236). Worldviews, according to Dilthey, have three dimensions: cognitive, affective, and practical:

Cognitive: They provide answers to important questions of the human condition and fit those answers together in relation to one another.
Affective: They guide our emotional responses to the human condition.
Practical: They function like a map to help us successfully navigate the human condition.

Through them, we attempt to articulate the largest existentially relevant "whole"—as opposed to a *complete* whole that literally includes an account of all facts about the universe—out of which to understand and live our lives.

From that largest "whole," that widest standpoint—*sub specie aeternitatis* (literally, "from the perspective of eternity")—we wonder whether a reality of such staggering magnitude, at the deepest level, cares about us: a concern about whether we matter. Does it have for us anything resembling a purpose: a concern about why we are here? We wonder how such infinitesimally small and fleeting creatures like ourselves, with our deepest hopes and fears, fit within such a reality: a concern about how to make sense of and fit our human lives together with everything else. Worldviews, in this way, center on the cluster of cares and concerns brought into focus by the Meaning Triad.

That our concerns about meaning are often cosmically focused is instructive. In the words of sociologist Peter Berger, in seeking life's meaning, many are attempting to locate it "within a sacred and cosmic frame of reference" of trying to plumb the connection "between microcosm and macrocosm" (Berger 1970: 27). This is an important reason why God, transcendence, and other ideas embodied and expressed in religion are so often thought to be lurking just around the corner from meaning. In locating the scope of human activity within a wider context, that wider context serves a role in determining the meaning of the thing located therein. If that wider context is an atheistic worldview—no God, no souls, no afterlife—one can see how worries about meaning are generated. If the wider context is a theistic worldview—God, cosmic purpose, cosmic care, souls, afterlife, perfect justice—one can see how this is plausibly more hospitable for meaning. Regardless, meaning is partly a function of *locating* our lives within a larger frame, context, or whole; and the widest of such "wholes" is the *cosmic* backdrop to human existence. Reflecting on our lives against this backdrop motivates substantial swaths of human questioning and concern over meaning.

> **Summary**
>
> Very often, when we inquire into something's meaning, we seek to "locate" it within a larger context. In this way, meaning is a part-in-whole relationship, where the meaning of the part is found in locating its place within a larger whole—the meaning of a word in the larger whole of the sentence; the meaning of the musical note in the larger whole of the composition; the meaning of life within the larger whole of the universe. Indeed, when we consider the conditions under which people often ask questions about life's meaning, many of those conditions include a cosmic focus: one in which those asking ponder their lives within a temporally and spatially vast, silent, and uncaring universe—*sub specie aeternitatis*, and not only or always *sub specie humanitatis*.

1.5 The "Loss" of Meaning: Meaning's Tilt Toward Transcendence

It proves difficult to fully and finally separate meaning from God, transcendence, and religion. Meaning is intertwined with them; and one loses something important about meaning when divorcing it from them. Albert Einstein (1879–1955) once said that "to know an answer to the question 'What is the meaning of human life?' means to be religious" (Einstein 1934: 11). Perhaps his statement is too strong. Others have theorized that religion itself developed as an answer to humanity's concern over meaning, and especially our anxieties over death.

Regardless of the precise relationship between meaning and God, the question of life's meaning appears tied to the perceived loss of a transcendence that secured deep versions of mattering, purpose, and sense-making. For a significant portion of human history, there was an expectation by many—nurtured in a way of looking at the cosmos—that the universe is the product of powerful, benevolent, personal, transcendent intentionality. Such a view of the world is hospitable to securing a unique kind of mattering, purpose, and sense-making—in a word, *meaning*—as part of the deep fabric of reality, because at the heart of reality are infinite Mind, intentionality, and value. Before a certain period in history, worrying and inquiring about meaning as such were not, by and large, on people's minds—partly because meaning, or the conditions of meaning, were already inherent in what was considered to be true about the world (e.g., see Young 2014).

Implicit in the background was an expectation that meaning resided in and flowed down from this meaning-hospitable setting. In the modern world, that expectation still lingered (after all, it is not the sort of thing that can be easily gotten rid of); but the expectation came under increased pressure as people began to wrestle with the potential implications of our growing understanding of the natural world in which we live. One thinks here of interpretations of, and reactions to, Copernicus (1473–1543) and Darwin (1809–1882). Though the historical story is complex, the development of the heliocentric astronomical theory of Copernicus and Galileo caused some to wonder about human significance and specialness in a vast universe in which the Earth was no longer thought to be at the center. This change from geocentrism to heliocentrism is likely a piece of the explanatory puzzle as to why people in modernity became increasingly concerned about life's meaning. Of course, Psalm 8 in the Hebrew Bible is just one example demonstrating that people prior to the sixteenth century already wondered about their place in a staggering cosmos:

> When I look at your heavens, the work of your fingers,
>   the moon and the stars, which you have set in place,
> what is man that you are mindful of him,
>   and the son of man that you care for him?
>
> (vs. 3–4; ESV).

Darwin's biological theory about the long, arduous, and suffering-riddled process of evolution prompted others to worry about whether humans are the product of caring creation and providence. This, too, is probably a piece of the explanatory puzzle of the modern human preoccupation with meaning. Though neither of these theories in and of itself need be thought of as requiring atheism, they are both likely important for understanding the rise of this view. Its ascendance in the modern world was itself accompanied by growing concerns over whether life has any meaning.

Here, it is worth considering whether asking for life's meaning, when framed by the abovementioned kinds of concerns, is largely rhetorical. In such settings, it may be that to ask, "What is the meaning of life?" is to engage in a kind of *rhetoric of lament* for an absolute, though "lost" cosmic meaning in which to live, move, have, and *interpret* our being (cf. Acts 17:28)—the kind of meaning that atheism seems ill-equipped to provide. In this way, it may be that the question in its traditional form becomes pressing precisely when this type of meaning appears to be lost, at the point when the question can no longer be answered.

Summary

Not everyone asks questions about life's meaning during times of crisis; but many do. We worry about meaning when "things" aren't going well: when we are dissatisfied with our job or our life; when sitting in an empty nest for the first time; when we get really sick; when someone we love dies; when contemplating our own demise. Historically, questioning life's meaning—at the cosmic level, *sub specie aeternitatis*—was (and continues to be) connected with a perception that

> "things" *aren't going well* at the cosmic level. Here "not going well" is simply to say that the reality of once-believed-in entities that themselves are thought to be part of the necessary architecture for meaning—like God, transcendence, cosmic purpose, souls, perfect justice, etc.—is now in doubt. Insofar as this is in doubt, meaning itself may be in doubt.

1.6 Absurdity: Meaning's Tilt Toward Existential Coherence

Absurdities do not make sense. They involve ill-fitting combinations of two or more things. As philosopher Rivka Weinberg says: "Absurdity occurs when things are so ill-fitting or ill-suited to their purpose or situation as to be ridiculous" (Weinberg 2015). Philosopher Thomas Nagel remarks that: "In ordinary life a situation is absurd when it includes a conspicuous discrepancy between pretension or aspiration and reality" (Nagel 1971: 718). Paradigmatic examples of absurdity are instances of logical or semantic absurdity, such as the following:

1. You are both reading and not reading this sentence at the same time and in the same sense.
2. I cannot type a sentence in English (even though I just did).

Such claims are absurd: they do not make sense. They are meaningless. They are grammatical and can be understood, of course. And yet they are nonsensical in an important way. Logical absurdity is not the only kind of absurdity, though. We often use "absurdity" more broadly to describe scenarios that exhibit other types of lack of fit, such as the following:

3. Demanding that your cat tell you the time.
4. Bringing a calculator to use for your philosophy exam.
5. Showing up to your concert with a baseball mitt instead of your violin.
6. Mowing your lawn during a tornado warning.

We can think of 3–6 above as exhibiting a kind of *practical* absurdity. Each is absurd for a similar reason to why 1 and 2 above are absurd. Each exhibits a lack of fit: a lack of fit between a cat's abilities and the sort of abilities needed to tell the time; a lack of fit between what a baseball mitt is for and what a concert is; and so on. This kind of practical absurdity is relevant to life's meaning.

It is not uncommon for people to claim that *life* itself is absurd. Such claims might be directed at the level of an individual's life and the parts of that life; but more often, charges of absurdity are directed at life *when viewed from the cosmic perspective*. They have as their focus a kind of normative and/or existential fittingness between things: between individual life or human life and the universe. At the personal level, someone might say, "It is absurd to spend so much of your time watching reruns on Netflix." Why? Because this sort of activity does not fit with what is ostensibly true about the world in terms of value. Some have said that human life itself is absurd; that it does not make sense at the cosmic level if our deep investments in creativity, personal moral advancement, and especially loving relationships all come to naught at death. The famous Russian novelist Leo Tolstoy (1828–1910) seems to have held this view. It is worth listening to him at length:

> So I lived, but then something strange began to happen to me. I began to experience moments of perplexity where life "froze," as though I did not know what to do or how to live, and I felt lost and became dejected. But this passed, and I went on living as before. Then these moments of perplexity began to reoccur more and more frequently, and invariably took the same form. When they came, the same questions kept coming to my mind: "Why? What is it for? What does it lead to?" ... While thinking about the management of my household and estate, which greatly preoccupied me at that time, the question would suddenly occur: "Well, you have five thousands [sic] acres of land, and three hundred horses—What then? So what?" I was absolutely muddled up inside, and did not know what to think. When thinking about how best to educate my children, I would ask myself: "What for?" Or when thinking about how best to promote the welfare of the peasants, I would suddenly say to myself: "But what does it matter to me?" And when I thought about the fame that all my literary works would bring to me, I would say to myself: "Very well, I will become famous. So what? What then?" ... My question—that which at the age of fifty brought me to the verge of suicide—was the simplest of questions, a question lying in the soul of every person. It was a question without an answer to which one cannot live, as I had found by experience. It was:

"What will come of what I am doing today or shall do tomorrow? What will come of my life? What is life for?" Differently expressed, the question is: "Why should I live, why hope for anything, or do anything?" It can also be expressed thus: "Does my life have any meaning that death cannot destroy?"

(Tolstoy 2006, 46–51).

Along with Tolstoy, it strikes many as—practically or existentially—absurd that what is most important to us has no ultimate, lasting traction in an atheistic world.

Shakespeare's (1564–1616) Macbeth laments that life "is a tale told by an idiot, full of sound and fury, signifying nothing" (Shakespeare, *Macbeth*, Act 5, Scene 2. Of note, some modern versions of the text replace "signifying" with "meaning"). One way to understand Macbeth's words is that he is lamenting that life does not make sense; that various aspects—especially those with existential gravitas—fail to fit together properly. Could it really be that no deep rhyme or reason frames the existentially profound stuff of life, as some twentieth-century thinkers have asserted? Does it unfold on a Samuel Beckett (1906–1989)-style stage, a kind of theatre of the absurd? Is life like Beckett's 35-second play *Breathe*, in which the curtain opens on a stage littered with junk; we hear a birth-cry, followed by a recording of somebody slowly inhaling and exhaling; and then the play quickly concludes with the curtain closing? To channel Bertrand Russell (1872–1970), are our joys, sorrows, and hopes—and all that induces them—simply accidental collocations of atoms that are here today and then quickly gone and forgotten forever? Surely, this is absurd; it makes no sense. No narrow logical norms are violated, of course; but a broader, existentially worrisome lack of fit surfaces.

Or take Albert Camus' (1913–1960) concept of the absurd: the profound discrepancy between the intense human desire for happiness and reason to coalesce and the utter silence of the universe to quench such desire. As individuals, many of our deepest desires remain unfulfilled amid cosmic silence (see "Pascal on Cosmic Silence" box). Camus calls this absurd. For both Shakespeare's Macbeth and Camus, life lacks an important kind of meaning—at least an existentially satisfying one. It is (cosmically) meaningless because its various parts do not (broadly) fit together. Some features of the universe—for example, deep longings for love to continue forever, and for ultimate justice to be served—appear not to fit with some other features of the universe if atheism is true—for example, death followed by a permanent dissolution of the human person and the ultimate "death" of the universe.

> ### Pascal on Cosmic Silence
>
> In his famous *Pensées*, French philosopher Blaise Pascal (1623–1662) wrestles with his place in an ancient, vast, and silent universe—one that seems wholly unconcerned with him. Below are some of his more provocative statements:
>
> - "When I consider the brief span of my life absorbed into the eternity which comes before and after – as the remembrance of a guest that tarrieth but a day – the small space I occupy and which I see swallowed up in the infinite immensity of spaces of which I know nothing and which know nothing of me, I take fright and am amazed to see myself here rather than there: there is no reason for me to be here rather than there, now rather than then. Who put me here? By whose command and act were this time and place allotted to me?" (Pascal 1995: 19).
> - "When I see the blind and wretched state of man, when I survey the whole universe in its dumbness and man left to himself with no light, as though lost in this corner of the universe, without knowing who put him there, what he has come to do, what will become of him when he dies, incapable of knowing anything, I am moved to terror, like a man transported in his sleep to some terrifying desert island, who wakes up quite lost and with no means of escape" (Pascal 1995: 59).
> - "The eternal silence of these infinite spaces fills me with dread" (Pascal 1995: 66).
>
> Do you share any of Pascal's sentiments? Why or why not?

For both Macbeth and Camus, being told a grand atheistic story or explanation of the cosmos would not suffice to render life intelligible on the fronts that really worry them. Despite providing sense-making in real, even powerful, ways, it does not allow for a fittingness between deep human longings and hopes and reality in the way that Macbeth, Camus, and countless others seem to want. For this reason, many think that an atheistic story of the universe is, at heart, an absurd tale told by an idiot. It does not make sense. Optimistic atheists, of course, will demur. **Pessimistic atheists** and theists have inflated expectations regarding existential fit, so the argument goes. They set the meaning bar too high. This rift reveals deep disagreement about both what needs to fit together and what is necessary for it to fit together.

An atheistic **metanarrative**, no doubt, makes sense of the world at one level. Atheism provides a kind of sense-making framework for situating life in the universe. It provides a type of intelligibility—a way of fitting together things that are part and parcel of the human condition. Even with this framework in hand, however, those who worry about life's meaning will think that life is absurd given atheism. For them, life still lacks an important kind of meaning. In terms of the sense-making aspect of the Meaning Triad conceived of cosmically, it fails to fit together properly. Why? Because deep human longings—especially along the mattering and purpose axes—and deep hopes for *ultimate* justice and a *lasting* place for love and felicity are stubborn. These longings do not fit (or at least do so in much thinner form) within an atheistic universe.

The human search for meaning is not so easily disentangled from our capacity to take up meta-perspectives; to set and evaluate our lives within wider frames—even cosmic ones—whether theistic, otherwise religious but non-theistic, or atheistic; and to ask what sort of sense they make and how they fit within the contours of those frames. I am skeptical that we can fully understand what is involved in the human search for meaning if we neglect this. And when we perceive that our lives and their various parts do not fit within such frames, we find ourselves entertaining the possibility that they are meaningless.

> **Summary**
>
> One way of thinking about meaning is in terms of something *making sense*. Things that make sense are meaningful; things that do not make sense are not meaningful, or meaningless. A way of thinking about what it means to "make sense of" something is in terms of things *fitting together* properly. If

something fits together properly with something else, we say it makes sense. Sense-making can be thought of narrowly—as in: it does not make sense to ask what is funnier than the funniest thing; or broadly—as in: it makes no sense to water your plants 30 seconds after you already watered them. The broad notion of sense-making has applications for life's meaning. Some are inclined to say that our lives in this universe fail to make an important kind of sense if atheism is true—their various parts do not appropriately fit with what atheism claims is true about us and this universe in which we live.

1.7 Death: Meaning's Tilt Toward the End[3]

Human preoccupation with meaning often tracks human preoccupation with death. It is a common though contested claim that death, as construed by atheism as involving the permanent cessation of human consciousness, renders life futile. It is worth examining this claim in greater detail. The intersection of futility and meaning also positions theism as more hospitable to deeper meaning. If atheism is true and death is the end—period—then life is futile, so the argument goes. It is not exactly clear what people mean by this, but the sentiment behind it is both intense and widely shared. Is such a strong pessimistic view reasonable? Is there something correct in thinking that life is, in some important sense, futile if death is the absolute end?

In order to investigate this idea, I must first be clear about what I mean by *futility*. In normal cases, something is futile when accomplishing or fulfilling what is aimed at or desired is impossible. Here are some examples. It is futile for you to try both to go to a concert and not go to a concert at the same time and in the same sense. It is futile to try to jump over the moon. Both are impossible, though in different ways. The first is logically impossible. The second is physically impossible. Futility in this way is similar to the concept of absurdity that I introduced earlier. They both involve a *lack of fit*—often between one's aspirations and a reality that does not cooperate with them. It is natural, therefore, to claim that trying to

---

3 Much of Section 1.7 borrows from Goetz and Seachris 2020.

accomplish futile tasks—like trying to write this book that you now read in five seconds—is absurd.

An important implication of the preceding account of futility is that the existential angst that accompanies some instance of futility is proportional to how you feel about that which is futile. The extent to which you are invested—for example, emotionally and relationally—in attempting to reach some desired end will affect how you respond to real or *perceived* futility (I emphasize "perceived" because, after all, you could be wrong about whether something is, in fact, futile). Say you have a passing curiosity to experience what it is like to dunk like LeBron James. It would be futile for most of us to attempt to dunk like LeBron. Though you might be slightly agitated about not being able to experience this, it is doubtful that you would experience soul-crushing angst. Contrast that with a situation where you have trained for years to run the Boston Marathon, but one week prior to the event you break your leg in an automobile accident. To try to run the marathon now would be futile. Given its central place in your life, you would naturally feel substantial existential angst at being unable to compete. Years of training would be unrewarded. Deep hopes would be dashed. A central life goal is now unfulfilled. How one feels about futility will thus vary, depending on circumstances. We can call this the *principle of proportionality*.

> **Principle of Proportionality:** The level of existential angst accompanying futility is proportional to the level of one's investment in some desired end and the relative desirability of that end.

How does this all relate to life's meaning? What might people have in mind when they say that life itself is futile if atheism is true and death is the last word of our lives and of the universe itself? The discrepancy here from which a sense of futility emerges is between central longings of the human heart and a world devoid of God and an afterlife, which is a world incapable of fulfilling such longings in any ultimate way. There is a stark incongruity between what we really want (even what we think we need) and an utterly silent atheistic reality that does not care.

There is also a discrepancy between the final state of affairs where quite literally nothing matters, and the current state of affairs where many things seem to matter—for example, one's happiness and the happiness of others, relationships, personal and cultural achievements, and scientific advancements, among other things. It seems hard to fathom that the things with such existential profundity to us are but a vapor in the grand scheme of things. We might also call this *absurd*, given that absurdity and futility involve a similar sort of incongruity.

Futility, then, connects to hopes and expectations about fulfillment and longevity. In some circumstances, we are inclined to think that a situation exhibits futility if it does not last as long as we think it should last, given the kind of thing that it is. If you are a veteran who served in Afghanistan (2001–2021), incurring trauma and loss, you will be inclined to think that your efforts were futile, given the collapse of Afghanistan's state and the suffering of the Afghan people following the 2021 US withdrawal from the country. You may not, however, think that your efforts were futile if the state lasts for many centuries.

Some say that an average human lifetime with average human experiences is sufficient to satiate core human longings, and for us to accomplish central purposes. Others, however, think that only eternity is long enough to do justice to those aspects of the human condition of superlative value—primarily, and especially, happiness and love, understood roughly as commitment to the true good or wellbeing of another. There are some things that have such gravitas and are so sublime that for them to be extinguished, even after billions upon billions of years, is truly tragic. Anything less than forever is less than enough time for them, and leads to a sense of futility. We want the most important things in life to last indefinitely. But if atheism is true, all will be dissolved in death; it will be as if none of this ever happened. If the important stuff of life that we are so invested in lasts only a short while, life itself is ultimately futile.

The preceding discussion of futility reveals that we often give the ending of something an important role in assessing that thing. With life's meaning in view, the worry is that life's meaning is jeopardized if, in the end, all comes indelibly to naught. Such worries have been articulated in what some call "final outcome arguments" (Wielenberg 2005). A final outcome argument is one whose conclusion is that life is meaningless (or its meaning is somehow threatened), absurd, or futile because of a "bad" ending, where "bad" ending tracks something like the atheistic idea that at death, we cease to exist; and where the prospects for ultimate justice are vanishingly thin. You can imagine weaker and stronger conclusions for such arguments, such as the following:

> **Slightly Bad:** A "bad" ending only slightly mitigates meaning.
> **Partly/Specifically Bad:** A "bad" ending threatens certain kinds of meaning but not others, and/or threatens meaning in certain ways but not in other ways.
> **Really Bad:** A "bad" ending completely destroys any and all meaning.

My own view is somewhere in the neighborhood of the "Partly/Specifically Bad" version. I can imagine life mattering in a certain way precisely because it is so short. The brevity of conscious existence and the possibility of it being extinguished forever *in the next moment* infuse our brief lives with a profound sort of specialness. On the other hand, such an ending would threaten meaning in other ways—for example, as our experience of intrinsic value in our relationships, in our joys and other pleasures, and in our interaction with goodness is extinguished forever. Such an ending would be mixed news for meaning; and I find the bad news much more lamentable than I find the good news consoling. Regardless, what all final outcome arguments have in common is that they give the ending an important role in evaluating life's meaning.

Why think that endings have such power? Many have argued that giving them this power arbitrarily privileges the future over the past. Thomas Nagel once said that: "[I]t does not matter now that in a million years nothing we do now will matter" (Nagel 1971: 716). Why should we think the future is more important or relevant than the past and the present when it comes to assessing meaning?

Contra Nagel, there are reasons why the future is important, and why how life ends is relevant for evaluating its meaning. Compare two very different endings to life and the universe, the first of which is the way it will all end if Bertrand Russell is right:

> **Atheistic Dissolution:** "That man is the product of causes which had no prevision of the end they were achieving; that his origin, his growth, his hopes and fears, his loves and his beliefs, are but the outcome of accidental collocations of atoms; that no fire, no heroism, no intensity of thought and feeling, can preserve an individual life beyond the grave; that all the labors of the ages, all the devotion, all the inspiration,

all the noonday brightness of human genius, are destined to extinction in the vast death of the solar system, and that the whole temple of man's achievement must inevitably be buried beneath the debris of a universe in ruins."

(Russell 1957: 107).

The second is how it will all end if St. John's vision on the isle of Patmos and recorded in the New Testament Book of Revelation is true:

> **Theistic Redemption:** "Then I saw a new heaven and a new earth, for the first heaven and the first earth had passed away, and the sea was no more. And I saw the holy city, new Jerusalem, coming down out of heaven from God, prepared as a bride adorned for her husband. And I heard a loud voice from the throne saying, 'Behold, the dwelling place of God is with man. He will dwell with them, and they will be his people, and God himself will be with them as their God. He will wipe away every tear from their eyes, and death shall be no more, neither shall there be mourning, nor crying, nor pain anymore, for the former things have passed away.'"
>
> (Revelation 21:1–4; ESV).

These, of course, are not the only accounts of how life and the universe might end. Rather, the point being made is that the way something ends—and these are two strikingly different endings to our lives and the universe—importantly bears on how one feels about life right now, informing either optimism or pessimism, or something in between. Think about these two endings and suppose you are asked which you would prefer to be the ending of your story. Do you really have no preference? I do—and what I suspect is a fairly widespread preference gives me reason to think that outcome matters; that the way the whole *story* of life ends is important for how we evaluate life here and now before the end. Let us now consider some reasons to think that outcomes and endings matter—not just for, say, games, but for life itself.

1.7.1 A Changing Past?

To where can we look to motivate and substantiate the central claim in final outcome arguments—that the ending of life is relevant for appraisals of life's meaning? One such place is in an initially counterintuitive idea: *a changing past*. Now, unless you think that time travel is possible, you will think that the past is fixed, settled. In a word, "past." There is no use crying over spilt milk, we say. Philosophers often talk about the necessity of the past. Once something has occurred, it cannot be altered. In this way, there is an asymmetry between the fixity of the past and the openness of the future; unless you are a determinist, in which case both the past and the future are fixed because *everything* is determined.

That said, the claim that the future can, in some sense, alter the past need not imply some strict change to events that have already occurred—for example, by making an event that occurred un-occur. The sort of change I have in mind is weaker, though still important: namely, that the future has the power to alter the *significance* of the past—a kind of meaning-altering influence. Here is how.

The description and significance of past events can change as context shifts through a dynamic relationship with later events. We can account for this change by distinguishing the *thick* past from the *thin* past. The thick past—the past as told by historians—makes use of descriptions of events in terms of the results and implications of those events. For example, "The Thirty Years War began in 1618" is a thicker description of events described thinly as "Various Protestant and Catholic states skirmished in and around 1618," because the former describes the events referred to in the latter in terms of how long the skirmish lasted (cf. Danto 1968). Though it is implausible to think that the thin (or the thinnest) past can change, the thick past changes in its significance and meaning as it enters into new relationships with later events. Consider the following scenario:

> **Touchdown Pass:** Notre Dame's quarterback throws a touchdown pass with one minute left in the final quarter of the game against the University of Southern California. The thick description of that touchdown pass—above and beyond a mere physical description of the ball's velocity, distance thrown, and so on—will change depending on whether Notre Dame goes on to win the game. If they do win, the thick past can now include the description that the quarterback threw the winning pass with a minute to go. If they lose, it cannot be the winning pass. Something about the past remains fixed, but something not entirely trivial changes given the outcome of the game. The future alters the significance and meaning of the pass—and the past!

In this scenario, nothing changes about the touchdown pass in the strict (or thin) sense after the game's outcome. A ball was thrown; it was caught; and a touchdown was scored. That said, as the future unfolds, complete with additional layers of description, the same event acquires new significance—indeed, new meaning. Later events, including outcomes, foist new properties onto earlier events, thus "altering" the past.

Significance and meaning evolve as events are situated within and framed by an expanding context. The touchdown pass thrown with one minute left in the fourth quarter means something different or accrues additional layers of meaning depending on whether Notre Dame wins the game. Winning passes are still *touchdown* passes in the thinner sense, and simply *passes* in a still thinner sense, and *objects with such and such velocity* in a still thinner sense and ... (you get the idea); but they are more in a thicker sense. They acquire new significance by virtue of when and under what circumstances they are thrown. Furthermore, it is not simply that they can now be described as "winning" passes; they acquire an emotional significance and added value that they would not have had otherwise. They acquire additional varieties of significance and meaning on other levels too, many of which are not fully actualized until the event is placed within even wider contexts. For example, the pass ignited the team in new ways that set the trajectory for an undefeated season. The preceding is a temporal version of a more general feature of part-whole relations in which some parts acquire new layers of significance in virtue of their relation to the whole. A line on a sheet of paper might represent a road in Mexico, part of a character in the English alphabet, or the right arm of a stick figure. What it *is* crucially depends on the whole of which it is a part (cf. Section 1.2.3).

The events of our lives—and our lives themselves, if placed in larger contexts—might be like that touchdown pass (or the right arm of that stick figure) in interesting ways. Winning a national championship, becoming a Rhodes Scholar, getting married, discovering a cure for cancer, enjoying treasured moments with loved ones, and so on do not cease being what they are because our lives end in one way as opposed to another. In this sense, they are akin to the *thin* past. However, the precise shape of the ending changes something about them—the kind of thicker descriptions that they can reasonably be given; how we evaluate them within the entire scope of the grand narrative of reality; and how we ultimately feel about them and our very lives of which they are a part.

This brings to mind former Phoenix Suns point guard Rex Chapman, who hit an improbable, running, off-balance, three-point basket to tie a playoff game with the Seattle Supersonics and send it into overtime back in 1997. In the overtime period, Seattle, not Phoenix, won the game. These were Chapman's words after the game: "It was great at the time, but we let the opportunity it gave us get away. I'm sure it was exciting to watch, but it's just a basket in a loss" (Lexington (KY) *Herald-Leader*, May 3, 1997).

Neither Chapman nor anyone else is arguing that the shot somehow lost some of its intrinsic greatness because the Suns eventually lost. It was an amazing shot. Nothing can change that. He, his teammates, and their fans would have felt great joy as the ball went through the net. No one doubts that. But, given the final outcome—a loss—that joy is muted. The significance of the shot is lessened. And the emotional connotations the shot initially acquired are reduced and supplanted by others, themselves then galvanized—especially the sadness accompanying the ultimate losing effort. Pessimistic atheists and **supernaturalists** have a Rex Chapman-like sense about life if atheism, along with its ending, is true. I think such sentiments are on target.

1.7.2 Narrative Ending

A second strategy to support the idea that later events can alter the characteristics and significance of what comes earlier—and, more to the point here, that endings are important for evaluations of life's relative meaningfulness—is through the idea of narrative ending. The way a narrative ends is important. A narrative's ending is not merely the last piece of narration in a succession of narrated events. In being the *last* word, it also contributes to indelibly structuring the whole, and in so doing affects the meaning of the whole in terms of both significance and sense-making. In virtue of being the end, it has the power to elicit a wide range of broadly normative responses on emotional, esthetic, and evaluative levels toward the story as a whole. The ending's power to "reach back" and influence in a final way the entire narrative is relevant here given the close connection that discussions of death and futility have with the meaning of life. Conclusions that the atheistic metanarrative suffers from cosmic futility, absurdity, or meaninglessness, for example, are saliently connected with claims about how it is all going to end on both the individual and cosmic levels.

Why think that a narrative's ending has such retroactive power? Is this simply an instance of arbitrarily prioritizing the later over the earlier? What gives the conclusion such potency to yield a settled stance toward the narrative as a whole? Embedded within his account of what narrative explanation is, philosopher David Velleman briefly articulates how the end shapes and galvanizes our perspective on the entire narrative, especially on the emotional level:

> What's more, the emotion that resolves a narrative cadence tends to subsume the emotions that preceded it: the triumph felt at a happy ending is the triumph of ambitions realized and anxieties allayed; the grief felt at a tragic ending is the grief of hopes dashed or loves denied. Hence the conclusory emotion in a narrative cadence embodies not just how the audience feels about the ending; it embodies how the audience feels, at the ending, about the whole story. Having passed through emotional ups and downs of the story, as one event succeeded another, the audience comes to rest in a stable attitude about the series of events in its entirety.
>
> (Velleman 2003: 19).

This is no small point. The ending marks the last word, after which nothing else can be said, either by way of remedying problems or destroying felicities that have come about within the narrative. If the last word is that hope is finally and irreversibly dashed, the end will be indelibly characterized by despair and grief. If the last word is that deep longings have been satisfied, then joy will be indelible at the end. Perhaps more importantly, one cannot backtrack into a narrative—for example, where the grief felt at a tragic ending is the final word—and expect that one's emotional stance toward any specific event within the narrative or the narrative as a whole will not now be affected by its ending. The ending relevantly frames the entire story, as it does our normative evaluations and emotional response to it. Recall Rex Chapman's three-point basket in that playoff loss!

The evaluative priority and indelibility of the final stance one takes toward a narrative because of the way it ends provide insight into the importance of apocalyptic accounts (apocalyptic: relating to the ultimate destiny of the world), whether atheistic or theistic, to how we appraise life. It is why so many have difficulty shaking conclusions of cosmic futility, absurdity, and meaninglessness on metanarratives where death has the final word, and happiness and love are eventually consigned to everlasting oblivion. In order to avoid ultimate meaninglessness, many see a practical, existential, and rational need for positing an ending where happiness, love, and other markers of human flourishing have a lasting place. The general point here, though, is that the way an individual life ends is important to us to the extent that that life is something like a lived narrative. If we view the history of the cosmos as a whole as a meta*narrative*, it potentially becomes clearer why many of us are so concerned with how it all will end. Neither atheist nor theist can wholly avoid the evaluative encroachment of the cosmos's ultimate ending into the present moment of their respective metanarratives. It really does make a difference whether Bertrand Russell, or St. John in Revelation (noted earlier), or someone else is right about the ending of life and the universe.

So, the ending of the story of life—on both the personal and cosmic levels—can retroactively influence and alter the mattering and sense-making meanings of what came earlier. And this point provides some reason to think that privileging the future—or, less ambitiously, simply claiming that it is relevant—in terms of its finality as an outcome may be neither arbitrary nor irrational, since mattering and sense-making meanings are malleable when something is placed in a larger context where later events come to bear on it.

It is worth noting that the ending's power over the events preceding and leading up to it is not simply an issue of its general temporal place as later in the narrative's timeline. This is one reason why it is misguided to charge those who give the ending such power with time bias. It is that the ending is the final, settled, indelible word that relevantly frames the entire ending and pre-ending context. It is the fact that it is *settled* by virtue of being last, not merely that it *is* last. Last "words" often possess deep significance in virtue of their finality:

- "Don't ask me again, and that is final!"
- A judge reading the verdict at the end of a trial: "Life in prison."
- The final grade you receive in a course.
- Your death.
- The heat "death" of the universe.

All of these are stark due, in part, to their finality. As the character Dr. Who says in Season Nine, Episode 11 of the beloved BBC series:

> It's funny, the day you lose someone isn't the worst.
> At least you've got something to do.
> It's all the days they stay dead.

If atheism is true, the settled word is that all life and love and progress and conscious experience will ultimately end in oblivion, tenuous prospects for transhumanism or secular immortality aside. The cosmic story, then, is that the rich technicolor of human existence is bookended on either side by utter silence. C. S. Lewis (1898–1963), the influential Christian writer and author of *The Chronicles of Narnia* stories, put it poignantly in another writing:

> If Nature is all that exists – in other words, if there is no God and no life of some quite different sort somewhere outside Nature – then all stories will end in the same way: in a universe from which all life is banished without possibility of return. It will have been an accidental flicker, and there will be no one even to remember it.
> (Lewis 1986: 74).

Though no atheist, Lewis here agrees with Bertrand Russell, whom I quoted earlier in this opening statement. If atheism is true, the ending is stark—as are its implications for the whole story.

Summary

Concerns about life's meaning are close companions to concerns about death and the ending of life and the universe in general. Many are wary of claims that life is rendered futile or absurd if, at death, our conscious, first-person experience is extinguished forever. That something *ends* does not automatically entail that it, in its pre-ending state, is worthless, valueless, absurd, futile, or meaningless. Yet there are reasons to think that endings—by virtue of being the *final*, definitive word—have the potency to either cast a long shadow over life or, alternatively, provide hope for a redemption that can wipe even the bitterest tears from our eyes.

1.8 Why Theism Is Better News: Meaning's Tilt Toward God

Meaning would be available in a Godless universe insofar as a Godless universe is possible. Why? As long as there are minds in that universe with sufficient capacities to generate mattering, purpose, and sense-making, the conditions for meaning are available, even if such minds are *finite* (see Section 1.2.5). An infinite Mind is not necessary for some manifestations of meaning just as an infinite Mind is not needed for water to be two parts hydrogen and one part oxygen; though I am quite sympathetic to the view that says if there were no infinite Mind, there would be nothing else in existence, including water and meaning.

As a theist, I do not think there would be finite minds—or anything else, for that matter—without the existence of an infinite Mind. In that sense, then, I do not think there would be any meaning without an infinite Mind, just as there would be no water if there were no God, because there would be nothing at all if there were no God. That said, I am happy to bracket this consideration, and agree that there could be meaning in an atheistic world provided that such a world contains finite minds with the relevant meaning-generating capacities. While real meaning is possible on atheism given this caveat, the news for meaning is much better on theism. How so? Ideas like *enhance, deepen, ultimate, fundamental, everlasting*, and *objective* partly capture how theism is better news for meaning. Theism uniquely positions the triadic conception of meaning—mattering, purpose, sense-making—at the very heart of reality, because an infinite Mind inhabits that place. It also provides conceptual space that atheism does not in which to situate additional interrelated aspects of the human concern about meaning:

Meaning's Tilt Toward the Cosmic: Concerns about meaning often are motivated out of cosmic concerns related to our place in the universe (see Section 1.4).

Meaning's Tilt Toward Transcendence: Concerns about meaning often are reactions to the perceived "loss" of, or doubt about, a transcendent realm (see Section 1.5).

Meaning's Tilt Toward Existential Coherence: Concerns about meaning often reflect worries that central features of human life fail to make sense in an important way on atheism (see Section 1.6).

We can add to this one additional aspect to our human concern about meaning:

Meaning's Tilt Toward the End: Concerns about meaning often accompany reflection on death and endings (see Section 1.7).

As we stare squarely at the end of life—our own, that of our species, and that of the universe—a theistic account of reality tends toward the *comic*; whereas atheism tends toward the *tragic*. Given the evaluative importance of endings, each ending is relevant to assessments of life's meaning. Atheism is insufficiently sensitive to the precise shape of the above four concerns, and to the prominent role each plays in generating questions about life's meaning (and meaningfulness).

As a result, I am sympathetic to the claims and conclusions of pessimistic atheists like David Benatar (2017) and Rivka Weinberg (2021), though Weinberg appears less pessimistic than Benatar. Both Benatar and Weinberg claim that the sorts of meaning available on atheism are mitigated by the loss of other kinds (or amplifications) of meaning that would be available if theism were true. It is lamentable that, if atheism is true, there is no loving, powerful, wise, guiding presence at the heart of reality. There is no ultimate prospect for loving relationships—which themselves possess a kind of infinite open-endedness—to last. There will be no perfect and definitive justice for the most morally repugnant ills of our world. The last word in such a world is full and final *dissolution*. Simulacra that speak to these human longings are available on atheism, but such longings receive definitive fulfillment on theism.

1.8.1 God and Mattering

We want the parts of our lives to matter. Too much triviality among what we choose to fill our lives with mitigates the extent to which they are meaningful. Many of us also want our whole lives to matter. Ways for our lives to matter include mattering in virtue of some inherent human dignity, mattering to ourselves, and mattering to our loved ones. These are, no doubt, ways to matter that are worth wanting. But there are deeper ways to matter—one of which is to matter cosmically, *sub specie aeternitatis*. If atheism is true, those prospects are bleak (though again, see Kahane 2013 for an alternative view).

Many of us worry about not mattering ultimately or in the grand scheme of things. Such concern is not assuaged if one is reminded that they are significant to themselves, or to their friends and family, or even to their culture or the entire human race. Neither is it assuaged by being reminded that they will "live on" in the memories of others for a few generations; or that their contributions to society will impact the culture for years, perhaps even centuries, to come. Why? Because they want their mattering to be deeper than merely in the traces of another human's memory which itself will soon pass. They want their mattering to be at least a part of the very reason the universe exists in the first place. Given atheism, this cannot be the case. An entire network of little "m" matterings does not add up to a big "M" Mattering. In this case at least, it really does look as though the whole is not greater than the sum of its individual parts. We can matter to ourselves and to others within the vast web of human relationships, but it does not follow that the whole human show matters on the cosmic stage. If atheism is true, there is no transcendent audience to whom we matter. The ultimate setting for the human drama is an empty house. That is worrisome. Here is the worry stated more specifically:[4]

Alone in the Universe? Mattering-to-God Worry

- We do not matter to someone responsible for the universe who can do something about the human condition because there is no such person.
- If we do not matter to someone responsible for the universe who can do something about the human condition, then we lack an important kind of mattering that would be worth having.
- Therefore, we lack an important kind of mattering worth having.

Many of us worry about ultimately not mattering from the widest perspective on reality because if atheism is true, there is no infinite, personal, powerful, loving presence responsible for it all—including us—who is at the heart of and occupies that widest perspective. There is no one who can ensure that we—with our happiness, our impacts, and our loving relationships—last as part of the deep

---

[4] Much of what follows in this section and the next is borrowed from Goetz and Seachris 2020: 85–88 and 25–31.

fabric of reality; as part of the metanarrative of the cosmos. We do not want our individual lives and the entire human saga—with all its tragedy, struggles for triumph, and joy—to fade away into oblivion forever unresolved. This would entail a kind of existential incoherence, and would threaten the meaning as sense-making portion of the Meaning Triad. We want all of this to matter to more than just ourselves—we want it to matter to someone who can do something about the human condition; who cares about our deepest needs, longings, and hopes concerning our wellbeing. We want to be the objects of care and concern to a necessarily existing and morally good *Someone* who is the answer to the question, "Why is it all—including and especially *us*—here?"

Sociologist Peter Berger poignantly captures the nature of this kind of worry about not mattering to someone at a metaphysically higher paygrade than ourselves. He has us imagine a young child being comforted by his mother after awakening from a nightmare:

> If reality is coextensive with the "natural" reality that our empirical reason can grasp, then the experience is an illusion and the role that embodies it is a lie. For then it is perfectly obvious that everything is not in order, is not all right. The world that the child is being told to trust is the same world in which he will eventually die. If there is no other world, then the ultimate truth about this one is that eventually it will kill the child as it will kill his mother. This would not, to be sure, detract from the real presence of love and its very real comforts; it would even give this love a quality of tragic heroism. Nevertheless, the final truth would be not love but terror, not light but darkness. The nightmare of chaos, not the transitory safety of order, would be the final reality of the human situation. For, in the end, we must all find ourselves in darkness, alone with the night that will swallow us up. The face of reassuring love, bending over our terror, will then be nothing except an image of merciful illusion.
>
> (Berger 1970: 56).

If atheism is true, there is ultimately nothing but silence on the cosmic stage concerning the human condition because the universe alone is ultimate reality. The cosmos does not care because it cannot care. We cannot matter from the *sub specie aeternitatis* perspective because that perspective is not occupied by a mind or person to whom we could matter. At the cosmic level, which is ultimate, there is no one who cares for us; no one who is concerned about us and our deepest joys and sorrows. This is unlike the situation according to theism, where a person with the attributes needed to guarantee our final wellbeing is at the heart of reality—a person who occupies the *sub specie aeternitatis* perspective. The best atheism can do on this count is a finite mattering grounded in the cares and concerns of finite minds—a network of little "m" matterings. According to atheism, we have a kind of significance, but only from the *sub specie humanitatis* perspective (again, however, cf. Kahane 2013).

The lesson here seems to be that our lives can have a personal, local, terrestrial kind of mattering. This is noteworthy. It is good news. Our lives are not totally insignificant. Our lives matter; they are important; they are special; and they are objects of care and concern ... *to us and those around us*. However, this does not deliver the deeper kind of mattering that many of us crave. For those with lingering concerns about cosmic mattering, the presence of terrestrial mattering will not be unmitigated good news. It will not be bad news, but it will not be the best news. In fact, it might not even be good enough news to block the conclusion that, despite some real humanly generated, terrestrial significance, there is a salient undercurrent of tragedy to the human condition if atheism is true. Countless humans want to be the object of care and concern to someone who can actually do something definitive about the human condition: someone who can finally right wrongs; who can bring ultimate justice; and who can guarantee a lasting place for happiness and love in the grand scheme of things. When you bury a child, is that it? In unfathomable pain, have you said goodbye to him for the final time? When grief is so acute that you feel as if you will be undone, is there anyone to whom this matters; who can bring everlasting *shalom*—deep peace and harmony—to the cosmic order?

The widespread human desire to matter deeply—all the way down—is not a megalomaniacal craving to be the most important thing in the universe; though, if we are honest, we are tempted to think this about ourselves. Rather, it is the longing to be cared for and ultimately to matter in the universe's story. We want to be children, not orphans in the cosmos. We would rather not be an accidental footnote in the cosmic narrative, "here [*merely*] because one odd group of fishes had a peculiar fin anatomy that could transform into legs for terrestrial creatures," in the words of famous paleontologist Stephen Jay Gould (Friend 1991: 33). If atheism is true, the *perspective*—unconscious matter in motion—that speaks first, longest, last, and likely loudest is one that does not care about us in the least. If theism is true, the *perspective*—infinite, powerful, loving Mind at the heart of reality—that speaks first, longest, last and definitely loudest includes *Someone* who both cares about us and can do something about our deepest hopes and needs. We are children, even in the grand scheme of things. As philosopher Philip Kitcher said: "Mattering to others is what counts in conferring meaning" (Kitcher 2014: 101). I think the most significant other to whom we need to matter is God.

If there is a God, a capital "S" *Someone* responsible for the cosmos, then many things matter in a very deep way (and quite possibly *everything*; cf. Ecc. 12:13–14). Returning to the epigraph at the beginning of this chapter from Marilynne Robinson's novel *Jack*, even the sparrow somehow matters in God's universe. The ordinary sparrow is "seen" by God and is God's object of attention. In Matthew 10:29, Jesus says: "Are not two sparrows sold for a penny? And not one of them will fall to the ground apart from your Father" (ESV). This kind of view, of course, must grapple with the traditional and sobering problem of evil which says the magnitude, distribution, and horrendous types of suffering—including of sparrows—are compelling evidence against the existence of a God who providentially attends to the creation. And yet this confirms the main point here: the fact that people worry about lost sparrows at all.

The point of this section is that though we can matter in real ways in an atheistic world, we matter in more fundamental ways with God in the picture. On theism, we are not an accidental part of the cosmic story, regardless of our small, fleeting place in the vast universe. On atheism, our existence is—in addition to being small and fleeting—radically contingent, unplanned, and precarious. In the words of the priest who has lost his faith in M. Night Shyamalan's wonderful 2002 film, *Signs:* "There is no one watching out for us ... We are all on our own." Being created, cared for, and guided by God deepens the kind and extent of human mattering. That is a benefit worth preferring.

1.8.2 God and Purpose

We can lead lives of purpose even if there is no God and no cosmic purpose or point to life in general. I have chosen to engage in this extended conversation on meaningful life with Professor Metz because I wanted the opportunity to explore this topic with him in a unique format. Taking this opportunity, in turn, partly structures how I choose to spend important chunks of my professional time in order to accomplish the goal of completing this co-authored debate. One can say the same about the numerous purposes to which we devote ourselves over the course of our lives. At one level, such purposes do not require any sort of cosmic or transcendent origin that assigns or bestows such purposes on us.

But theists insist that there is a cosmic purpose—a reason why the universe exists and why humans in particular exist. There is a point to our existence, and this affects what we should see as the highest end to which we aspire. Our highest end—that for which we exist—is the fundamental purpose around which we ought to orient all else. While this overarching purpose is foundational, it allows ample space for a myriad of personal expressions in terms of emphases, vocations, and so on. One might choose to cultivate the life of the mind vocationally in academia. Another might find deep joy in using one's hands to create beauty as a materials artist. Another might thrive in a trade vocation. Another still might "feel God's glory" in running fast as Eric Liddell did in the movie about his life, *Chariots of Fire* (1981).

If theism insists that there is an overarching point to human life, what is that point? Why do we exist? To what end? For what purpose? One prominent strand of theism—Christian theism—has described our purpose with variations of this common theme: *to glorify and enjoy God.* One will find this in, for example, the reformed theological tradition as well as the Roman Catholic tradition. Not inconsistent with this view, one thinks of the Eastern Orthodox concept of *theosis*, in which the end toward which human life aims is communion, consummation, and participation within God's intra-Trinitarian life. In all of these views, the goal of human life is a kind of intimate communion with the source and fountain of all life, truth, goodness, beauty, and joy—communion with God Himself. And since that source is essentially good, the purpose of human life would be essentially good and good for us. It would be what promotes full human flourishing, as humans fulfill and embody what they are supposed to be by nature.

A specific way of thinking about the purpose of life on Christian theism is in terms of perfect happiness, where the meaning of the word "perfect" is often either taken for granted, replaced with words like "blessed" or "eternal," or implied by such terms as "beatitude" or "felicity." Thus, in the early Middle Ages, Saint Augustine (354–430) wrote that: "We wish to be happy, do we not? ... Everyone who possesses what he wants is happy ... Therefore ... whoever possesses God is happy" (Augustine 2008: 52–3). Not too long after Augustine, Boethius (480–524) wrote *The Consolation of Philosophy*, in which his interlocutor Lady Philosophy reminded him that:

> The whole concern of men, which the effort of a multitude of pursuits keeps busy, moves by different roads, yet strives to arrive at one and the same end, that of happiness ... In all of these things it is obviously happiness alone that is desired; for whatever a man seeks above all else, that he reckons the highest good. But we have defined the highest good as happiness; wherefore each man judges that state to be happy which he desires above all others ... And you also, earthly creatures that you are, have some image, though hazy, in your dreams of your beginning; you see, though with a far from clear imagination yet with some idea, that true end of your happiness. Your natural inclinations draw you towards that end, to the true good ...
> (Boethius 1973: 233, 235, 241).

And a few centuries later, Saint Anselm (1033–1109) affirmed the idea that God created us for the purpose that we be happy:

> It ought not to be doubted that the nature of rational beings was created by God ... in order that, through rejoicing in him, it might be blessedly happy ... Man, being rational by nature, was created ... to the end that, through rejoicing in God, he might be blessedly happy ... God ... [made man] for the purpose of eternal happiness.
> (Anselm 1998: 315–16).

Saint Thomas Aquinas (1224/25–1274) agreed with Augustine, Boethius, and Anselm. According to Aquinas, "the ultimate end of man ... is called felicity or happiness, because this is what every intellectual substance desires as an ultimate end, and for its own sake alone" (Aquinas 1975: 102). Because "all creatures ... are ordered to God as to an ultimate end" (Aquinas 1975: 97), and "the highest good for man ... is felicity" (1975: 113), it follows that "man's ultimate felicity consists only in the contemplation of God" (Aquinas 1975: 125). French Reformer John Calvin (1509–1564) also believed we were created for the purpose that we be perfectly happy. According to him, in order that God "may encourage us in every way, he promises present blessings, as well as eternal felicity, to the obedience of those who shall have kept his commands" (Calvin 2008: II.8.4). Indeed, because the "holy patriarchs expected a happy life from the hand of God (and it is indubitable that they did), they viewed and contemplated a different happiness from that of a terrestrial life" (Calvin 2008: II.10.13). And, wrote Calvin: "He who confesses that there is nothing solid or stable on the earth, and yet firmly retains his hope in God, undoubtedly contemplates a happiness reserved for him elsewhere" (Calvin 2008: II.10.15).

More recently, C. S. Lewis added his voice to the vast weight of the Christian tradition when he affirmed that the purpose for which God created human beings is that they be ultimately or finally perfectly happy. In his book *The Great Divorce*, which is about a fantastical bus trip from Hell to Heaven, Lewis had one of the ghostly heavenly visitors say, "I wish I'd never been born ... What *are* we born for?" To which a spirit answers, "For infinite happiness ..." (Lewis 2001a: 61). Lewis wrote elsewhere that infinite, complete, or ecstatic happiness is the life of the blessed; and he stated that we must suppose "the life of the blessed to be an end in itself, indeed The End" (Lewis 1992, 92). He maintained that a Christian "believes that men are going to live forever, [and] that they were created by God and so built that they can find their true and lasting happiness only by being united to God" (Lewis 1970: 109) (for a sustained account and defense of the view that God created humans for the purpose of our perfect happiness, see Goetz 2012).

Having been assigned a purpose from someone else, however, is morally problematic in many instances. For example, atheist philosopher Kurt Baier (1917–2010) writes that:

> To attribute to a human being a purpose in [the sense of the purpose of an artifact] is not neutral, let alone complimentary: it is offensive. It is degrading for a man to be regarded as merely serving a purpose. If, at a garden party, I ask a man in livery, "What is your purpose?" I am insulting him. I might as well have asked, "What are you *for*?" Such questions reduce him to the level of a gadget, a domestic animal, or perhaps a slave. I

imply that *we* allot to *him* the tasks, the goals, the aims which he is to pursue; that *his* wishes and desires and aspirations and purposes are to count for little or nothing.

(Baier 2000: 120).

Regardless of whether one is a theist, it seems fair to say that Baier's position is not obviously compelling. Perhaps in some contexts it would be offensive or degrading to ask a person about his or her purpose. But this is not always the case. We often ask others questions like, "What do you do for a living?" or "What's your role in the business?" and no offense is taken (Mawson 2016: 117–120). Perhaps Baier would assume no offense is taken in cases where we ask these questions because those whom we ask had a choice about their line of employment and the purpose that comes with it. What Baier thinks is problematic about the case of our being something like artifacts created by God is that we had no choice about either being created by God or having the purpose given to us. But even here, one might wonder about the cogency of Baier's reasoning. While it clearly would be degrading and objectionable if the purpose of one's life were to serve as food for intergalactic travelers, it seems just as clear that there might be an acceptable and ennobling purpose of life.

Theists believe that having a purpose of life as a created being is a good thing. A criticism of their belief comes from the pen of French existentialist philosopher Jean-Paul Sartre (1905–1980). Sartre argued that there is actually a benefit that comes from not being an artifact created by God (Sartre 1973). Being an artifact implies having an *essence* or *nature* that is fixed and not open to being freely chosen by the artifact itself. Loosely speaking, Sartre's point is that an artifact is stuck with its nature, whether it likes it or not. For example, a pencil's nature—which includes its size, shape, weight, etc.—is chosen by its artificer. In Sartre's catchy terminology, the pencil's *essence precedes its existence*: the concept of the pencil in the maker's mind determines *what* the pencil is (its essence) before it exists. The pencil has no say in the matter. The same point applies to any artifact. Thus, being a person and having the essence that comes with the purpose for which a person is created is fixed in the mind of God before the person exists. The individual has no choice about the matter. Sartre believed that this is something which is deeply problematic because it limits a person's freedom and autonomy.

The Truman Show (1998)

Baier's and Sartre's worries about humans having a purpose given to them are reminiscent of the movie *The Truman Show*, in which an insurance salesman (played by Jim Carrey) discovers that his life is actually a reality television series. The story of his entire life, from birth onwards, is largely authored by the show's creator; and everyone, except poor Truman, is in on what is happening. In one sense, the purpose of Truman's life is to be entertainment for a worldwide audience, despite his own sense that he has autonomy, and that his life is filled with authentic relationships.

- An important question is whether and to what extent having an essence *prior to one's existence* is like the case of Truman. What do you think?

But once again, one might wonder whether being an artifact and having a purpose of life is always problematic. Whether it is problematic might again very well depend upon what the purpose of life is. As I have already pointed out, if it is that one be food for intergalactic travelers, then one would naturally be bothered by having an essence prior to one's existence. But if one's purpose is that one be perfectly happy, then it is not obvious why one would and/or should be bothered by the fact that one has no choice about one's essence. If Sartre were free to choose his essence because, in his terminology, his *existence preceded his essence*, what would he choose that it be? Could one take him seriously if he were to respond that he wanted to be free to choose not to have the essence that he be perfectly happy, or as happy as he could be? Would he choose as his essence that he be less than as happy as he might be, or that he be miserable? True, people sometimes choose a course of action that they believe will make them temporarily unhappy (e.g., they sometimes choose the dentist's chair or the operating table over losing a tooth or long-term disability). They do not choose such a course of action for its own sake, however, but because they believe pursuing that course of action stands a good chance of making them happier in the long run. Could anyone choose to be unhappy in the long run for its own sake? Could anyone choose to have the purpose that he or she be unhappy as an end state? If not, then the fact that one lacks the freedom to choose one's essence—which comes from being an artifact with the purpose that one be happy—might not be all that bad, if it is bad at all. Freedom of choice might be a good thing to have in some circumstances; but to regard it as a good that is superior to the good of happiness seems at least questionable.

1.8.3 God and Sense-Making

In Section 1.6, I discussed how atheism can be perceived as a threat to a certain kind of cosmic existential coherence: a threat to life not—*broadly*—fitting together in the right way. I will not rehash that discussion here. Instead, I want to argue that, on atheism, the "story" of the cosmos—especially with human cares and concerns as our starting point—is ultimately tragic because it fails to make a certain kind of existential sense.

Take a narrative kind of sense-making. On one such view, meaningful life—*sub specie humanitatis*—is largely a matter of having enough life aspects that are meaningful in virtue of cohering in clusters of humanly constructed interlocking narratives. In the absence of God and transcendence, none of those narratives through which we make sense of our lives and their events will contain elements that give human life any kind of cosmic point. Insofar as some of us lament the prospect of there being no such narrative, the advice might then be to seek narratives that get one and the various aspects of one's life as far beyond parochial concerns as possible. Narratives that help us transcend limits in this way perhaps do a better job of satiating our hunger for meaning than those whose scope is narrower, even though I personally think such hunger is saliently generated by cosmically oriented pangs. If a cosmic narrative sense-making frame with a point for human existence is not available, we might ensure that among our interlocking narratives through which we make sense of our lives are ones that have a deeper traction—even if only *sub specie humanitatis*—at the level of family, community, culture, and even the entire human race. In these ways, our lives could still be grounded in narratives that extend far behind and well beyond us, even on atheism.

Still, in shifting to an exclusively terrestrial focus, I worry that we lose something important to what concern over life's meaning is often all about—and, some would say, metaphysically and normatively important to the kind of meaning that many want. To borrow again from sociologist Peter Berger, in seeking life's meaning, many are attempting to locate it "within a sacred and cosmic *frame of reference*" of trying to plumb the connection "between microcosm and macrocosm" (Berger 1967: 27). God, transcendence, religion, and the like give our lives and their parts a deeper traction within a "sacred and cosmic frame ..." This project of locating, framing, contextualizing, and situating our lives and their existentially weighty aspects is a project of *sense-making*—one whose focus is squarely on questions and concerns about origins, purpose, mattering, value, suffering, and destiny. It is also laden with complex emotional and existential baggage that defines the shape that sense-making takes in this context. And insofar as this sense-making pursuit has an ineliminable cosmic element, the human search for meaning will continue to stubbornly intersect with questions about transcendence, spirituality, religion, and God.

Not everyone is comfortable with such strong connections between meaning and God. Some think that requiring conditions of *cosmic* mattering, purpose, and a kind of broadly existential sense-making sets the meaning bar too high. Why think that we need all of that in order to have *real* meaning? Even if there is no meaning *of* life, there can still be meaning *in* life (see Section 1.3). In the words of Lucy from *The Lego Movie 2*: "Everything's not awesome, but that doesn't mean that it's hopeless and bleak." We can find meaning in human pursuits, relationships, joys, and limited impacts.

Atheistic objections notwithstanding, many philosophers and non-philosophers alike think that ultimate, cosmic meaning is what most of us really want, and that such meaning is hard (near impossible) to come by if the space-time universe is all there is—in other words, if there is no God and human beings are wholly material things that cease to exist in any noteworthy sense at death. With religious believers in numerous traditions who insist that God is necessary for ultimate meaning, many pessimistic atheists agree. The human predicament—without God—has a salient undercurrent of tragedy if there is no cosmic significance, purpose, or existential fittingness to human existence; and especially if there is no reason for rational hope that the last words in the universe are life, love, full and ultimate justice, and everlasting felicity. For many, this tragic undercurrent undermines the prospect for deep and ultimate meaning.

Atheism omits two elements of the explanation of what is true: ultimate, perfect justice, and a lasting place for love. Both of these, when combined, require an afterlife. I cannot speak for all, since not everyone claims to have a desire to live forever in loving relationship within a community; but many do. This is a deeply engrained longing that many of us have. For such, the idea is *absurd*—in that broader, existential sense—that our lives are but flickers in a vast darkness; that all of our joys, loves, relationships, and accomplishments eventually will be swallowed up and obliterated by a silent, uncaring universe that was here long before we were born and will remain long after we are gone. Very few, if any of us, will ever make the history books. But even those who do will in the end be forgotten, as even those history books and the last traces of memory disappear from the universe forever. More generally, our earthly lives appear to be insignificant when compared with the immense canvas of a 15-billion-year-old cosmos that is, by some calculations, a sphere of nearly 100 billion light years across. Add to this that the universe is ultimately silent and oblivious to human cares and concerns, and you have a potential recipe for serious worries about the meaning of human life, both individually and collectively, relative to the cosmos. Elsa Dutton, one of the central characters and main narrator from the 2021 hit mini-series *1883*, poignantly captures the indifference of the universe: "The world doesn't care if you die. It won't listen to your screams. If you bleed on the ground, the ground will drink it. It doesn't care that you're cut" (Episode Four, "The Crossing"). In such a universe, there is no ultimate justice for the little child murdered, whose last moments of conscious existence were sheer terror. In such a universe, those who were the recipients of untold oppression and who never experienced justice on this earth are forever cut off from experiencing the definitive righting of wrongs. In such a universe, the last time you say goodbye to your closest, cherished loved ones with whom you have encountered the deepest and most sublime of moments, will be the *last* time ... forever.

Many human hearts contemplate this possibility and respond by claiming that life is absurd; it does not make sense if this is the way the world is ... and ends. Pessimistic atheists join theists and others who think that the resources of theism—or at least transcendence—provide a more hospitable context for humans to be able to say that life, ultimately, makes sense. In terms of sense-making, my fellow theists and I have our own profound sense-making challenges related to *fitting* together the realities of pain and suffering with a powerful, wise, loving God that we claim exists (for serious, substantive treatments from a theistic perspective of what has come to be called over the centuries, "The Problem of Evil," see Adams 2000 and Stump 2010 for academic audiences; and Bowler 2021 and Wolterstorff 1987 for wider audiences). Again, consider the words of *1883*'s Elsa Dutton:

> I told myself when I meet God it will be the first thing I ask him: Why make a world of such wonder then fill it with monsters? Why make flowers and then snakes to hide beneath them? What purpose does the tornado serve?
> (Episode Four, "The Crossing").

None of the above material in Section 1.8 moves toward actually defending that the theistic explanation of the cosmos is true; rather, it simply claims that its being true would be better news for us than atheism. It is the kind of explanation that we can (and should) rationally hope is true—partly because it is better news for humanity's place in this cosmos. And it is better news for humanity's place in the cosmos partly because of the ending it provides. In the Christian theistic ending to the cosmic story, our tearstained cheeks will be wiped gently by God Himself in the person of Jesus, whose own tearstained cheeks and nail-scarred hands redeem those who turn from sin and place their trust in Him. Through his life, death, resurrection, ascension, and returning consummation, all wrongs will be forever righted in a new Heavens and Earth where all things are made new in a fully redeemed metanarrative (cf. Rev. 21:5), because, as the Eastern Orthodox ascetic St. Paisios is alleged to have said: "[N]o matter what happens, God will have the last word." It will be like the very end of the last book in C. S. Lewis's *Narnia* series:

> Then Aslan turned to them and said:
> "You do not yet look so happy as I mean you to be."
> Lucy said, "We're so afraid of being sent away, Aslan. And you have sent us back into our own world so often."
> "No fear of that," said Aslan. "Have you not guessed?"
> Their hearts leaped and a wild hope rose within them.
> "There *was* a real railway accident," said Aslan softly. Your father and mother and all of you are—as you used to call it in the Shadowlands—dead. The term is over: the holidays have begun. The dream is ended: this the morning."
> And as He spoke, He no longer looked to them like a lion; but the things that began to happen after that were so great

and beautiful that I cannot write them. And for us this the end of all the stories, and we can most truly say that they all lived happily ever after. But for them it was only the beginning of the real story. All their life in this world and all their adventures in Narnia had only been the cover and the title page: now at last they were beginning Chapter One of the Great Story which no one on earth has read: which goes on forever: in which every chapter is better than the one before.

(Lewis 2002: 227–28).

Anything less is lamentable at best, tragic at worst.

> **Summary**
>
> While meaning—indeed, *real* meaning—can be found in an atheistic universe as long as there are finite minds with sufficient cognitive capacities like our own, God allows for deeper, more ultimate expressions of meaning; we might say an *amplified* and *eternal* meaning. The presence of God in the cosmic story addresses more clearly and directly our desires for cosmic, existential coherence and ultimate justice, among others.

1.9 Summary

I here close my opening statement with a brief summary of my main claims and conclusions about both the meaning *of* life and a meaningful life or meaning *in* life:

Meaning's Foundational Place: Human questions and concerns about meaning are some of the most basic ones we have.
Meaning's Triadic Nature: The concept of meaning primarily centers on the triad of mattering, purpose, and sense-making.
Meaning's Cosmic Dimension: Human questions and concerns about meaning often have an important cosmic element, and are tied to the perceived loss of cosmic forms of mattering, purpose, and sense-making.
Meaning's Religious Dimension: Human questions and concerns about meaning, therefore, often intersect with religious

ideas—it is difficult to untangle meaning from God, religion, spirituality, or the transcendent more generally.

Meaning's Mortal Dimension: Human questions and concerns about meaning closely intersect with questions and concerns about death and ending.

Intrinsic vs. Extrinsic Meaning (1): One's life can be intrinsically meaningful in virtue of *what one is*—binary meaning; and extrinsically meaningful in virtue of *what one does*—non-binary, gradient meaning. Extrinsically understood, meaningfulness is on a spectrum, and lives can be more or less meaningful.

Intrinsic vs. Extrinsic Meaning (2): Therefore, one either has intrinsic meaning or one does not; whereas extrinsic meaning comes in degrees, and one can have more or less of it. The framing of this current debate tracks the latter, extrinsic sense of meaning.

God Enhances Meaning: Meaningful life is significantly enhanced, both intrinsically and extrinsically, if there is a God and an afterlife where objective value and our interaction with objective value continues indefinitely. Such realities would ground a more fundamental, ultimate, and everlasting expression of the Meaning Triad.

Tragic vs. Comic Meaning: Therefore, though meaningful life is possible on atheism, there is a salient undercurrent of tragedy on this view; whereas a theistic conception of reality is ultimately comic—at least when the ending is in view.

Chapter 2

Making Life Meaningful Without God or a Soul

Thaddeus Metz

Contents

2.1 Introducing an Earthly Approach to Meaning 70
2.2 What We Are Talking About 75
2.3 What Is Central to Life's Meaning 87
2.4 Moderate Supernaturalism 120
2.5 Rebutting Nihilism; Or, Yes, Your Life Has Meaning in It 130

2.1 Introducing an Earthly Approach to Meaning

When people enquire into life's meaning, they usually do so seeking to answer one of three questions: "What does it mean to talk of 'the meaning of life'?"; "What would make life (perhaps mine in particular) meaningful?"; and "Is (my) life in fact meaningful?". In this opening statement, I provide answers to all three questions—answers that in some cases substantially differ from those offered by Professor Joshua Seachris.

My answers are all earthly—by which I mean secular or, in the Anglo-American philosophical lingo, instances of **naturalism**. They are focused on what can be done in the **physical** universe and are not religious—or at least not in the ways normally associated with the Judeo-Christian-Islamic tradition. In this opening statement, I argue that God and a soul are, upon reflection, much less relevant to thought about meaning than is often supposed by those from Western cultures. That is, I reject **supernaturalism**: the view that **spiritual** conditions are central to what makes life meaningful.

DOI: 10.4324/9781003436386-3

Note that naturalism and supernaturalism are broad accounts of what would confer meaning on life, and they do not imply metaphysical claims about whether **God** and a **soul** in fact exist. Probably, most naturalists are **atheists**, who deny that a spiritual realm exists; and most supernaturalists are **theists**, who roughly hold that one does. However, those are not the only combinations of claims about meaning and metaphysics available. It is consistent to be a supernaturalist who is an atheist—that is, to believe that God and a soul are central to what would make life meaningful, but to deny that they exist. Conversely, it is not inconsistent to be a naturalist who is a theist—that is, to hold that God and a soul exist, but that they are not central to life's meaning, which is to be found mainly or perhaps even solely in the physical world. It might be more difficult to defend the more unusual combinations of claims about meaning and metaphysics; but the current point is that they are **logically possible**—that is, it is not a contradiction in terms to accept them.

Atheism, Theism, Naturalism, Supernaturalism

Consider the table below, which represents four different combinations of philosophical views. Explain why the positions in boxes 1 and 4 are not tautologous (i.e., why it is not redundant to speak of both "atheism" and "naturalism"). In addition, explain why the positions in boxes 2 and 3 are not contradictory (e.g., why it is logically possible to hold both atheism and supernaturalism). At the moment, in which box are you inclined to place your own views?

1 Atheism-Naturalism	2 Atheism-Supernaturalism
3 Theism-Naturalism	4 Theism-Supernaturalism

Some believe that whenever we think about life's meaning, it should—or even must—be an intensely personal or "**existential**" exercise. By this I have three different things in mind, none of which the reader should expect to encounter in my contribution to this debate with Professor Seachris.

First off, there are those who hold that thought about meaning is always about the meaning of one's own life. When one is young, one thinks about which choices to make in the future; and when one is old, one looks back (perhaps on one's deathbed) to appraise the choices one made in the past.

However, it is simply not true that thought about meaning is always "first-personal" in these ways. I care about the meaningfulness of my children's and students' lives, and not merely because I expect their lives to influence mine in some way. In addition, it is reasonable to think that a government could be concerned about whether there is enough meaning in the lives of its citizens. Protecting natural wilderness, funding the search for extraterrestrial intelligence, and sending athletes to the Olympics are all plausibly done out of a concern to promote meaning in other people's lives. In this debate, I do not focus on my own life, and instead write about human life in general—presumably including yours.

For a second respect in which some believe that discussion of life's meaning must be intensely personal, some maintain that whenever one addresses the topic of meaning in life, one must do it expressively—say, by exuding passion. Because the topic is so vital, some hold that one would be doing it an injustice if one were not emotionally engaged when considering it. I recall that a graduate student once gave my first book on life's meaning a poor public review because it lacks feeling.

However, I confess that my approach, for philosophical purposes, is indeed a dispassionate one. For me, philosophical enquiry into life's meaning is not qualitatively different from other sorts of philosophy. Talking a lot about one's feelings is not central to determining whether one has free will or what makes a belief justified (you're not going to get a high mark on an essay if that's your approach). Similarly, I doubt that doing so is key when considering what, if anything, makes human existence significant. Although I do indeed care about whether my life and my children's lives are meaningful, I do not think that expressing my care would reveal much about whether, say, your life is meaningful or how the lives of citizens could become more so with certain political interventions. Instead, in this debate I focus strictly on **argumentation**, aiming to provide evidence in support of various claims about life's meaning. That is, I evaluate controversial claims and draw conclusions about the nature of life's meaning by appealing to premises about what is meaningful and what is not that are, by comparison, less controversial (even if not utterly certain), and that I expect most readers will accept.

For a third respect in which some believe that discussion of life's meaning should be intensely personal or existential, there are those who want guidance about how to live their lives. Perhaps when addressing meaning in life, I should be providing advice to readers, many of whom surely hanker for it. Some readers might be reading this debate with Professor Seachris in search of concrete suggestions about pitfalls to jump over and opportunities to grab.

A couple of philosophers have recently written books like that (Landau 2017; Williams 2020), but I do not really provide advice about how to live here. That is largely because what I have to offer is not so much about which means one should take in order to live meaningfully, but rather about what living meaningfully involves as an end in itself. Advice is often about how to steer the course of one's life, whereas I, to continue the metaphor, address the nature of the proper destination. If all we have is this earthly existence of approximately 80 years, which kinds of lives would plausibly exhibit some meaning in them? Is meaning indeed possible, despite the apparent facts (i.e., from a scientific point of view) that our lives are brief and make no different to the enormous cosmos? Would it be much better, so far as meaningfulness is concerned, if God and a soul existed? These are the kinds of questions I answer here with argumentation, and I hope readers find this project of interest. Upon ascertaining what a life of meaning would look like, readers can then take the next steps on their own to consider how to achieve it.

In the following, I begin by working to clarify what this debate between me and Professor Seachris is about—that is, what he, I, and presumably you upon reflection mean by the phrase "life's meaning," as distinct from other values such as happiness or morality (Section 2.2). Among other things, I point out that when we speak about "life's meaning," we are not *by definition* thinking about God and a soul as characteristically conceived by monotheists.

Supernaturalist or spiritual conditions such as these could in principle be relevant to answering the question of life's meaning, but I show that the question is not essentially about them. Instead, when we wonder what, if anything, makes life meaningful, I maintain that most of us are considering whether there is something more valuable than our own pleasure and desire satisfaction; or whether we are connected with something greater than ourselves; or whether there is something that merits pride about our lives; or whether our lives constitute a good life-story. Religious accounts of these features are, of course, possible and even common; but they are not the only accounts conceivable.

In the following two sections, which constitute the bulk of this opening statement, I address the question of what makes human lives meaningful—particularly those of individual persons, but also the life of the species. Here, I further deny that God and a soul are essential to a good answer, and instead argue that one can live quite meaningfully in a world in which no spiritual realm exists. What is sufficient for a life to be meaningful, I argue, is to exercise intelligence in certain ways in the physical world, even supposing there are no imperceptible agents behind the scenes (Section 2.3).

In fact, I point out that many religious philosophers have lately accepted the point that—at least when it comes to an individual life—it is possible for it to be meaningful if neither God nor a soul exists. Instead, supernaturalist philosophers these days tend to argue that spiritual conditions are essential, not for a meaningful life as such, but rather for a life with a *great* amount or kind of meaning. That, I accept, is a more compelling view; but I also provide some reason to doubt it and key arguments for it (Section 2.4).

Finally, I take up the question of whether there is any good reason to think that all our lives are meaningless (2.5). Some philosophers believe in **nihilism** (or pessimism), which in the present context is the view that our lives amount to nothing or that no one's life is meaningful. I provide reasons to doubt a major rationale for this view, which appeals to the desirability of a cosmic meaning; and I also point out that it is the supernaturalist who is driven toward nihilism. If God and a soul are central to what would make a life meaningful, and if we lack strong evidence that they exist, then only bad news follows. However, I conclude that we have reason to think there is good news for many of us.

Summary

The main aim of this opening statement is to advance a comprehensive and basic account of life's meaning that is naturalist—that is, which does not make spiritual conditions such as God and a soul central to what confers meaning on life. Advancing the view that certain physical conditions are principally what would make life meaningful does not commit one to atheism—the metaphysical view that spiritual conditions do not exist. I not only articulate a naturalist theory of life's meaning, but also seek to argue for it—mainly by showing that it accounts well for judgments that I expect readers to share about which aspects of life are meaningful and which are not.

2.2 What We Are Talking About

In this section, I clarify the terms of the debate—that is, I define phrases such as "life's meaning" and (what I take to be) synonymous phrases such as "significant existence" and "life that matters." After drawing a key distinction between which sort of human life might be the object of our enquiry (Section 2.2.1), I point out how meaning-talk is equivalent to talk of neither subjective happiness nor moral rightness (Section 2.2.2). Then, more positively, I suggest what thinking about life's meaning does essentially involve (Section 2.2.3), contending that it consists of a variety of overlapping ideas regarding purpose, contribution, pride, narrative, and still others. Next, I draw a distinction between a life insofar as it matters and one with what I call "anti-matter" in it—that is, features that reduce its amount of meaning (Section 2.2.4); after which I conclude by considering what role a meaningful life should play in our decision-making (Section 2.2.5). If indeed meaningfulness is distinct from happiness and rightness, the question arises as to which of these values is most worth choosing, supposing one has some options.

2.2.1 The Bearer of Meaning: Individual or Species

The first thing to address is the sort of life in which we are interested. Of course, we mainly want to know about the meaningfulness of human life, and not so much a worm's life. Or at least that is the focus of my debate with Professor Seachris. However, there are different human lives that could be considered (as my colleague points out in Section 1.3, with the following distinction meant to align with his).

For much of the medieval and modern period, Western philosophers and related thinkers such as theologians were substantially interested in what might confer meaning on human life as a whole. Was humanity created for a reason? Does anyone out there care about us, or is the universe instead indifferent to our presence? What should the human race be striving to achieve? These days, many English-speaking philosophers put such questions under the heading of the **"meaning of life"** in a narrow sense, where the "of life" indicates that we are referring not to any one of our lives, but rather to human life as such (if not all life or things in the universe).

In contrast, Anglo-American philosophers now tend to use the phrase **"meaning in life"** to pick out thought about what, if anything, confers meaning on the life of an individual human person. Philosophical attention in the West shifted at a certain point, so that, for at least the past 100 years or so, the focus has been on the life of a person and not *Homo sapiens*. One reason for the shift is probably that many philosophers came to doubt that God exists; not seeing how the human race in general could be meaningful in the absence of God, they turned to consider whether particular human beings might have meaning in their lives. Another reason for the shift is likely "the rise of the individual" or the "spread of the open society" in Western culture, in which people have roughly come to think that their identities and fates in life are properly determined by themselves, as opposed to by their membership in a group, or by some authority such as a monarch or a church. Individualist values such as creativity, uniqueness, self-expression, authenticity, autonomy, and pleasure were not salient in Europe in the centuries before the Enlightenment, when Christendom reigned. Along with the spread of such values in the West has come systematic philosophical enquiry into the meaningfulness of a person's life.

Notice that focusing on the individual does not necessarily mean that religious considerations are irrelevant. After all, for all that has been said so far, it might be that the individual's life is meaningful insofar as it fulfills a purpose God has assigned to him or her, after which the individual enters Heaven. Despite the shift from enquiry into the human species to that of particular persons, it is important to appreciate why supernaturalism has remained a viable theoretical contender of what would confer meaning.

Although meaning in life has received the lion's share of attention from Western philosophers over the past century, my colleague Professor Seachris has been a prominent voice in the literature arguing that the meaning of life (in the narrow sense defined above) deserves much more consideration than it has received of late (Seachris 2009, 2013b, 2016). I think he is right about that. One can consider whether the life of an individual matters or how it could, while also considering the same about the life of the species. In fact, one need not think there is any evidence of God's existence in order to take seriously questions about whether humanity matters or how it might come to do so. Even if God does not exist, should we wish that God did exist, since then someone would care about all of us? Could the human race have a purpose in some sense without God having created us for one? Could *Homo sapiens*, as distinct from individual members, make meaningful achievements in an atheist world? These questions are coherent and deserve answers; and so I provide accounts of meaning both in and (to a lesser extent) of life in my debate with Professor Seachris.

Which Things Can Have Meaning in Life?

The difference between what is meant by "meaning in life" and "the meaning of life" is about the **bearer** of meaning—whether it is a particular human or humanity in general whose life has or lacks meaning. A very large majority of enquiry by contemporary English-speaking philosophers has addressed one or both of these bearers. However, it is worth asking whether other bearers are possible. For example, could a group of certain human persons—such as a government, choir, or sports team—be meaningful beyond the meaning ascribed to its members? Could some animals—say, dogs—have meaning in their lives? It is literally only in the past few years that philosophers have begun to pose and systematically answer such questions (e.g., Purves and Delon 2018; Thomas 2018; Metz 2019a).

2.2.2 What "Life's Meaning" Does Not Mean

Nearly all contemporary philosophers have come to agree that when we are thinking about life's meaning—whether that of an individual or the species—we are not *essentially* thinking *merely* about values such as happiness or rightness. We might be, but not necessarily. For about 200 years in Western philosophy, most **normative** thinkers held—at least implicitly—that when it comes to individual decision-making, there are only two major values: namely, an individual's self-interest (**happiness**) on the one hand, and how much to promote her self-interest relative to the interests of others in a morally sound way (**rightness**) on the other. However, these days many of us have come to think that meaningfulness is a major value that is distinct from happiness and rightness, in part due to the influential work of philosopher Susan Wolf (2010, 2015).

Most twenty-first-century Western people think of happiness in terms of subjective wellbeing, which means that it depends on the subject's positive state of mind. Common views are that happiness consists of feeling pleasure, getting what you want, or approving of your life (or all three in combination). However, when we are thinking about what is or could be meaningful, we are not necessarily thinking about **subjective** factors; and in fact, we more often seem to be considering **objective** ones—conditions that are not constituted by our minds. That is obviously true if we are considering the meaning of life—for instance, whether the human race was created for a reason and has a purpose assigned to it that it should fulfill. When addressing meaning in life, though, it is also the case that feelings, desires, and emotions are not so central, even if they are indeed relevant. More specifically, when we think about what might make an individual's existence significant, we are often drawn toward activities as ways of living that go beyond our attitudes. For instance, most of us think that it can be meaningful to help other people—whether family and friends on the one hand, or strangers through justice or charity on the other. For a second example, creativity for many of us can be an uncontroversial source of meaning—particularly when we make beautiful music, literature, or paintings. For a third, many readers will find it significant to become knowledgeable—whether in the form of obtaining self-understanding and wisdom, or improving one's "book-smarts" about facets of the world.

One might reply that people choose to engage in these activities simply because they like doing them or enjoy them. However, let us test the hypothesis that "meaning in life" just means doing what one likes or feeling good. There are two sorts of **counterexamples**—that is, exceptions—to this general claim that many philosophers have found convincing.

First, we can imagine cases in which there is *meaningfulness without happiness*. Think, for instance, of making sacrifices for other people. In the extreme case, we can imagine someone giving up her life, and hence her happiness, so that other people will survive and have lives worth living. Less extreme, consider a nurse who cares for patients by, say, cleaning up bedpans and changing dressings on nasty wounds; her work would be meaningful if she were not happy doing it (even if, perhaps, it would be more meaningful if she were into it). In supposing her work would be meaningful, there is no **logical contradiction**—that is, inconsistency—simply by virtue of the meanings of the terms involved akin to speaking of a "square circle." However, there would be such a contradiction if "meaning in life" *by definition* meant subjective wellbeing, and so we can conclude that it does not mean that.

Furthermore, we can imagine cases in which there is *happiness without meaningfulness*. The standard thought experiment here is called the "Experience Machine": a virtual reality device that gives you as many pleasant experiences as you would like while you are in it alone (Nozick 1974: 42–45). If you spent your entire life in the Experience Machine, it would be a very happy one; but it is implausible to suggest that it would be a meaningful life. If you want to say that it would be meaningful, then you are probably using the word "meaningful" in a dramatically different way from how I, Professor Seachris, and most other contemporary philosophers are using it. Few of us would choose to spend our entire lives in an Experience Machine; and, if you would not, that probably shows that you value something else in life besides your own happiness. A good candidate for that other value is meaningfulness.

Similar thought experiments apply to the relationship between morally right action and meaning in life; we see that when we think about meaning, we are not necessarily thinking about morality. One influential example of *meaningfulness without rightness* from the philosophical literature is artist Paul Gauguin (1848–1903), who is reported to have abandoned his wife and children to refine his artistic talent in the French Polynesian islands. Supposing this in fact happened (there is some debate about that), it can be plausibly described as a situation in which a person did the morally wrong thing but acquired a meaningful existence thereby.

In addition, think about an example of *rightness without meaningfulness*. Suppose you agree to perform a boring, repetitive task over which you have no control in exchange for a wage. If you accept and live up to that labor contract, you are not wronging anyone else; but for all that has been said, the odds of you engaging in meaningful work are low. If the labor is such as to preclude growth, creativity, the exercise of a skill, self-expression, and the like, then meaning is unlikely to come from it. To be sure, the labor might have the effect of meeting other people's needs and acquire some meaning thereby. However, the point is that simply performing a permissible action is not necessarily meaningful. Perhaps the point is stronger if we think about the unusual (but entirely possible) case of someone who spends an entire day walking in a circle in his front yard. That need not involve treating anyone immorally, but it would hardly be a good candidate for meaning.

A good way to see that meaningfulness is not by definition equivalent to either happiness or rightness (or even both) is to reflect on those whose lives come to mind as having been particularly meaningful. Of course, Gandhi (1869–1948), Mother Teresa (1910–1997), Nelson Mandela (1918–2013), and Martin Luther King Jr (1929–1968) are admittedly salient, where they (or at least our stereotypical understanding of them) plausibly embodied moral value beyond the call of duty. However, not all exemplars of meaningful lives involve morality at all. Consider visual artists such as Wassily Kandinsky (1866–1944) and Pablo Picasso (1881–1973); writers such as Toni Morrison (1931–2019) and David Foster Wallace (1962–2008); or musicians such as Beethoven (1770–1827) and John Coltrane (1926–1967). Think, too, about philosophers such as Socrates (470–399 BCE) and Immanuel Kant (1724–1804); as well as scientists such as Charles Darwin (1809–1882), Albert Einstein (1879–1955), and Jane Goodall. If the reader agrees that there was substantial meaning in these lives, it is implausible to think that it is conceptually exhausted by virtue of subjective well-being or morality.

Note that even if talk of "life's meaning" does not mean one and the same thing as happiness or rightness, there could be overlaps between these properties. Indeed, below I discuss a number of ways in which a moral life could be meaningful, which is perfectly consistent with denying that we necessarily have morality in mind when thinking about meaning.

2.2.3 What "Life's Meaning" Means

So far, I have argued that the concept of meaningfulness is not one and the same as the concept of happiness or rightness. When we are enquiring into meaning, we are not thereby thinking merely about subjective wellbeing or morality. Again, there could of course be overlaps between these properties—for instance, it is reasonable to suppose that a meaningful life would usually not be an utterly immoral or miserable one. However, the point of the previous section was that a meaningful life is not *by definition* one that is moral or happy; it conceivably need not include either of these properties, or at the very least could also include something else.

Now, what else? Something else on which Professor Seachris and I agree is that there is probably not just one idea that philosophical enquirers always have in mind when thinking about the meaning of life or the meaning in a life. Instead of a **monist** understanding of what "life's meaning" means, he and I favor a **pluralist** approach, according to which it is about a number of similar ideas.

Let us think about why getting an education might matter, to see the plausible variety of respects in which it could. Earning a higher degree would involve realizing a valuable *purpose*. The achievement would merit *pride* on your part; and the hard work it would take to do so would be *admirable*. The understanding you would have obtained would involve higher *faculties beyond your animal nature* of pleasure and desire. Your comprehension of some of humanity's best thinking about important topics would have *connected you to something greater* than yourself. In virtue of your knowledge, the world might *make sense* to you in a way it did not before. If you came up with a novel insight, you would have *made a difference* to our understanding. If you used your degree to get a job and thereby support a family, you would have *acted out of love*. If you were the first to get a bachelor's degree in your family, and your children went on to obtain even higher degrees, your *life-story would be compelling*.

I submit that reflection on higher education reveals a variety of respects in which it could *prima facie* count as meaningful. Note how the group of features intuitively captures the value of getting a degree insofar as it would confer meaning on your life and that it does not connote considerations of happiness or morality. My suggestion is that, when those who are philosophically inclined are thinking carefully about meaning in life, they have in mind a *cluster* of ideas, not just one. If a thinker appealed only to, say, what involves achieving a valuable purpose, she would be missing potential dimensions of meaning. Similar remarks apply to an array of other activities, such as finding a partner and having children together, designing graphics for a computer program, or protecting wildlife. The point is not that a specific meaningful activity will always be meaningful in a variety of ways; it is rather that activities can be meaningful in a variety of ways, and that sometimes a specific activity will be too. What goes for meaning in life applies to the meaning of life; the species could also have a meaningful life in a variety of ways, not merely, say, in virtue of having been created for a reason.

Note that in expounding the concept of life's meaning, I have said nothing about God and a soul. The reason they have not even been mentioned is that they are most relevant to providing a substantive account of what could make a life or the human race meaningful, not to indicating what we invariably mean by the phrase "life's meaning." If talk about "life's meaning" *by definition* meant an ensouled life in touch with God, then it would be logically contradictory to try to think of a meaningful life in a purely physical universe! However, that condition is not a contradiction in terms akin to speaking of a "married bachelor"; it is conceptually possible for life to be meaningful without any spiritual realm. (Even so, for all that has been said so far, argumentation might lead us to the view that, in fact, if we want meaningful lives, we should want God and a soul to exist.)

The naturalist and the supernaturalist can agree that when we are thinking about life's meaning, we are thinking of a collection of features such as: meriting pride; transcending one's animal self; acting on reasons of love; making a contribution; connecting with something great; authoring an interesting life-story; finding the world to make sense, etc. *What they really disagree about is what our lives must be like in order to exhibit such features*, with the supernaturalist roughly holding that spiritual conditions must exist and that we must orient our lives in the right way toward them, and the naturalist denying this. Before considering arguments for and against supernaturalism, there is one more aspect of the concept of life's meaning I need to spell out.

Is Meaning in Life about One Thing?

I have suggested a pluralist approach to what "life's meaning" means; but some other philosophers hold a monist one, according to which all thought about life's meaning can be reduced to a single idea. One recent suggestion is that whenever we think about meaning, we merely have in mind doing what merits pride or admiration (Kauppinen 2012). Another monist suggestion is that the concept of meaning is nothing other than the thought of acting on reasons of love (Wolf 2016). Still another is that talk of "life's meaning" solely connotes making a contribution (Martela 2017). Can you think of plausible counter-examples to these proposals—that is, apparent exceptions to these general claims? For instance, can you think of a case in which there might be meaning in a life but nothing that merits pride, or in which there seems to be meaning but no loving behavior?

2.2.4 The Concept of Anti-matter

So far, I have analyzed only the positive dimensions of meaning. A large majority of philosophers agree that meaningfulness is a **final** (or **intrinsic**) value—that is, something good for its own sake and not merely as a means to something else. We want money merely because of its **instrumental** value, solely because of what it can bring us when we exchange it on a market. However, meaning is different from money in that most of us want it (at least partially) because of it "in itself," apart from what else it can do for us.

Insofar as meaning is valuable for its own sake, we can—at least broadly speaking—think of its amount in terms of positive integers. Some activities are more meaningful than others, where the greater the meaning, the higher the score. Even if no one can specify an exact score for the activity of, say, helping an old lady cross the street, one can often rank degrees of meaning—acknowledging, for instance, that helping her would be meaningful, but not nearly as meaningful as having discovered the origin of our species or of freeing a country from racial domination.

However, there are some activities that are well represented with a negative number, in that they reduce the meaning in a life. Suppose that you instead robbed an old lady as she sought to cross the street.

Giving her a swift kick and then grabbing her handbag would make your life *less* meaningful on balance than it had been before you did such things. It is not merely that you *would not gain* any meaning from behaving in that way, as you might if you simply on occasion had eaten too much chocolate; instead, I submit that you would thereby *lose* some meaning. In the proverbial book of life, whatever would make your score go down in respect of meaning I call "**anti-meaningful**" or (a bit playfully) "**anti-matter.**"

Some useful ways of thinking about the concept of anti-matter is in terms of the opposites of the concept of what matters (from Section 2.2.3 above). Instead of what merits pride, anti-matter is what merits shame. Instead of acting out of love, one acts out of enmity. Instead of a compelling life-story, one's narrative is abhorrent or pathetic. Instead of prizing one's higher faculties, one treats one's animal nature as most valuable. Instead of making a contribution, one takes things backwards—say, by fostering confusion, ugliness, and harm.

In suggesting that anti-matter exists, I am maintaining that talk of "life's meaning" has both a positive and a negative dimension, similar to the way several other values do. For example, it is possible to be a good person or exhibit virtue on the one hand, and to be a bad person or exhibit vice on the other. It is possible to be happy on the one hand, and miserable on the other. It is possible to feel pleasure on the one hand, and pain on the other. In all three of these cases, there can be the presence of a negative—a disvalue—that is more than merely the absence of the positive. I think that meaning has a similar structure.

Value Theory

Can you think of a value that does *not* have a negative correlate—that is, where there can be only the presence of a positive value or its absence, and not also the presence of a corresponding disvalue? If you can, is there any reason to think that meaningfulness is like this, instead of like virtue/vice and happiness/misery?

If so, then one needs to be aware of both what matters and what anti-matters when deciding how to live or appraising the overall meaningfulness of a person's life. An important question is precisely what would make a life anti-matter, parallel to the question of what would make a life meaningful. However, the question of anti-matter's nature is quite under-developed in the field (but see Metz 2013: 63–64, 71–72, 234–235; Campbell and Nyholm 2015), and I also do not say more below about it; I focus more on the positive as opposed to the negative, on what to strive for rather than what to avoid.

One interesting issue pertaining to the nature of anti-matter, which should be discussed at some point, is whether it can come into one's life passively. While I think it is clear that, if anti-matter indeed exists, certain ways *one acts in relation to others* can reduce the meaning in one's life, it is not so clear whether *being acted upon by others* can also do so. Calling other people racist epithets can plausibly reduce the meaning in the life of one doing the insulting, but can it also reduce the meaning in the life of one insulted? I suspect so; it appears to me that other people not only can harm us and treat us immorally, but also can make our lives less meaningful. Sometimes the way we are treated can make our lives less worthy of esteem, make them more meriting of shame, make our life-stories less attractive, or make our lives more bewildering. Or so I put forth for consideration.

2.2.5 The Worth of Life's Meaning

Above I pointed out that, for nearly all philosophers, life's meaning involves something desirable—and, furthermore, desirable for its own sake. It is a final or non-instrumental value, meaning that it is good for reasons beyond serving as a means to something else that is good. In addition, I argued that meaningfulness is a value that differs, at least conceptually, from happiness and rightness. In the light of these considerations, one naturally wants to know whether one of these evaluative/normative categories is most worth choosing. What should one do when one has to pick between meaningfulness and happiness, or between meaningfulness and rightness? It could be, for instance, that meaning is indeed distinct from subjective wellbeing, but that the latter is always preferable to the former (a view that many philosophers would call "hedonism" or "welfarism").

Some of the discussion above provides a bit of guidance. Start with happiness, and consider those exemplars of meaningfulness: the Einsteins, Picassos, and Mother Teresas—at least in our stereotypical understanding of them. I presume most readers would ideally like to have lives like these: that were as admirable, that had life-stories as attractive, that had made as much of a positive difference. Furthermore, I take it one would still want to have a life akin to theirs, on the supposition that they were not particularly happy *and* not particularly miserable either. If so, then happiness is not always the most choice-worthy compared to other goods; it can be reasonable to trade off some subjective wellbeing for the sake of meaning. This point was also suggested by the Experience Machine thought experiment. If you would not spend the rest of your life in one (supposing one existed), then you implicitly think there is something worthwhile about life beyond happiness and for the sake of which we should leave some happiness behind.

That said, we might well not want a meaningful life if it were utterly miserable. A life full of agony and frustration would not be worth picking, despite the gains to meaning—at least for many of us. Hence, all together, these reflections suggest that most readers probably want a minimum amount of happiness in life, a floor beneath which we do not go; but that we think it would be reasonable to give up the prospect of lots more happiness for the sake of lots more meaning.

I believe similar points apply to rightness in relation to meaningfulness. Many of us would continue to want the life of an Einstein, Picasso, or Mother Teresa, even supposing that involved a less than perfect moral life. Suppose these individuals were by and large moral, but on occasion also engaged in wrongdoing, specifically to advance their otherwise meaningful projects. Imagine Einstein had plagiarized a few ideas when he was getting started, but then went on to do original work. Suppose Picasso had been a philanderer, but that his romantic exploits had inspired some of his paintings. What if Mother Teresa had made some people better off against their will—say, by tricking some of them into taking life-saving medication that they would not have taken otherwise? Stealing, cheating, and deceiving are wrong, let us grant. Even so, there would remain much to admire in these lives, and many of us would find them worth choosing for that reason.

Yet if it were the case that the behavior were much more immoral than these cases, then most of us would begin to doubt that meaning was worth the price. Again, a moral floor is suggested: we should not become serial killers, even if it would somehow result in lots of meaning. Perhaps the murderer in the movie *Seven* had a meaningful life-story or had been creative in a way that is admirable in some respect (although, of course, even more detestable in other respects). However, where some minor to moderate wrongdoing is involved, there could be situations in which one has most reason to do wrong, when lots of meaning would be the unique result.

What these reflections also show, if the reader is sympathetic to them, is that meaning is not always the most choice-worthy value. One might have initially been tempted to think that whatever is meaningful is alone what makes life worth living or that meaning is (perhaps by definition) the most important value that takes precedence over all others. However, if one would not want a life of either meaningful misery or meaningful evil, then meaning is not the be-all and end-all. In all likelihood, some kind of balance among values is appropriate.

> **Summary**
>
> Talk of "life's meaning" is ambiguous between the life of an individual human person and that of the species as a whole; and in this book, I address both. In either case, when we have meaning in mind, we are thinking of any one of several different but related ideas, such as what merits esteem or admiration, how to transcend our animal nature, how to achieve particularly valuable purposes, how to make sense of our existence, and how to make a positive difference. One should also recognize a disvaluable correlate to meaning—that is, what reduces it—which is well understood in terms of what merits shame, what makes life bewildering, and how to make a negative difference. Although the value of meaning is good for its own sake and often worth striving for at some cost to one's subjective wellbeing or moral virtue, it is not the only thing good for its own sake and there are probably times when other values should be chosen instead of it.

2.3 What Is Central to Life's Meaning

In this section, I begin by advancing a number of claims I expect Professor Seachris and readers to share with me about when there is meaning in a life and when there is not (Section 2.3.1), after which

I try to provide a comprehensive principle that plausibly indicates what the differences are between them (Section 2.3.2). According to this theory, a life is more meaningful the more it exercises intelligence in positive, intense, and sophisticated ways—ideally ones that involve advancement. Next, I provide reason to doubt an **extreme supernaturalism**, according to which nothing in the physical realm could make a person's life meaningful unless there were also a spiritual realm (Section 2.3.3). An earthly existence could be enough for your life to matter, so I argue. Then I consider the meaning of life—that is, whether and, if so, how humanity might be meaningful—and offer reasons to think that neither God nor a soul is necessary for that either (Section 2.3.4). It is only in the following major section (Section 2.4) that I consider a powerful reply from the supernaturalist: namely, that even if a spiritual realm is not necessary for a meaningful life as such, it is for a life with *great* meaning. Such a **moderate supernaturalism** is more plausible, I accept, than the extreme version considered in this section.

2.3.1 Intuitions about Meaning in Life[1]

Let us suppose that we have an individual who not only does charity work, but also has advanced social justice in some way—perhaps by winning a major court case that assisted a less-privileged community. He also goes out of his way to help others by making podcasts to teach them a useful skill, like how to hire a lawyer. Furthermore, let us imagine that this person is highly educated and has obtained a few postgraduate degrees. This person reads a lot and has come to understand much about human nature and society. Let us assume that he has made some discoveries in his field of law and has published books to share his findings with scholars and the broader public. Add in that he knows not merely about others or his world, but also about himself; he is a reflective individual who has spent time going through psychotherapy, and as a result, he has come to understand himself in ways he did not before. He has overcome some major blind spots, better understands his motivations, and now accepts his desires instead of pretending they do not exist. This individual is by the same token pretty good at understanding others. He can empathize with them and see the world from other

---

1 Many of the following intuitions are drawn from Metz 2021a.

people's points of view. He has close friendships, good collegial relationships, and loving ties with his spouse and children—maybe even his grandchildren. Still more, suppose this individual has a home that he has filled with beautiful artifacts; and in his leisure time, he tends to be creative by writing poems and tending a garden.

Let us call this a "rich life." Indeed, it would be an unusually rich life, which I want to compare with other sorts of lives. For examples of what I will label "poor lives," consider some **hypothetical** cases of meaninglessness, most of which other philosophers have suggested over the years. These are situations that have not existed and might never exist, but that are possible. Recall the case of a life spent in an Experience Machine. No such virtual reality device exists (yet); but thinking about what we would do and why if it did exist reveals something about our values, including that we do not think it would be a meaningful life, and that there is something other than pleasant experiences we think is choice-worthy. Another classic thought experiment concerns Sisyphus, a mythic figure from ancient Greece, famously addressed by Albert Camus (1913–1960) in his influential book *The Myth of Sisyphus* (1955). Sisyphus is imagined to have treated some of the gods disrespectfully; as punishment, Zeus—the king of the Greek gods—made him roll a heavy stone up a large hill for eternity. Every time Sisyphus got the rock to the top of the hill, it would roll back to the bottom; at which point Sisyphus would roll the rock back to the top, only to see it fall back down again, *ad infinitum*. Other hypothetical cases of meaninglessness include: a human being who: strives to maintain exactly 3,732 hairs on his head (Taylor 1992: 36); lines up balls of torn newspaper in neat rows (Cottingham 2003: 21); or has perfected her prowess at long-distance spitting (Wolf 2010: 104). Lastly, consider someone who believes things such as that the world was created 5,000 years ago by the Flying Spaghetti Monster and that gravity consists of its numerous tentacles keeping things from flying away.

Some readers might be uncomfortable with hypothetical cases. If they will never exist in the real world, why should we care about them? Most philosophers believe that reflecting on merely possible worlds can reveal important things about our **actual** world, which the Experience Machine seems to do in a compelling way. Consider an analogy in respect of morality. No intelligent Martians exist and nor have any visited Earth. However, suppose hypothetically they did. Would they have moral status—that is, would we have some obligation to treat them well for their own sake? If you answer "yes," then you are committed to denying that being a member of the human species is necessary for moral status. It is not the fact that a being is human—or at least, not only that fact—that can entitle it to moral treatment; or so we learn by reflecting on a merely possible situation.

While hypothetical cases can be revealing of what we value, we need not appeal only to them in order to illustrate what lacks meaning. Consider someone who spends a lot of time alone watching reruns of sitcoms. Think of someone who spends much of her life sunbathing while drinking daiquiris. Reflect on the case of someone who has been in solitary confinement for many years, without access to books, the internet, other people, or the ability to draw or write. Contemplate someone who has become addicted to drugs. Suppose that a person has suffered a major brain injury and will remain in a severe coma for the rest of her life. Imagine someone whose life is substantially focused on food, gorging himself on chocolate, milkshakes, and pizza to the point of getting so large he cannot pass through his bedroom doorway. Ponder on someone who spends his money on flashy things merely to impress others and make them jealous. Reflect on the life of someone who strives to become the person who can put the greatest number of toothpicks in his beard.

These are actual cases of poor lives—yes, even the last one![2] They illustrate lives or stretches of life that lack meaning—at least by comparison with the rich life above. In labeling these lives "poor" and pointing out that they lack meaning, I am not suggesting that the *people* are worthless or do not equally count from a moral point of view. Instead, I am claiming—as per the definitions above (Section 2.2.3)—that what these people are doing does not merit pride on their part, is not admirable, does not make a contribution, does not connect with something greater, does not involve a beautiful life-story, and so on.

Another point to make is that some of the activities put forth as meaningless are in fact worth doing, at least on occasion. I, for one, eat lots of chocolate and still enjoy watching reruns of the HBO series *Veep*. Even so, I do not suppose that my life is more meaningful by virtue of these things. They are sources of happiness, but they

---

[2] https://www.buzzfeednews.com/article/gabrielsanchez/bizarre-guinness-world-trending-records-2020.

do not add to the "meaning score" in the book of my life. It is consistent to hold that a certain way of life is worth living and to deny that it is significant. Meaning isn't everything (recall Section 2.2.5).

Some readers will want to question my pronouncements, suggesting that what appears meaningful in the first life might not be, and that what appears meaningless in the other cases might in fact be meaningful. However, such suggestions typically involve changing the cases from what I had initially intended to convey.

For instance, suppose someone has developed his ability to empathize with others, but has done so merely in order to be able to torment them more efficiently. Upon knowing more about how others feel, this person has been able to make them feel worse than he would have otherwise! Then, I agree, the empathy would not confer meaning. All that suggests, however, is that activities often do not *unconditionally* confer meaning—that is, regardless of what else is going on in the life. That is consistent with them being intuitively meaningful *under certain conditions*, which is all I invite the reader to accept. In the original scenario, I was imagining a "normal" situation in which a person empathizes with others so as to come closer to them, not to inflict greater pain on them. In the former circumstance, I presume the reader will agree, there is some meaning—even if there is not in the latter.

Similarly, suppose someone was addicted to drugs, but then used that experience to encourage others to avoid becoming addicted. Then, I accept, there is some meaning here. However, it is not the addiction *per se* that is meaningful, but rather the helping others; the addiction "in itself" lacks meaning, even if the use to which it is later put has meaning. In the original scenario, I had imagined merely the addiction, and had left aside later aspects of the person's life. Framing the case in that way, I presume the reader will again agree with me, this time that meaning is lacking.

So, yes, an interlocutor could change the cases, so that the intuitive presence of meaning changes. However, I simply request the reader to reflect on the cases I had had in mind! My suggestion is that if we stay focused on those, then nearly all readers will agree about ones that exemplify meaning and those that do not. Furthermore, I can point out that when a reader does change a case, so that meaning is then gained or lost, there is agreement again between us about when there is meaning and when there is not—I accept that it is not meaningful to cultivate empathy in order to be able to torment others better! In sum, we encounter a substantial consensus about whether quite a large number of activities are meaningful or not.

In the following, I draw on these comparatively uncontroversial judgments about particular cases in order to evaluate more controversial claims—especially principles that are general. To use philosophical terminology, I often argue for or against theories of life's meaning by appealing to such "**intuitions**." Supposing that the first life is rich in meaning, while the other lives or stretches of life lack meaning (or at least do not have as much as the rich life): what is it about the rich life that is so meaningful? Is there one thing that person's various ways of living have in common? It would be intellectually fascinating to find a compelling **theory** of life's meaning—that is, a basic principle that appears to capture all (and only) the ways that life can be meaningful.

In addition, if the theory were defended by showing that it accounts well for our comparatively uncontroversial judgments, then it could sensibly be used to resolve harder cases in which there is substantial controversy. Is marathon running meaningful? Can a boring activity be meaningful? If one has benefited others but did not try to do so (and also did not try to harm them), does one get some meaning credit thereby? There is currently a lack of consensus about how to answer these kinds of questions; but we might be able to answer them with some confidence if we knew what separates intuitions about when there is meaning from those about when there is not.

The Status of Intuitions When Doing Philosophy

Some students, as well as professional philosophers, are uncomfortable evaluating theories by the extent to which they entail and explain intuitions. One reason that has been offered is that our intuitions are often culturally relative. It is unlikely that all societies share the same intuitions about what is meaningful and not across the board, which might suggest that philosophers should not rely on them to draw any conclusions. One solution to this problem might be to find those intuitions that are indeed universally held and focus on using those to appraise theories. Can you think of any intuitions about life's meaning that are probably shared by all cultures? Another solution might be to do philosophy with the aim of justifying beliefs only to those in one's society, not necessarily across cultures. A third reply that has been made is that it could be that some societies know more about certain matters than others—so that, for example, the moral intuitions of a number of white people living under South African apartheid were skewed, but those of many people outside that society were less so (at least in regard to race). A good question is: is there any way to evaluate a general principle except by seeing how well it fits with particular cases that seem less controversial than it? How else might we ascertain which philosophical theories of life's meaning (or of other topics) are justified without appealing to intuitions?

2.3.2 A Naturalist Theory of Meaning in Life

A well-defended theory of meaning in life would offer a comprehensive account of what is meaningful as opposed to meaningless that does a good job both of entailing that the rich life is meaningful whereas the poor lives are not, and of explaining why. So, the question at hand is thus: what (if anything) do all the intuitively meaningful elements of the rich life have in common and is lacking in the poor lives without meaning? Roughly, what makes it the case that the rich life merits pride and admiration whereas the poor lives do not?

My proposal is that the exercise of intelligence is central to meaning in life. The rich life at its core involves the use of a person's rational nature in effortful, complex, and progressive ways, whereas the poor lives do not.[3] There might be more to meaning in life than that; however, that constitutes a lot of it.

Psychologists are probably in the best position to analyze what intelligence or rationality is in detail. For the sake of this debate, I presume the reader can identify instances of it as a mental operation distinct from the instinct and conditioning that are typical of the animal kingdom. Language and labor are quintessential sites of rationality.

---

3 I first advanced this sort of approach in some detail in Metz 2013: 200–239.

Intelligence and Rationality

One way to think more about what intelligence and rationality are is to consider what human persons can do that animals cannot. Someone might answer that we can play tennis, while giraffes, dogs, and turtles cannot. That is true; however, it would be more revealing to think about which general mental capacities we have that enable us to play tennis. What are some of them?

I should point out that I have a broad notion of what counts as intelligence, so that it is not merely cognitive, but also emotive. Emotionality includes feelings, and for that reason is often distinguished from rationality; but consider the expression "emotional intelligence," which has become common. I take that phrase literally. It is possible to be more or less aware of one's own emotions as well as those of others, and to take them into consideration when acting.

In addition to knowing about and responding to emotions, I believe that simply *having* certain emotions can be an instance of intelligence. Consider sympathy, in which one feels good when others flourish and feels bad when they fail. That requires having the idea of another person's state of mind as distinct from one's own, inferring what she is experiencing on the basis of signs, and then having a feeling similar in kind and degree to what she is experiencing. That all involves judgment, and so is quite different from, say, feeling hungry or in pain—states that we pretty clearly share with many animals.

There is some evidence that apes and possibly other animals sympathize, or at least empathize—that is, become aware of what others are feeling—even if they do not come to feel similarly, as we do when we sympathize. Presumably, though, humans can sympathize more robustly than typical animals. For instance, we can apprehend another's personality, and we can act for another's sake at some cost to our own pleasures and desires; in contrast, it is unlikely that many animals are capable of that sort of awareness and motivation. I submit that when we exercise this higher capacity, we can exhibit some meaning in our lives. Remember that part of what makes the initial life above rich involves sympathy. I described this person's life as including awareness of other people's perspectives and emotions, close friendships, and loving ties. Sympathy includes such an awareness, while friendship and love include sympathy (even if they are not one and the same thing as it).

Another respect in which intelligence or rationality can be emotional concerns esthetic engagement. When we make a work of art, we are often interpreting something about our lives in a way that expresses our emotions; and similarly, when we apprehend a work of art, we are often interpreting it by allowing it to elicit emotions in us. Think about what went into composing Samuel Barber's (1910–1981) *Adagio for Strings*[4] or Arvo Pärt's *Cantus for Benjamin Britten*,[5] and consider what goes into your listening to them. These works matter—and some meaning accrues to the lives of the composers who made them—in part because of the emotions they thereby express and convey, as well as the emotions they draw out of us. Our lives, too, are plausibly more meaningful for understanding—in part by being moved by—such masterpieces. I did not above imagine the rich life to include making or listening to music; but I did invite the reader to imagine that the man had acquired works of art on the one hand, and wrote poems and tended a garden on the other. Creating patterns and presenting them in ways that are beautiful and emotional intuitively together constitute a meaningful process and are, I submit, clear forms of intelligence.

The other aspects of the rich life exemplify intelligence in more straightforward ways—ones that require little explication by comparison. I had supposed the man to have obtained higher degrees, to have come to understand much about human beings, and even to have made intellectual discoveries. The exercise of the intellect to understand the world is a patent use of rationality. So is the exercise of the intellect to understand oneself. Recall that I had imagined that, over time, this man had become more aware of what drives him, and in that respect had become wiser. Finally, beyond theoretical reason, the man had been using his practical reason in a variety of intuitively meaningful ways, including by instructing others through making podcasts and publishing books, doing charity work, advancing justice through the law, and engaging in collegial relationships. Being helpful toward others, and doing so for their sake, are also kinds of intelligent behavior, in which one judges it

---

4   https://www.youtube.com/watch?v=uMr-WNV0tlw.
5   https://www.youtube.com/watch?v=eRyb5vVHDJ4.

appropriate to set aside one's subjective wellbeing in order to enable others to live better and acts in accordance with that judgment—which is quite different from acting on instinct or automatically in response to positive stimuli.

Although rationality is present in all the meaningful aspects of the rich life, I need to be more careful about that, in a few ways. First, the rich life is rationality oriented in ways naturally described as "positive," as opposed to "negative." After all, a serial killer could act rationally in the sense of simply exercising his intelligence effectively; he could be quite clever in how he captures his victims and evades the police. So, I must qualify the respect in which the intelligence is used, so that it is employed in a respectful, constructive, or supportive manner. Instead of killing a person, one feeds someone who cannot feed himself (or, better still, teaches him how to feed himself). Instead of stealing from others to feed a drug addiction, one goes to rehab, gets clean, and then counsels other drug addicts. Instead of destroying a work of art in a museum with a can of spray paint, one creates an artwork that merits being put in a museum. Instead of using one's intelligence to spread unjustified and false conspiracy theories, thereby impairing others' rationality, one engages in journalism that reveals the truth about how society operates.

Second, rationality must normally be exercised with some effort in order for meaning to accrue. It is not easy to get a higher degree, rear children, or write a book. And if desirable consequences did somehow come easily, most of us would judge there to be less meaning in the life of one who produced them. To see the point, consider the hypothetical case of the Result Machine (Nozick 1974: 42–45). This thought experiment is similar to the Experience Machine in that it is extremely powerful (and non-existent); however, it is different in that, instead of producing any desirable experience one might like for oneself, it produces any desirable result in the world. If all one had to do in order to publish a book were to press a button, the meaningfulness of doing so would be gone—or at least much less than if one had written it oneself. Perhaps one should in fact press the button, and perhaps it would not be utterly pointless to do so. However, there would be much less in which to take pride; one's life-story would not be as compelling; one would not have really transcended one's animal nature, etc.

Third, at least in cases where there is a lot of meaning, reason is employed in intricate ways that make some kind of advance.

There is a progression, as opposed to deterioration or even repetition. Several examples from the rich life include having won the court case, obtained the higher degree, published the book, come to understand himself, reared his children to adulthood, and created a beautiful garden. These are accomplishments, realizations of a long and sophisticated deployment of intelligence. The point about avoiding repetition is important—for it shows that it is not simply avoiding a decline that is essential for meaning, or at least a substantial degree of it. Consider the movie *Groundhog Day*, in which the protagonist continually relives the same day. After initially foundering for a while, he does grow, learning how to play the piano and to ice sculpt. His skills improve and so he changes, despite the rest of the day being the same. However, at a certain point it appears that he has maxed out his talents and he just repeats the same piano playing and ice sculpting; and his life then does not seem meaningful—or at least not as much as when there had been development.

Return to some of the famous lives mentioned above as exemplars of meaning; they are well understood as having exercised rationality that is positive, effortful, and developmental. Nelson Mandela strategized against autocratic and racist institutions in South Africa for about 50 years (including during 27 years in prison), eventually helped topple them, and became the country's first democratically elected President. David Foster Wallace battled with depression; but despite that, he honed his ability to write and eventually produced *Infinite Jest*, his creative, hilarious *magnum opus* about contemporary life in the West that spans more than 1,000 pages (with 350-plus footnotes), is recognized as being one of the 100 best English-language novels of the twentieth century, and has sold more than 1 million copies. Although few of us will achieve such feats, upon seeing the structure that these lives display, we can emulate them to some degree—even if it means at the level of, say, helping to organize a soup kitchen in one's neighborhood or publishing a poem in a local journal.

Now, consider the poor lives, and how they are well understood in terms of the absence of the exercise of rationality that builds, overcomes obstacles, and accomplishes something. Recall a number of the cases. A life spent in the Experience Machine is not *doing* anything; nothing is a result of deliberation, decision-making, or willpower. Similar remarks apply to the person who is permanently comatose, to a lesser degree the person in solitary confinement, and even to the sitcom rerun watcher and the sunbather. Sisyphus is using brute force to push the stone up the hill; there is no accomplishment consequent to planning, ingenuity, and dedication. Similar remarks apply to the overeater. Addictions are, probably by definition, respects in which the ability to act in accordance with reasons is short-circuited. And then, belief in the Flying Spaghetti Monster is not merely false, but also unjustified, given what we know about the world; and so it is a failure to exercise theoretical intelligence.

If this analysis is approximately true, we have learned something important (yup, I think meaning-conferring) about meaning in life: namely, what all (or, more carefully, at least many) meaningful aspects of a person's life have in common in contrast to the meaningless ones. We started with a wide array of intuitions of what is meaningful (the rich life), and what is not (the poor lives), and have apparently found a common denominator: the presence or absence of using one's intelligence in constructive, robust, and progressive ways.

Intelligence Theory of Meaning in Life

Can you think of any plausible counterexamples to the intelligence theory of meaning in life advanced above? According to it, a human person's life is meaningful if, and only if (or just insofar as), she exercises her rational nature in positive, effortful, and developmental ways. Are there any apparent exceptions? One sort of exception would be a case in which there seems to be meaning, but not the exercise of rationality in these ways. Another sort of exception would be a case in which there is the exercise of rationality in these ways, but not meaning. Try to come up with any such counterexamples, whether hypothetical or actual.

Notice that I have said nothing about God or a soul. Not a peep. This is a clue that they are not necessary to understand how a life could be meaningful. However, before arguing against those who would maintain that they are somehow implicit in the above analysis, I first indicate how the theory I have suggested differs—and in plausible ways—from the most popular one held by naturalist philosophers over the past 25 years or so.

It has been articulated and defended with care by Susan Wolf (2010, 2015, 2016), a professor of philosophy for a long time based at the University of North Carolina, Chapel Hill. In her influential terms, "Meaning arises when subjective attraction meets objective attractiveness" (Wolf 2010: 62). By "subjective attraction," Wolf usually has in mind love; but we could broaden it to include an array of other positive mental attitudes, such as enjoying, wanting, or liking. By "objective attractiveness," Wolf usually means something that is worth loving; but again, a broader notion will suffice in terms of what merits being enjoyed, wanted, or liked. For Wolf, meaning comes from both conditions, never one on its own. If one enjoys, wants, or likes a project that is not objectively worthwhile—or if one engages in an objectively worthwhile project but fails to enjoy, want, or like it—then no meaning arises.

There are **subjectivists** who maintain that simply getting what one wants is enough for meaning; but Wolf powerfully objects that some things are not worth wanting, such as torturing innocent persons for the fun of it or, as above, developing one's ability to spit long distances. There are **objectivists** who maintain that simply doing what one ought to love to do is sufficient for meaning, regardless of whether one in fact loves it or is otherwise attracted to it. However, here Wolf points out that a life full of being bored by and alienated from—and perhaps even hating—what one is doing does not look meaningful. Hence, one sees why her **hybrid** approach, essentially including both subjective and objective conditions, has been so compelling to the field.

The Subjective-Objective Distinction

The subjective-objective distinction is a recurrent one in philosophy. For something to be objective in general is for it to be independent of the human mind and yet possibly known by at least some human minds. The fact that the Earth is round is objective. It was round even when people thought it was flat, and these days many of us know that it is indeed round. People coming to the realization that it is round did not make it round; it would have continued to be round even if they had not thought that it was round. And those who believe the Earth is flat are making a mistake. When something is objective, there is a

> fact of the matter about which our beliefs can be more or less correct. In contrast, for something to be subjective normally means that something is dependent on a human mind for its truth. Do carrots taste good? It depends entirely on the subject—that is, on whether the particular person eating them likes them or not. There is no fact of the matter about whether carrots taste good beyond how the subject is affected. If a person did not like the taste of carrots, he or she would not be making any sort of mistake; similarly, if a person did like the taste of carrots, he or she would not be making any sort of mistake. Now, is meaningfulness more like the roundness of the Earth or the taste of carrots?

My approach does not neatly fit this schema. It might look as though any naturalist theory would have to be either subjective, objective, or hybrid; but that is not true. My view is something "in between" objectivism and Wolf's model. Before explaining that, note that I find Wolf's criticism of subjectivism to be convincing; it is not enough simply to like or even love an activity for it to confer meaning on your life. You might "find it meaningful," or it might be "meaningful to" you; but you could be mistaken. This does not mean that anyone should stop you from doing something you think is meaningful but that in fact is not; forcing you to live a certain way might well be counterproductive and fail to foster any more meaning in your life, beyond any moral objections to paternalism. However, insofar as the reader found the characterizations of the rich life and the poor lives compelling, it is difficult to hold subjectivism—for a person could be attracted to the poor lives, instead of the rich one, and then we could not avoid the conclusion that her existence is significant.

I do find Wolf's criticism of objectivism compelling in some regard, but not to the same degree as her criticism of subjectivism. Whereas Wolf believes that subjective attraction is a **necessary** condition for meaning in life, I think it is instead a **contributory** condition. That is, I hold one's life could acquire *some* meaning from an activity toward which one is *not* attracted, but that one would often acquire *more* meaning if one *were* attracted. Basically, I believe meaning can come from sacrifice, from giving up one's happiness and related positive mental states for the sake of others.

For instance, I did not enjoy, want, or like (uh, let alone love) changing my infant son's dirty diapers, but I did it anyway because it was important to care for his needs. Even if I had hated changing his foul nappies, I would have acquired some meaning for having done so (and would have acquired some anti-matter in my life if I had avoided doing so—say, letting him risk getting a rash by waiting until someone else did the labor). Perhaps I would have acquired some additional meaning from changing disgusting diapers had I been "into it." However, a cheery disposition or passion to take care of one's son by cleaning up poo that he cannot clean for himself does not seem essential for it to be something that merits pride, makes a difference to someone else's life, or involves acting out of love.

Another reason I favor my theoretical account of meaning in life relative to Wolf's hybrid model is that it is more specific. Wolf and a large majority of those who have held her sort of view have avoided providing an account of which activities are objectively attractive or worth loving. They are able to point to some that are and some that are not; but, as mentioned above, I think it would be philosophically revealing and useful to have a principled way by which to distinguish between them. I have offered such a principle with the view that meaning in life (at least largely) consists of exercising one's rational nature in positive, effortful, and developmental ways.

2.3.3 Three Challenges from Extreme Supernaturalism

The theory advanced in the previous section is naturalist: it contends that central to, and sufficient for, meaningfulness is living in a purely physical universe in a certain way. Some lives could exemplify meaning, according to my approach, even if neither God nor a soul exists. Indeed, as I pointed out, I had not mentioned anything about a spiritual realm when distinguishing between meaningful and meaningless conditions or explaining what makes them that way.

However, some friends of what I am calling "supernaturalism" will maintain that, upon reflection, the conditions that I indicated would be meaningful could be so only on the supposition that God and a soul exist. Recall that by the word "supernaturalism," I mean the view that God and a soul are central to life's meaning. That is different from theism—the metaphysical claim that God and a soul exist—and also is not meant to suggest anything about ghosts, witches, or extrasensory perception (which I would instead label "paranormal").

Furthermore, notice that supernaturalism is the view that meaning mostly, if not exclusively, would come from relating to God in the right way and one's soul being in the right sort of state, which differs from the view that meaning would come from the mere *belief* that God exists or that one has a soul. The present religious theory is not that having faith provides meaning, regardless of whether there is a spiritual realm or not; it is instead that an actual spiritual realm is crucial for life's meaning.

Focusing, for now, on meaning in life, probably most supernaturalists would accept our intuitions about what is meaningful and meaningless (2.3.1). And many would find something appealing about the idea that our rational nature is what helps to account for the difference between them (Section 2.3.2). However, some of them would contend that more is needed in order to have an adequate theory. What follow are three major rationales for thinking so. In catchwords, they appeal to God's purpose (Section 2.3.3.1), free will (Section 2.3.3.2), and just deserts (Section 2.3.3.3). After providing objections to these rationales for extreme supernaturalism about meaning in life, according to which our lives would be utterly meaningless without God and a soul, I provide a reason to reject extreme supernaturalism itself (Section 2.3.3.4).

2.3.3.1 God's Purpose

First off, some supernaturalists would point out that, beyond meaning in life, I also appealed to a number of other values, such as morality, enquiry, and creativity. For a long while, philosophers have abbreviated these values as "**the good, the true, and the beautiful**." "The good" stands for beneficence: doing what is expected to make other people's lives go better—say, through friendship, charity, or justice. "The true" means knowledge and related kinds of intellectual reflection—whether that means coming to understand (or at least hold reasonable beliefs about) oneself, others, or the environment in which we live. "The beautiful" signifies making and apprehending works of art in the first instance; but it potentially includes anything that is creative, such as humor or the way one dresses. These three higher values were at the heart of the rich life (Section 2.3.1).

Now, where do these values come from? Perhaps lower values of pleasant experiences and desire satisfaction, which animals can enjoy, are possible in a purely physical world. However, it seems that the intuitively higher values of the good, the true, and the beautiful must have come from God. After all, notice that the good, the true, and the beautiful correspond to God's three defining properties of being morally perfect, knowing everything, and being all-powerful. According to some religious thinkers, when we give to others, improve our understanding, and are creative, we are realizing divine capacities that God has put into us and wants us to actualize. As one influential supernaturalist, John Cottingham, has put it:

> We need, as the religious mode has it, to complete the work of creation: our autonomy, our rationality, inescapably require us to do something more with our lives, to grow, to learn, not just physically but intellectually and aesthetically and morally, to orient ourselves progressively and ever more closely towards the true, the beautiful, and the good.
> (2005: 42–43).

That sounds very much like something I could have said in the previous section—except, of course, for the part about the need to "complete the work of creation."

According to Cottingham, morality, enquiry, and creativity have patterns or rules that we ought to follow, where only God, our Creator, could be their source. Think about morality in particular. In order for a moral life to be a meaningful life, it seems that morality must be universally binding—that is, it must include rules that apply to all human persons. Otherwise, morality would be arbitrary and unimportant by comparison, like the norms of etiquette. The norm of eating with a fork, knife, and spoon does not apply to all human persons, but only those in a certain society who have adopted that convention; and arguably for that reason, it is not so weighty. It does not matter too much if one eats with one's hands instead of uses cutlery, even if one lives in a society where cutlery is the norm. In contrast, it seems to matter a great deal if a person, regardless of which society she belongs to, goes beyond the call of duty to help others, or if she violates her duty by harming them for trivial reasons. Where else could a set of moral rules that applies to all of us come from, except from a holy being standing apart from and above us and issuing commands to the entire species?

It is this **Divine Command Theory** of the source of morality that normally informs the supernaturalist view that one's life is more meaningful the more one fulfills a purpose that God has assigned.

If there were no God, then one's life would have zero meaning; or if there were a God but one failed to fulfill the purpose God had assigned, then again, one's life would be meaningless. The standard version of this view is not that having been created by God for a reason is sufficient for our lives to be meaningful, for then everyone's life would be equally meaningful. Instead, the usual idea is that people's lives vary in the degree to which they are meaningful, by virtue of the extent to which they have in fact freely done what God intended them to do. That, in turn, involves living up to commands to realize one's divine nature—in the first instance, by living morally, but also by acquiring knowledge and being creative.

The "Euthyphro Problem"

The standard objection to the Divine Command Theory is often called the "**Euthyphro problem**," named after a dialog in which the puzzle was articulated that was written long ago by Plato (428–348 BCE), the ancient Greek philosopher. The objection takes the form of a dilemma. Does God command certain things because they are right and forbid certain things because they are wrong; or, in contrast, are they right because God commands them and wrong because God forbids them? Suppose the former is the case, and that certain actions are wrong by some standard independent of God's will. In that case, the fact that God has told us not to do them seems irrelevant, for they would be wrong regardless of whether God had forbidden them or not. Next, suppose the latter is the case, so that certain actions are right simply because God has instructed us to do them and wrong simply because God has said not to do them. In that case, it appears that it would be right to be cruel to babies for the fun of it, if God told us to act in that way. However, such an action could never be right, regardless of what any authority has instructed us to do. It is tempting to reply that God would never command us to be cruel to babies for fun; but why not? You cannot say that God would not command us to act that way because it would be wrong, because then we have returned to the first horn of the dilemma, in which there is a standard of right and wrong independent of God's will.

Evaluating this argument about where higher values come from would take a lot of space. It would take us far into the field of **meta-ethics**—a field that enquires not into how to tell the difference between right and wrong, but rather into what makes it the case that anything is wrong (or right) at all, and how to know what is wrong (or right). Particularly over the past 40 years, there have been a variety of ways in which philosophers have sought to make sense of how a universal morality might be possible, aside from being what God commands us all to do or not to do, and these approaches have eclipsed the Divine Command Theory. There are forms of rationalism, according to which moral rules are constructed by our own powers of reason; **realism**, according to which there are concrete moral properties in the physical world (e.g., injustice) that we know exist because they best explain certain events in the world and judgments we make of them; and non-naturalism, according to which there are abstract moral properties or propositions that are causally inert but that we can nonetheless apprehend. Furthermore, there is quite a variety within each of these major categories.

I cannot, in my opening statement—which must focus squarely on issues of meaning—argue that one specific view is preferable to all the rest, let alone that it is better than the Divine Command Theory of where a universal or objective morality and other higher values come from.[6] Instead, what I do here is provide a reason to doubt that God is the best explanation of them. Specifically, what I suggest is that it is in fact for many of us incoherent to hold that God is the source of morality and other higher values.[7]

On the one hand, most supernaturalists and readers claim to know that some actions are wrong to perform, regardless of the society in which one lives. For instance, I presume you will agree that it is impermissible for anyone to be cruel to people just for fun (i.e., be a bully), or to kill innocent people without their consent in exchange for money (be a "hit man").

On the other hand, few supernaturalists and readers claim to *know* that God exists; and in fact, most will readily admit that they do not know that God exists. Many supernaturalists and readers might have faith in the existence of God, or hope that God exists;

---

6 Although I note that I have defended realism in, for example, Metz 2019b; and I also sketch a form of realism in Chapter 6 of this book.

7 I have advanced this argument in Metz 2013: 88–97.

but that is, of course, not to have knowledge of God's existence, which requires evidence. Such evidence has been hard to provide—particularly given the possibility that the physical universe (or at least multiverse) has existed forever (just in the God way is imagined to do), and given the horrific amount of suffering in it that humans and animals undergo (which God would presumably prevent if He existed).

These two considerations render it incoherent to claim to know that morality depends on God. If you claim to know there are immoral actions but claim not to know that God exists, then you cannot consistently claim to know that immoral actions are constituted by facts about God. Instead, if you say that you know some actions are wrong but say you do not know whether God exists, then you are committed to saying that actions are wrong because of something other than God's commands.

In reply, some might maintain that they know God exists. If you reasonably claimed to know that God exists, then it would indeed be coherent for you to hold that God's commands constitute moral facts that you also reasonably claim to know exist. However, do you in fact know that God exists? What evidence do you have that would make it reasonable for you to claim to *know*? Among other things, that would mean having a terrific explanation of why God would let a three-year-old orphan suffer from terminal cancer or allow a deer to get burned alive in a forest fire. Have you got one? Consider that around 3 *billion* animals died or were harmed in Australia's terrible forest fires in 2020.[8] Why would God—by definition, someone who knows everything, is morally perfect, and is able to do anything—permit such a thing? The classic "**problem of evil**" cannot be avoided if one wants to claim to know that God exists. It's a real problem.

Another way to reply to the incoherence argument is more complicated (for one who has made the following reply, see Wielenberg 2016: 29). Someone might try to argue that one might now plausibly claim to know that God exists, precisely in the light of knowing that a God-based account of wrongness is true and that wrongness exists. One could claim to apprehend strong evidence of God's existence if one were sure both that some actions (e.g., murder) are immoral for any human person to perform and that if some actions

---

8 https://www.bbc.com/news/world-australia-53549936.

are immoral for any human person to perform, then God exists. However, I believe that such a move is unpromising, since it is the God-based account of morality that is in question. I have presented an argument for the *conclusion* that actions are wrong because of something other than God's commands. If my interlocutor now comes along and *asserts* the opposite—that is, claims that actions are wrong only because of God's commands—this "begs the question" against my argument. At best, it provides a reason to believe that God exists—and hence to doubt a premise of the incoherence argument—only by asserting that the conclusion of the argument is incorrect. The claim that only God could make wrongness possible is, however, a highly contested claim in need of philosophical defense, not an uncontroversial premise to be used to draw a conclusion about the existence of God.

In sum, many twenty-first-century educated people are skeptical about the existence of God, but not about the existence of right and wrong—which combination of perspectives drives us to deny that God's existence is essential for something to be right or wrong. It appears that quite a few readers are committed to thinking that higher values such as a universal morality can and do exist without God, and hence that meaning is possible without fulfilling a purpose that God has given to us.[9]

2.3.3.2 Free Will[10]

Consider now a second argument that philosophers have made for thinking that some spiritual conditions are essential if our lives are to be at all meaningful. By this approach, we could not have a free will, which is needed for a meaningful life, if we did not have a soul—that is, an immortal, spiritual substance. Note that this is mainly an argument for thinking that a soul is necessary for meaning in life, not so much that God is. One might suspect that a soul could exist only if God existed; but many religious thinkers in South and East Asia believe that we have a spiritual element that survives the death of our bodies (e.g., being reincarnated or experiencing *nirvana*), while denying that the God of the Abrahamic

---

9 I say more about how a purely physical world could conceivably ground objective values in Chapter 6.
10 Much of this section borrows from Metz 2020: 256–257.

faiths exists. Even if it might be possible (*contra* Descartes) to have a mind that were material and felt pleasure/pain, specific kinds of mental states perhaps could not be made of mere matter so as to make our lives matter (so to speak).

The German Enlightenment philosopher Immanuel Kant maintained, for instance, that if we were merely physical beings subject to the laws of nature like everything else in the animal, vegetable, and mineral kingdoms, then we could not act according to good reasons and could not be autonomous. Instead, we would be causally necessitated to act at any given time by the prior state of the natural world, widely known as the thesis of "determinism." If all our actions were determined and could not have been otherwise, then it appears that we would lack the freedom to choose: to act according to good reasons; to abide by moral rules; to help realize God's plan; or indeed, to do anything that merits pride or admiration.

It appears that the only way we could transcend the deterministic causal laws of the material world is if we had some spiritual essence that is independent of them and stronger than they are—that is, a soul. If our selves were constituted by an indestructible, non-physical nature, then we could understand how it is invariably within our power to do the morally rational thing, regardless of what might have happened before to us, where lacking such a freedom would seem to render our lives meaningless. Such a view is suggested in the following eloquent passage by a theologian:

> The moral spirit finds the meaning of life in choice. It finds it in that which proceeds from man and remains with him as his inner essence rather than in the accidents of circumstance and turns of external fortune ... (W)henever a human being rubs the lamp of his moral consciousness with moral passion, a Spirit does appear. This Spirit is God ... It is in the "Thou must" of God and man's "I can" that the divine image of God in human life is contained.
>
> (Swenson 2000: 27, 28).

The "I can" signifies a person's inherent ability to make the morally justified choice in any given situation—which, as per the previous discussion of Divine Command Theory (Section 2.3.3.1), might be to obey God's will. If we lacked that power, so that it was beyond our control whether we did the right thing or not, then our lives would be senseless, so the argument goes.

The point arguably applies not just to moral choices, but also to esthetic or epistemic ones. If we lack free will because everything we do is necessitated by a prior state of the natural world, then we get no credit for making an artwork or acquiring knowledge. We are then not the authors of our lives, and no meaning accrues to us.

One major way that critics have responded to this argument is to explain how the relevant kind of choice would be possible in a purely material world—one where there are no souls. Philosophers have striven to show that one could indeed act rationally, freely, and morally, in the important senses, if we were a part of nature in the way that everything else on Earth appears to be (e.g., Dennett 1984, 2003). It is worth keeping in mind how often the scientific method has been able to replace the spiritual with the physical. People used to believe that angels held planets in their orbits and gods were responsible for lightning; but these days cosmologists and meteorologists, respectively, can identify the physical causes of these events. The kinds of decisions that we intuitively think make our lives important are probably analogous to these events, and it is plausible to expect that they too have a material basis.

Space precludes recounting these kinds of materialist explanations of free will in detail, which would take us far into the field of metaphysics. However, briefly here, note that for many contemporary philosophers, even if we could not have acted otherwise than we do, so long as the causal chain runs through our brainy-bodily selves in a certain way, that is enough to ascribe actions to us and for us to count as free. Roughly speaking, so long as our choices are a product of our internal deliberation—even if that deliberation is itself ultimately causally determined by other things—we have free will. Note that there is an intuitive difference between, say, you deciding to steal money simply because you want it and, hypothetically, a mad scientist manipulating your brain with radio waves to make you steal money, or someone slipping you a drug that makes you steal it (cf. Frankfurt 1969). You would be free and responsible in the first case, but not in the latter two—even though in all three cases, your behavior would be causally determined by a past state of the world.

There is another way to criticize the present argument for thinking that an immortal soul is essential for meaning. That is to grant, for the sake of argument, that only a spiritual aspect of us could enable free will, but to question whether it must persist *forever* in order to do so. At this stage, let us suppose that only something utterly different from the natural world could intervene into it by making a moral choice. Suppose, in particular, that it would have to be a powerful force in order not to be determined by the laws of nature. Even so, there is a gap between that idea and the concept of a soul, as something indestructible or at least destined to continue without end. It seems that a spiritual substance could influence nature without being influenced by it and yet not be the sort of thing that is eternal. Just imagine that God did exist and were to assign it an expiration date.

2.3.3.3 Just Deserts

The previous arguments for (an extreme) supernaturalism were that realizing God's purpose for us is necessary for our lives to be meaningful, since only God's will could ground higher values pertaining to meaning in life, such as a moral system that applies to all human persons; and that the only way we could act so as to live morally—or more generally, to act for good reasons—is by having a soul that is not determined by the laws of nature. The argument explored here is that a spiritual realm is necessary in order to respond justly to people when they live up to such a moral system and when they fail to do so. Basically, the idea is that life is pointless if the wicked are not punished, the innocent who have been harmed are not compensated, and the virtuous are not rewarded, where such punishment, compensation, and reward are possible only if we survive the deaths of our bodies. Like the previous free will argument, in the first instance the just deserts reasoning is intended to show that having a soul is necessary for meaning, not quite that God is.

One might suspect that one's soul could receive its just deserts only if God existed and judged it. However, again, many religious thinkers—particularly in South Asia—deny that the Abrahamic God exists, but believe that we have a spiritual element that survives the death of our bodies and is subjected to *karma*—an impersonal force imposing burdens consequent to wrongdoing. In reply, one might contend that, even if punishment of the wicked were possible in a world without God, reward of the upright would not be; perhaps the only fully just way to reward those who have been good would be for them to unite with a personal creator of the universe in Heaven. If so, then the logic of the just deserts argument would show that both God and a soul must exist in order for life not to be pointless.

Consider an example to illustrate the three different lines of argument for thinking that meaning in life requires certain spiritual conditions. The previous two arguments involved the claims that God's commands alone make it wrong for anyone to be cruel to others for fun and that a soul is essential to be able to avoid acting cruelly, and hence immorally. In contrast, the present argument includes the claim that, if someone acted cruelly to others for fun, then justice—and hence meaning in life—would require that they undergo some kind of punishment and that the victim receive some kind of compensation; those conditions, in turn, require an afterlife and hence a soul that would survive the deaths of our bodies.

You could consistently hold one argument without the others. For instance, you might think that God would alone make possible the good (morality), the true (enquiry), and the beautiful (creativity), but that neither God nor a soul is needed for justice to be done (or perhaps that justice is not needed for a meaning in life). Or you might think that the good, the true, and the beautiful can exist without a spiritual realm, but that meaning requires perfect justice to be done, where a spiritual realm that includes a soul is necessary for that.

Many supernaturalists do, however, advance all three arguments: God alone could make the moral rules; only with a soul (perhaps that has come from God) could we be able to live up to the moral rules; and only with a soul could we receive our just deserts for having broken the moral rules (perhaps via God's judgment). That combination admittedly forms a tight and interesting package of philosophical claims—indeed, a compelling narrative, as Professor Seachris would put it—although I have been evaluating one piece at a time.

The idea that life would be meaningless if the good suffered and the bad flourished is an old one, harking back to Ecclesiastes, a book from the Hebrew Bible (*Tanakh*) that was composed more than 2,000 years ago. In this text, the author bemoans the apparent fact that every human person dies along with the death of her body, contending that it is a grave injustice such that "all is futility" (1.2) and "all the happenings beneath the sun" are akin to "the pursuit of wind" (1.14). In particular, the author of Ecclesiastes often conceives of justice in terms of what we deserve as something determined by our efforts, noting how often we do not get what we deserve for what we have done. He has in mind the claims that those who have chosen poorly receive benefits they do not deserve, and that those who have chosen well receive burdens they do not deserve.

One example involves the unfairly universal distribution of the burden of death:

> For the same fate is in store for all: for the righteous, and for the wicked; for the good and pure, and for the impure ... That is the sad thing about all that goes on under the sun: that the same fate is in store for all.
> (9.2–9.3; see also 2.14–2.16, 3.17).

Here, the suggestion is that, regardless of how well or poorly we have treated others, our lives all end up the same in the absence of an afterlife: namely, terminated. That seems unfair, and hence to rob our moral choices of significance.

There are myriad additional examples of undeserved conditions to be found in Ecclesiastes. Those who are oppressed do not get comforted (4.1). One works hard to build up wealth, only to see it squandered (5.12–5.13) or someone else enjoy it and not oneself (6.2). A good or upright person suffers harm, while a wicked person flourishes (7.15, 8.14). A man "who is pleasing to God" is not chosen by a woman, who instead selects a man who is displeasing to God (7.26). Still further, the author remarks:

> I have observed under the sun that
> The race is not won by the swift
> Nor the battle by the valiant;
> Nor is bread won by the wise,
> Nor wealth by the intelligent,
> Nor favor by the learned.
> (9.11).

And for two more examples: "He who digs a pit will fall into it; he who breaches a stone fence will be bitten by a snake" (10.8).

Life does seem to be in vain or absurd insofar as the upright, the courageous, the wise, the educated, and the hardworking do not flourish, whereas the wicked, the cowardly, the foolish, the ignorant, and the lazy do flourish—and, still worse, insofar as the latter receive the goods that the former had labored to produce (2.12, 2.18–2.21)! Our existence appears pointless if the kinds of lives we lead do not correlate with our efforts. Since that sort of justice is clearly not done in this earthly world, in order for our lives to be meaningful, there has to exist another world in which desert is meted out. That is, we must have immortal souls that are able to survive the deaths of our bodies, and God must give them what they deserve in an afterlife. The contemporary philosopher most known for advancing this position is the influential Christian philosopher of religion William Lane Craig (2009a, 2009b, 2013).

I find it hard to deny that there must be more to this life of ours if justice is going to be done in full; and further, I accept that life is not as meaningful as it could be in the face of this kind of injustice. However, why believe that there must be an *eternity* beyond this life in order to make things right? When we think of a soul, we are imagining a spiritual substance that contains one's mental states and that will never perish. Heaven is understood as eternal bliss and Hell as eternal damnation. It does not appear, though, that we could do anything to deserve either Heaven or Hell; those are not required by justice. For example, if someone wrongfully breaks my arm, I deserve some compensation; but I do not deserve an infinite amount of it in the form of happiness that never ends. In addition, the arm-breaker deserves some punishment; but he also does not deserve an infinite amount in the form of suffering that never ends.

The general point is that finite deeds undertaken on Earth seem to lack any infinite value or disvalue and that deserved responses to them—that is, ones that are proportionate or fitting—could also be finite. In order for justice to be done, we often would need more time beyond the 80 or so years that we tend to have on this planet; but we would not need to be immortal.

One might suggest that the only way for us to survive the deaths of our physical bodies would be to have a spiritual self that is indestructible. However, recent work in the philosophy of mind and personal identity strongly suggests otherwise. Imagine that the contents of people's minds were uploaded into a computer upon their bodily deaths on Earth and then downloaded into new bodies on another planet where they received their just deserts. Why wouldn't another few hundred years there suffice to right the wrongs? Of course, we are not in a position to transfer people's mental states from one brain to another. However, the point is that there is a possible physical world in which we could; and in that world, it appears that we could survive the deaths of our bodies. This provides reason to doubt that having a soul is necessary for an afterlife.

> **Soul and Self**
>
> Many of us are inclined to identify ourselves with something mental. We tend to think that we could survive even if all the cells in our body were to change over the years, or even if we were somehow able to switch bodies altogether. There are then two natural candidates for which sort of mental thing our selves might be: either a particular soul or a particular consciousness. A soul is understood to be a spiritual substance that can contain a certain stream of consciousness, but that could contain some other one. Imagine that you have a soul and that it gets "possessed"—say, by a demon. So, suppose that this soul comes to house a different personality with different memories. How would you describe the situation? Would you still be present, since the previous soul is there; or would you no longer be present, since the previous consciousness is gone?

Another way to question this argument for thinking that God and a soul are necessary for meaning in life is to contend that it is precisely the presence of certain kinds of injustice that offers some of us an opportunity to obtain meaning in our lives. Consider Nelson Mandela, who, as noted above, struggled for some 50 years against racist oppression in South Africa and played a major role in overturning it. Not too shabby when it comes to meaning! From this perspective, the presence of undeserved harm does not render everyone's life unavoidably futile, but rather can be what gives some lives a point.

Finally, it is worth remembering that, although there is overlap between morality and meaning, it is only partial. By this I mean that there are conditions of life that are intuitively meaningful but that have little, if anything, to do with living up to moral norms and receiving one's just deserts for having done so. Certain kinds of enquiry and creativity are good candidates.

2.3.3.4 This World Can Be Enough

In this section, I have considered three arguments for the view that exercising intelligence in certain ways in a physical universe is perhaps necessary to make life meaningful, but is not sufficient on its own. In addition, according to these three rationales, God and a soul have to exist—roughly in order to make a universal morality possible; to make it possible for us to abide by it; or to make it possible for justice to be done according to how well or poorly we have done so. I have provided reason to doubt all three arguments: morality, free will, and justice could be realized in the absence of any spiritual realm, or so I have tried to show.

Intuitively, so could meaning in life. Suppose, for the sake of argument, that neither God nor a soul exists. Even if that were the case, surely the lives of Einstein, Mother Teresa, Mandela, and the like were meaningful—more meaningful than those who merely spent their time tending to a drug habit or watching sitcoms alone. This sort of thought experiment, where we imagine that there is no spiritual realm and then appear to encounter meaning nonetheless, has been powerful enough to convince even many religiously inclined philosophers in the post-war era that meaning does not require God or a soul (e.g., Quinn 2000: 58; Audi 2005: 334, 341–342; Mawson 2016: 5).

That does not mean, however, that the debate between naturalists and supernaturalists is over. Instead, as I discuss in the next major section (Section 2.4) below, supernaturalism has changed, so that the claim these days is usually not that God and a soul are necessary for meaning in life as such, but rather that they are essential for a *great* meaning. Before considering that position, though, I first want to articulate a naturalist account of the meaning of life, in the specific sense of what would make the human race significant.

2.3.4 A Naturalist Theory of the Meaning of Life

It might seem as though, even if naturalism is plausible as an account of meaning in life, it is a non-starter in regard to the meaning of life. By "meaning of life," recall, much of the field now means the specific idea of what, if anything, would make humanity—and not just a given human person—important (Section 2.2.1). Key questions include whether the human race was created for a reason; whether anyone cares about it; and whether it has a purpose it should fulfill. It seems that we are driven straight into the arms of God if we are going to ascribe meaning to humanity. Surely, only God could have created the human race for a reason; only God could be the sort of being who loves us all; and only God could ascribe a purpose that applies to all of us.

A tempting initial reply from the naturalist is to point out that it would be possible for these things to be done by aliens with lesser powers than God. One can imagine that an advanced race of extraterrestrials created us for a reason, continues to care about us and wants us to flourish, and has ascribed a purpose to us. Why think God is in fact essential for these kinds of meaning?

However, a powerful response is that it is not just any agent who could confer meaning on the human race, but rather only a perfect person. It would matter to have been intentionally created by the source of the entire universe, not so much by aliens who had tinkered with DNA in a laboratory. It would matter to have a holy being take an interest in us, not so much extraterrestrials who have planted undetectable satellites around the Earth to listen in and observe. It would matter to realize a purpose ascribed to us by someone who is morally perfect, not so much one from more limited beings who might, say, want a human race version of *The Truman Show*, or for us to serve as food for them when they stop over on their way to another solar system.

I accept that if we had to choose between God or aliens, God would be preferable. Aliens could create, care for, and ascribe a purpose to us, but not in a meaning-conferring way—or at least not to the same degree. However, I can believe that God would *enhance* the meaningfulness of humanity compared to what aliens could do, while denying that God would be *necessary* for humanity to be meaningful. I conclude this major section by pointing out that the human race could be meaningful without God.

Think, first, about the significance of having come from a certain source. At the individual level, to speak bluntly, most of us want to be the intended product of a loving union among our parents, not the unintended by-product of a one-night stand. However, even those whose conception was accidental can have lives that are meaningful—and indeed, meaningful to the same degree as anyone else's. Much depends on which choices they make in life. Consider Einstein, for example. As one scholar remarks: "In judging whether his life was meaningful, no one would ever ask 'Was his existence intended?'" (Trisel 2012: 400). Analogous remarks apply to the collective level, I submit. It could well be that, given atheism, humanity "is a freak of nature—a blind product of matter plus time plus chance. Man is just a lump of slime that evolved rationality" (Craig 2013: 163). Even so, that rationality could be sufficient for humanity to be meaningful, if exercised in the right way.

I believe broadly similar remarks apply to the idea that God could alone care for us as a whole in a meaning-conferring way. Even if that were true, it seems as though humanity could still have a point and be significant if it were alone in the universe, but developed in a certain way. Again, an analogy with the individual level seems powerful. I accept that a person's life would be somewhat more meaningful if others loved him;[11] but I deny that being loved is essential for a meaningful life. Meaning can come to a person in other ways—for example, by being loving as opposed to being loved.

In fact, *more* meaning would arguably come from being the one who loves others as opposed to the one whom others love. (That's arguably one lesson to learn from the life and (bodily) death of Jesus.) That is particularly true if one does not even know that one is loved by others—and note how difficult it is for us to know whether God exists and hence whether God cares about us. If God loves us, we cannot really know that (even if many of us have faith or hope that God does).

If this analysis has been correct, then whether humanity is meaningful or not depends, crucially, not on whether it was intentionally created or is cared about, which are passive conditions, but instead on the choices humanity makes—something active. And I suggest that what it would make sense for the human race to feel proud about or what would make a good life-story for it involves its exercise of intelligence in positive, effortful, and developmental ways. For example, imagine that human beings—perhaps through some organization such as the United Nations—were to strive collaboratively to overcome poverty, unemployment, oppression, discrimination, and climate change. These meaningful achievements would be properly ascribed to humanity—or at least to it at a certain point in time. For another example, if many countries around the world cooperated in order to communicate with another intelligent species in the universe, then, again, meaning would plausibly accrue to human beings.

The careful reader will have noticed some hedging in this naturalist approach to the meaning of life.[12] In particular, it grounds

---

11 A good question is whether this point is a counterexample to the intelligence theory advanced above (in Section 2.3.2). I suspect not, if what it is that people love is, say, one's character, as opposed to one's looks.
12 The next few paragraphs borrow from Metz 2022a.

the claim that humanity *at a certain stage* would be meaningful, not so much that the human species, as something stretching over hundreds of thousands of years, would be. That might seem to be a problem; but it is, upon reflection, difficult to see how the human race as a whole could ever be the agent responsible for fulfilling a purpose—even God's—or making an achievement. Suppose that humanity at a certain time defeated evil, created global justice, met intelligent aliens, or loved God properly. Why attribute any of those accomplishments to all members of the human race, as opposed to principally those human beings who were at least alive at the time they were effected? Why think that the species, which includes members who lived more than 50,000 years ago, gets the meaning credit?

I do not mean to suggest that literally only those alive at the time of, for example, realizing a just world could obtain meaning from it; for the lives of those who had intentionally contributed to the relevant aim but perished before seeing it realized would be made more significant upon its realization. I am also open to the idea that it could be sensible to attribute a feature to the species, despite not every single individual member exhibiting it. The trouble is that many, and probably most, members of the species neither would have intended to realize the relevant aim—whether that is global justice or love of God—nor would have done anything substantial to contribute toward its realization. What grounds the attribution of such meaningful achievements to the entire group of human beings?

One might point out that we often ascribe meaning to the life of an individual in the light of certain actions that he took only at a particular stage. For example, there are those who would maintain that Winston Churchill's (1874–1965) life had substantial meaning in it because of some of the decisions he made during World War Two. By analogy, perhaps the life of humanity as a whole can be meaningful because of what some of its members did at a certain stage.

However, I am concerned that an important disanalogy is the lack of mental and causal relations among a sufficient number of human beings to give credit to the whole for the actions of only some at a particular time. Churchill's life formed a unity, by virtue of continuities among psychological and bodily events, such that the meaningfulness of what he did at a particular time is sensibly ascribed to his life as a whole. I find it hard to identify relevantly similar continuities among, say, the first *Homo sapiens* from several tens of thousands of years ago in Africa, an isolated clan in the

Amazon jungle living 300 years ago, and people in twenty-first-century Tokyo.

> ### Ascribing Credit (or Blame) to Humanity
>
> I have argued that any large-scale accomplishment, such as defeating evil, should be ascribed not to the human race as a whole, but rather to some subset of it that is nonetheless much larger than an individual. However, sometimes we do speak in ways suggesting that humanity deserves the credit for accomplishments. Consider, for instance, the famous description of landing on the moon as "one giant leap for mankind." Can you think of additional cases in which we speak in ways ascribing a success (or a failure) to the species? Should we take such ascriptions literally, or are they best understood as metaphors for some large part of humanity at a given time?

Hence, I do not think that it is a problem with my account of the meaning of life that it does not ascribe it to literally every member of the human race. More problematic, I believe, is the fact that this account is not, on the face of it, as compelling a life-story as a possible supernaturalist account—one that I am sure Professor Seachris accepts. My account lacks any connection with a grand plan for everything that exists in the cosmos, and it is consistent with the eventual death of the human species—a presumably unwelcome ending. While I submit that I have provided reason to doubt that supernaturalist conditions are necessary for humanity to be meaningful, the door remains open for the supernaturalist to claim that a greater sort of meaning would be available to the human race if, and only if, God and a soul existed.

> ### Summary
>
> The main aim of this section was to articulate and defend a naturalist theory of meaning in life. According to it, one's life is more meaningful the more one exercises one's rational nature in positive, effortful, and developmental ways. I argued that this comprehensive and basic principle accounts

well for intuitive respects in which there is meaning in the rich life, and in which there is not in the poor lives. Next I addressed the supernaturalist suggestion that, in order for our intelligence to confer meaning on our lives, some spiritual conditions must exist, too—whether they be a moral purpose assigned by God, a soul that would give us free will, or just deserts for our virtue that could come only with an eternal afterlife. I basically replied that the relevant purpose, freedom, and justice could obtain in a purely physical world, and then argued that a thought experiment reveals that most of us believe that a meaningful life is possible in the absence of anything spiritual. Finally, I extended the intelligence theory to account for what could make humanity meaningful—at least a major part of it at a given point in time.

2.4 Moderate Supernaturalism

For hundreds of years, Western philosophers debating about life's meaning focused on the claim that God and a soul are necessary for life's meaning of any sort or to any degree. Supernaturalists held what I label the "extreme" view that if there is no spiritual realm, then all our lives are meaningless, whereas naturalists strove to deny that claim. However, since around the start of the twenty-first-century, there has been a shift in the nature of the debate. These days, many (not all) supernaturalists are "moderate" in their approach—by which I mean that they grant that some meaning would be possible in an atheist world but maintain that a greater meaning could come only in a theist world.[13]

Typical is the following statement from T. J. Mawson, based at the University of Oxford and one of the more prominent religious philosophers about life's meaning currently writing:

> [According to extreme supernaturalism—ed.] if we are in fact in a Godless universe, everyone's life – from that led by Gandhi to that led by that wastrel youth who lives at the other end of your street ... is entirely meaningless. Gandhi and the wastrel each score a flat zero. But that is a hard teaching. Who can believe it? ... [I]t might well be true that Gandhi's life is more

---

13 This distinction was first articulated in Metz 2019c.

meaningful than that of the wastrel even if there is no God. But, if there is no God, then there's some deeper or more permanent sort of meaning that even Gandhi's life lacked because all our lives lack it.

(Mawson 2016: 5; see also 17).

Mawson is claiming that it would be incredible to think that Gandhi's life had literally no meaning in it on the supposition that there is no God with a purpose for him to have realized and he did not survive the death of his body. We have to believe that Gandhi's life was significant for having helped to end colonial rule in India by using substantially non-violent means. However, Mawson maintains that Gandhi's life would have had a much better sort of meaning if God and a soul existed—indeed, a meaning that would never end.

In this section, I critically discuss two major reasons for thinking that a much greater meaning in life and meaning of life would be available if the world were the way that Christians, Muslims, and (some) Jews believe. Let us suppose: God exists and made the physical universe with a plan in mind; God also created us for a purpose that dovetails with this plan—something like worshipping God, overcoming evil, or developing features in us that approximate the divine; we have immortal souls that will outlive the deaths of our bodies; God will judge our souls based on the extent to which we have fulfilled God's purpose for us; if we adequately fulfill God's purpose, God will give us eternal bliss in Heaven; and if we do not, God will send us to Hell, understood as eternal damnation. According to at least one philosopher, this kind of supernaturalist narrative would be better than its naturalist rivals, perhaps even providing "the best story we have about life's meanings" (Quinn 2000: 66; see also Seachris 2016).

Why think so, exactly? In the rest of this section, I consider two different arguments for thinking that we should wish for the world to be like this if we want our own lives and that of the species to be maximally meaningful (Sections 2.4.1–2.4.2). I provide some criticism of them, after which I offer a reason to doubt moderate supernaturalism itself (Section 2.4.3).

2.4.1 Sharing a Temporary Life with God

One rationale that has been advanced explicitly in support of moderate supernaturalism is that our lives could enjoy a much greater meaning if God existed and we became part of God's life. Although some theologians understand that concept quite literally, the more common view—which I address here—is that meaning would come from sharing a life with God, where God could have existed without us.

Sharing a life with God, here, does not mean enjoying an afterlife in His presence—the sort of rationale that is considered separately below (Section 2.4.2). Instead, the thought is that, by living a certain way while on Earth, our lives can have a "cosmic significance ... instead of a significance very limited in time and space" (Swinburne 2016: 154). Without God, our lives could be meaningful in only "a local and temporary sense" (Cottingham 2016: 136).

For example, if we were to help realize God's plan for the universe while on Earth, then our actions would seem to have a much greater importance by virtue of their role in a benevolent project that is as large and long-lasting as one can get for covering "the whole universe and all its inhabitants" (Swinburne 2016: 154, and see also 156–158; and Quinn 2000: 58–65). In partnering with God to fight evil, our lives would acquire a much greater meaning because of the massive spatiotemporal scope of the endeavor in this world.

For another example, consider the eternal effect of so acting on God's mind. In particular, consider God forever fondly remembering what one did to help to realize God's purpose—something eloquently emphasized by Cottingham:

> The sense that our acts are eternally subject to divine evaluation ... seems deeply to enhance their significance [as] a source of joy to a being of supreme wisdom and love. This amplifies and as it were confirms the meaningfulness that they already had on earth, and protects them against the erosions of time and contingency, shielding them against the backdrop of impermanence against which nothing in the long term matters very much.
>
> (2016: 135; see also 131–134).

Notice again what I am calling the "moderate" approach: Cottingham appears to accept that meaning would be available on Earth without God but suggests that a permanent meaning would be possible by pleasing God. Cottingham continues by saying that if "our acts are eternally subject to divine evaluation ... our contribution ultimately and eternally matters" (Cottingham 2016: 135).

These rationales could sensibly apply to either meaning in life or the meaning of life. That is, any one of us as individuals or the human race as a whole (or of course both) could have a more significant existence if we played a role in God's plan and God were pleased because we had done so (Quinn 2000: 64–65; Mawson 2016: 57–64).

One major criticism of this rationale for moderate supernaturalism is that the opportunity for greater meaning with a spiritual dimension would bring in its wake a corresponding opportunity for greater "anti-matter"—which, recall (2.2.4), means conditions that would reduce meaning in life. If the prospective gains with God would be much greater, then so would the prospective losses, making it unclear whether a world with God would be more desirable in respect of meaning than a world without. Specifically, if one's fulfilling God's purpose and God's being pleased about that would produce a much greater significance for one's existence than would be possible in a world without God, then, by the same token, one's frustrating God's purpose and God's displeasure at that would reduce the significance of one's life to a correspondingly greater degree. With God, the stakes are higher—and it is not obvious that one would come out ahead, as opposed to lose much more than one could ever lose in a world without God.

The point of the present criticism is not that the chances of a life empty of meaning would increase in a world with a spiritual dimension. It is rather that the chances of a life full of anti-matter—a negative score as opposed to a zero—would increase with it, supposing, for the sake of argument, that the chances of a meaningful life would increase with it. It is therefore unclear whether a spiritual realm is in fact desirable for living meaningfully.

2.4.2 Enjoying Eternal Life with God[14]

The previous argument was that an eternal significance could come to one's life from fulfilling God's purpose, even if one did not live forever. Simply participating in a plan for the universe or pleasing God would be enough. In contrast, the present argument is that an eternal significance could come (either also or instead) from one's living forever in Heaven consequent to one's having obeyed God's will.

---

14 Some of this section is borrowed from Metz 2021b.

Consider the following quotations from Craig:

> (I)f theism is true, we have a sound basis for moral accountability ... Evil and wrong will be punished; righteousness will be vindicated ... [T]he moral choices we make in this life are infused with an eternal significance.
>
> (Craig 2009a: 31).

> In the absence of moral accountability, our choices become trivialized because they make no ultimate contribution to either the betterment of the universe or to the moral good in general because everyone ends up the same. Death is the great leveler.
>
> (Craig 2009a: 38).

> [T]o believe that God does not exist and that there is thus no moral accountability is quite literally de-moralizing, for then we should have to believe that our moral choices are ultimately insignificant, since both our fate and that of the universe will be the same regardless of what we do.
>
> (Craig 2009b: 184).

Notice the qualifications. Speaking of "eternal" significance invites comparison with a less than eternal significance. Talk of an "ultimate" contribution or of something being "ultimately" insignificant suggests a less than ultimate significance. This reasoning is therefore naturally read as supporting a moderate supernaturalism (even if it might not be Craig's own view), according to which meaning is possible in the world as known particularly well by science, but an eternal or ultimate one is not, and requires a God who rewards good and punishes bad in the course of judging one's soul. In any event, that is how I shall interpret the above quotations.

Craig is not explicit when advancing this reasoning about how it is that God would hold us morally accountable—that is, respond to our choices by giving us what we deserve. However, the picture is presumably the common one among monotheists mentioned above, according to which God sends the souls of those who have exhibited moral virtue (whether in the form of faith or works) to Heaven, where they will enjoy eternal life with God; and God sends the souls of those who have exhibited vice to eternal damnation in Hell. If, and only if, there is such judgment can one's moral decisions make an eternal or ultimate difference and have a corresponding meaning, so the argument goes.

Now, I submit that the objection I made to the previous rationale for moderate supernaturalism applies to this one with comparable force. It was that along with the prospect of a greater meaning would also come the prospect of a greater anti-meaning. *If* moral accountability requires the prospect of eternal life in a Heaven (which we of course might doubt: see Section 2.3.3.3), then it also requires the prospect of eternal life in a Hell—which would presumably make one's life anti-matter, and to a degree much greater than it could in a world without God and a soul. Hence, it is again not clear that supernaturalism would be preferable, given an interest in living meaningfully. Simply pointing out that Heaven would be on offer is not enough to support supernaturalism, since Hell would be a possibility, too. One might not be inclined to think of Hell in terms of what is anti-meaningful; but it is a reasonable approach—it would not merely be punishment, but suffering imposed because of one's badness that is furthermore unredeemable and serves no purpose such as, say, preventing a greater suffering on the part of oneself or someone else. Getting tossed into Hell would merit great shame.

The Risks of an Afterlife

Imagine that a society created a lottery in which you could either win a fortune with which you could live out your days in comfort or completely lose your freedom, becoming someone's unconditional slave for the rest of your life. Many of us think it would be wrong for a government to permit such a lottery, let alone to create and run it. And if such a lottery happened to exist, many of us would not want our children and friends to purchase a ticket. What might be a plausible difference between this lottery and a theistic world, in which you would face the prospect of either eternal bliss or eternal damnation? If we prefer to avoid such a lottery, should we analogously prefer not to live in a world as standardly conceived by Christianity and Islam? You might think that, in the theist world, you would have a choice of whether to go to Heaven or Hell, which makes it different from the lottery case. However, is there not always the risk of making the wrong choice? And might the decision of whether to buy a lottery ticket be analogous to having a choice?

At this point, the moderate supernaturalist might respond by denying that moral accountability on the part of God would involve sending anyone to Hell. Hell is out of fashion these days among philosophers of religion. Many of them have come to doubt that God would send anyone to Hell, when that is understood as damnation that does not end. What follow are some of the most salient considerations from the past 30 years or so (from the likes of Adams 1993; Kvanvig 1993; Kershnar 2005; Buckareff and Plug 2017; and Mawson 2019).

First off, a compassionate, loving God might well impose penalties; but they would be ones that would be lifted upon having done some good, such as reform of the wayward individual and reconciliation between him and others, including God. Such a God would not impose suffering merely for the sake of suffering.

Furthermore, even an angry, vengeful God would not judge that any one of us should go to Hell, since nothing we can be or do would deserve such a penalty. Humans would deserve an eternal punishment only if they did or were something infinitely bad, and we may reasonably doubt that infinite disvalues are possible in an earthly life.

Still more, even if infinite disvalues were possible in an earthly life, it would not follow that eternity is needed to give people what they deserve. Supposing that one could do or be something infinitely disvaluable in one's 80 or so years here, then a response proportionate to this deed would require merely a finite amount of time.

Lastly, even if infinite disvalues were possible during an earthly life, and even if only an infinite punishment would be proportionate to them, it is implausible to think that God would create such horrible beings in the first place. Of course, free will has some final value; but it is hard to think that the specific sort that would produce the kind of vice or wrongness that warrants eternal damnation would be worth such a cost.

Let us suppose, then, that universal salvation would be on the cards in a world with God and a soul. If so, then there would not be the prospect of anti-matter from Hell. And so, it appears the objection is avoided. However, a new and ironic problem arises, since universal salvation would mean, quoting Craig, that "our choices become trivialized because they make no ultimate contribution to either the betterment of the universe or to the moral good in general because everyone ends up the same" (2009a: 38). If we all are destined for Heaven, then it would be the case that everyone's lives end up the same, regardless of the choices they have made while on Earth!

Of course, some would take a detour on the route to Heaven; some bad people would require time away from God—perhaps even in the form of punishment—in order to become the sort of people on whom God would bestow the gift of eternal bliss. However, such a finite amount of time would not detract from the overall supreme quality of life that would come to everyone; for a life of never-ending goodness would be, if not literally an infinity of well-being, then so enormous as to make the punitive detour amount to nothing by comparison. And hence all lives would end up the same, regardless of the moral choices we make.

One might be inclined to think that, in the way one is tempted to imagine circles of Hell, there would also be circles of Heaven, with some concentric circles coming to closer to God than others (cf. Jeremiah 17:10; Matthew 16:27, 19:28–29; 1 Corinthians 3:7–15; 2 Corinthians 5:10; and the Qur'an 30:38–39, 56:1–11, 83:18–28). Some people's faith has been stronger; some of their virtue higher; some of their works better.

However, even if that were true, it would not make any difference to people's quality of life, on what I take to be the standard understanding of this sort of infinity among mathematicians since Cantor. Two lives of infinite goodness would both be "countable" infinities and hence the same, in the sense that for any unit of value in an eternal life, it could be put into a one-to-one correspondence with the natural numbers.[15] The amount of goodness in two infinite lives would be the same, or so is suggested by the views of contemporary mathematicians.

In sum, I believe that trying to defend moderate supernaturalism by appeal to eternal life consequent to one's moral choices encounters a dilemma. On the one hand, if one could wind up in either Heaven or Hell, then it is not clear that God and a soul offer any expected advantage relative to an atheist world, since although Heaven would involve eternal meaning, Hell would involve eternal anti-meaning. On the other hand, if there were no prospect of Hell and everyone would wind up in Heaven, then one's moral choices would make no difference, undercutting the logic of the argument

---

15 For one clear exposition, see Barrow 2005: 55–74.

according to which there must be differential responses to righteousness and evil for a great meaning to obtain.

2.4.3 A Reason to Reject Moderate Supernaturalism

There are many objections in the philosophical literature to the notion that immortality would foster meaning in life, even when conceived as living in God's presence. Some maintain that living forever would get boring and hence become meaningless. Others say that meaning depends crucially on authoring a compelling life-story, and that an infinite life could not facilitate that since such a narrative must have an end. Still others contend that if we lived forever, nothing would seem precious to us and we would not be motivated to get anything done without, well, a deadline. Still others maintain that our lives would unavoidably become repetitive, which would substantially drain them of meaning.

Of these arguments, I find only the last one particularly strong. However, I do not pursue it here, instead advancing a different sort of reason to doubt that a world with God and a soul would offer a greater meaning, while also making sense of the intuition that a meaningful life would be possible in a purely physical world. Recall that both of the above arguments for moderate supernaturalism appeal to the idea that a spiritual realm would offer us an eternal significance, as opposed to a finite and indeed quite short one available in an earthly life. My criticism is that there is a tension between advancing a moderate supernaturalism on the one hand, and holding that God would make possible an eternal significance on the other.

The greatness of a life that eternally matters must dwarf any meaning lacking this feature, making it difficult to explain how a merely earthly life without God and a soul could, by comparison, be meaningful. However, the defining point of moderate supernaturalism is that such a life could indeed be meaningful—remember the case of Gandhi above.

In terms of time, if God would afford our souls significance for an eternity, then no earthly life of about 80 years can compare, and hence the supernaturalist cannot account for the intuition that such a life could be significant. Furthermore, if a life with eternal significance would bring an infinite amount of meaning in its wake, then consider that no life with a finite amount of meaning could compare, and again the supernaturalist cannot account for the intuition that such a life could be meaningful. To be sure, by the present position, an 80-or-so-year life would not be a "flat zero" in terms of the amount of meaning in it. However, it would, compared to eternity or infinity, come about as close to zero as is mathematically possible for a positive number, which fails to capture the judgment that a life can be meaningful absent God and a soul.

The moderate supernaturalist who invokes eternal significance needs to explain how we can avoid thinking that its value would ridiculously outweigh that of an earthly lifespan, reducing it to next to nothing by comparison, thereby leaving us unable to capture the intuition that an earthly life—such as that of Gandhi, or Mother Teresa, or Einstein, or Mandela—could ever count as meaningful. For these lives to have been meaningful involves the claim that they, among other things, have warranted reactions such as pride from a first-person perspective, and admiration and awe from a third-person perspective. It is difficult to see how that claim can be sustained if we are comparing these lives with those that have an eternal or infinite meaning. They simply are not impressive enough by comparison. Moderate supernaturalism is no longer really moderate, upon appealing to eternity.

A moderate supernaturalism that appeals to standard monotheistic ideas involving eternal significance is just one form; and there could be other kinds of moderate supernaturalism that avoid the objection I have raised (as well as the other *prima facie* problems with immortality mentioned at the start of this section). For example, I am open to the idea that a maximally meaningful life would be one with an afterlife that does not last forever. In that case, we could affect other people's quality of life for better or worse and receive our just deserts for having done so, without people's lives turning out to have an infinite value that makes the life of a Gandhi amount to nothing by comparison. This would be an unusual version of moderate supernaturalism to hold, but seems to me worth developing.

Summary

Even if the previous section successfully showed that a meaningful life is possible in a purely physical world, it still seems attractive to hold a moderate supernaturalism, according to which a spiritual realm is necessary not for any meaning at all, but rather for a much greater amount or kind of meaning.

> On the one hand, a grand and eternal meaning could come from participating in God's plan for the universe and God forever remembering that fondly. On the other hand, an infinite significance could come from uniting with God in Heaven forever. Against both rationales, I argued that, if God and a soul would offer the chance at a greater meaning, they would by the same token offer the chance at a greater anti-meaning—for example, in the form of displeasing God or winding up in Hell. Finally, I provided a reason to doubt not the arguments for moderate supernaturalism, but the present version of moderate supernaturalism itself. I argued that an appeal to eternal or infinite meaning is "too big" to invoke, since it makes it difficult to make sense of the intuition that an earthly life such as Gandhi's could be meaningful—that is, warrant reactions of pride and admiration, make a positive difference, or author a compelling life-story.

2.5 Rebutting Nihilism; Or, Yes, Your Life Has Meaning in It

So far, I have addressed two of the big three questions that are normally posed about life's meaning: what we are talking about when discussing it, and what would make life meaningful. What remains to answer is the third question: whether any of our lives or whether the human race is in fact meaningful. Nihilism (or sometimes pessimism) is the claim that no one's life is meaningful, and in this section I briefly provide reason to doubt an influential argument for it.

Notice that rebutting nihilism does not necessarily mean showing that all lives have meaning in them. To reject the claim that no one's life has any meaning in it does not commit one to accept the claim that everyone's life has meaning in it, or at least not the claim that everyone's life is meaningful—that is, full of meaning. I do not think that all lives are meaningful. Plausible cases, I submit, are, someone who has been a serial killer since his teenage years and a three-year-old orphan who gets cancer, suffers horribly for a year, and dies. I might want to grant that there is some meaning in even these lives; but I do not believe there is enough for them to be characterized as meaningful on the whole. Instead, in the following I aim to rebut reasons for thinking that no one's life is meaningful, or that no one's life has any meaning in it at all.

Throughout this discussion, we have been supposing that some lives do have meaning in them. In particular, the intuitions about what *would* confer meaning on a life, such as those pertaining to the rich life (Section 2.3.1), were also, in effect, intuitions about what *does* confer meaning on a life. Nihilists claim that these judgments are misguided; they say that our lives are missing certain features that would make it possible to obtain meaning from the good, the true, and the beautiful.

One argument for nihilism that had been influential was, interestingly, an appeal to extreme supernaturalism. Holding that God and a soul are necessary for life to be meaningful (as per Sections 2.3.3.1–2.3.3.3), and then failing to find evidence that God and a soul exist, thinkers such as Leo Tolstoy (1828–1910) (1884) and Camus (1955) were forced to conclude that our lives are meaningless. In the modern era, when many have become skeptical of being able to know that there is a spiritual realm, the view that life has meaning only if God and a soul exist prompts many to doubt that anyone's life has meaning in it.

Another reason many religiously inclined philosophers have opted for moderate supernaturalism is that it enables them to avoid a nihilist conclusion in the face of the difficulty of proving that God and a soul exist. Recall that, according to the moderate version of supernaturalism, life can be meaningful without God and a soul, even if a much greater sort of meaning is unavailable without them. Hence, it can be coherent for the moderate (but not the extreme) supernaturalist to hold both that we do not know whether God and a soul exist and that we do know that some lives are meaningful.

There are other rationales for nihilism that do not appeal to the non-existence of a spiritual realm, or at least not explicitly. Probably the most influential one invokes what is often called the "*sub specie aeternitatis*," Latin for the point of view of the universe or the perspective of eternity. Human persons have the ability to view their lives in relation to the entire cosmos—that is, in relation to all times and all places. When one takes up this most external standpoint on one's life and views one's puny impact on the world, nothing of one's life appears to matter. As one generally pessimistic philosopher, the South African David Benatar, points out:

> Earthly life is thus without significance, import, or purpose beyond our planet. It is meaningless from the cosmic perspective ... Nothing we do on earth has any effect beyond it. The

evolution of life, including human life, is a product of blind forces and serves no apparent purpose. We exist now, but we will not exist for long ... (N)othing we do makes any difference beyond our planet or in cosmic time.
(Benatar 2017: 36, 50; cf. Nagel 1986: 208–232).

What one does in a certain society on Earth over 80 years or so just does not amount to anything, when considering the billions of temporal years and billions of light-years that make up space-time.

Benatar and others sympathetic to the deliverances of the point of view of the universe tend to admit that a human or terrestrial sort of meaning is possible. However, they often add in the claim that the cosmic perspective is more important or more justified than a limited one. For instance, in one text Benatar notes that, for many of us, the point of view of humanity is more valid for judgments of meaning than an individual's perspective, since an individual might deem it important, say, to count blades of grass on a lawn. If you hold that claim, then, by analogy, Benatar suggests, you should consider the point of view of the universe "more reliable" than judgments of meaning from the standpoint of humanity (Benatar 2006: 83). Similarly, two philosophers have recently said: "In virtue of being more encompassing, the cosmic point of view can claim to present your life in a truer or more rational light than any more mundane point of view it contains" (Persson and Savulescu 2019: 235). If the point of view of the universe is more reliable, accurate, or rational than any other point of view, and if our lives are meaningless from the former perspective, then a robust form of nihilism follows.

What might cosmic meaning look like? What are we missing, exactly? One possibility involves God and a soul as characteristically conceived in monotheist religious traditions (Benatar 2021: 32–33). However, Benatar denies we have evidence that they exist; and, in any event, at this point in this chapter I want to consider non-religious grounds for holding nihilism. A second possibility, then, does not involve serving a spiritual Creator, but instead more limited, embodied aliens. Here is Benatar's most explicit comment on what meaning from the point of view of the universe would amount to: "I can tell you what it would take for our lives to have cosmic meaning. Part of what it would take is for there to be an extra-terrestrial population and for our lives to have significance from their perspective" (Benatar 2021: 15). For us to have significance from their perspective would centrally involve having some positive effect on their lives. In addition, Benatar maintains that cosmic meaning would plausibly involve us living for much, much longer than humans ever have or plausibly could.

Now, I am sympathetic to the claim that some real meaning would come from interacting with, and especially meeting, intelligent alien life.[16] I have been moved by films such as *Close Encounters of the Third Kind*, *E.T.*, *Contact*, and *Arrival*—where my emotional reactions are, I think, tracking a sense of significance, as opposed to some other value such as happiness, moral virtue, or beauty.

However, I have wept no more intensely at these kinds of movies than I have at other ones. Films about establishing a romantic connection (between humans) in the face of obstacles, and about protagonists struggling to overcome and make something of their lives, have also affected me—and in comparable, if not stronger, ways. If the reader's emotions are similar to mine, that is evidence that they believe that meeting smart extraterrestrials would matter, but to no more a degree than certain human engagements.

There is some additional *prima facie* evidence that substantial meaning would come from interacting with intelligent alien life: namely, in that it seems appropriate for governments to spend some tax money searching for evidence of it. Concretely, I, for one, believe that it has been right for the United States to spend public resources on The Search for ExtraTerrestrial Intelligence (SETI) project.[17] The hope has been to detect not just communication from an extraterrestrial source, but also a signal to which we could respond. The idea that spending taxes on such aims is apt is probably best justified by the propositions that government ought to foster meaning in people's lives and that interacting with self-conscious beings elsewhere in the cosmos would be pretty meaningful. It would not just be the science and technology that aliens might be able to share with us—for I submit that the government should spend some resources to make contact with intelligent life, even if this species were about as advanced as we are, or even if it were much more advanced than us, but we were unable to benefit from its knowledge for whatever reason (e.g., because we are too dumb).

---

16   The next few paragraphs borrow from Metz 2022b.
17   National Aeronautics and Space Administration, "SETI: The Search for ExtraTerrestrial Intelligence," https://history.nasa.gov/seti.html.

However, I do not think that finding evidence of intelligent alien life is so more important as to mean that the SETI project should receive the *lion's share* of a government's budget. And I presume the reader agrees with me. If so, then we have some reason to doubt the claim that meeting alien persons would confer a *much* greater meaning on our lives than human projects—a claim to which Benatar is committed by virtue of holding that cosmic meaning is the most valid sort and that cosmic meaning would involve engaging positively with extraterrestrial populations.

Which kinds of personal sacrifices would you make in order to interact with alien persons? Would you ditch your spouse and children to join the crew of a starship with warp drive in hot pursuit of a (much) more attractive instance of E.T.? Some readers would, but relatively few—suggesting that, for most, meaningful ties with humans count for more. In addition, of those who would leave their families behind, for many of them it would be a very difficult decision—suggesting that meaningful ties with humans and those with aliens are of comparable importance. Would the prospect of, say, romance with one who lives across the galaxy really matter so much more than with one's spouse on Earth?

I submit that these reflections indicate that, while many of us would find substantial meaning in relating to intelligent aliens, that sort of meaning would not overshadow the sort available on Earth. Upon comparing the human point of view with the point of view of the universe, many favor the former—or at least find the two of similar importance in respect of the spatial dimension of cosmic meaning. The difference we can make to humans matters an awful lot, and for quite a few readers would matter more than the difference we could make to faraway aliens.

Meaningfulness and Eternity

A cosmic meaning would involve doing something that, in the ideal case, not only ranges over a huge array of space, but also spans an enormous amount of time. I have focused on the spatial aspect, providing reason to doubt that extraterrestrial engagement would be all that important compared to an earthly life. What about the temporal aspect? It is tempting to think, with Benatar, that with more time could

> come more meaning. However, some philosophers maintain that an eternal or extremely long life of billions of years would get boring or have to repeat itself, either of which would be anti-meaningful. Would living for that long inevitably become boring or repetitive (or both)? If so, would that necessarily undercut the prospect of living meaningfully?

To sum up, I do not deny that living meaningfully from the standpoint of the universe would be worth doing, but question whether it would be more important than living meaningfully from the standpoint of humanity. Insofar as the latter perspective has a validity comparable to the former, and insofar as many of our lives are indeed meaningful from the standpoint of humanity, we do not find reason to believe nihilism. So, yes, dear reader, your life can be meaningful. In fact, by my account of meaning in life (Section 2.3.2), it is so, in part, by virtue of having read this book and thereby exercised your intelligence to learn about a fundamental feature of human life.

Summary

Nihilism is the view that no one's life is meaningful, or that everyone's life is at least lacking an important kind of meaning. A major rationale for nihilism in the modern West has been extreme supernaturalism, according to which God and a soul must exist for anyone's life to be meaningful and we lack evidence that they do exist. Another rationale for nihilism appeals to meaning from the point of view of the universe or a cosmic meaning, which in principle appears compatible with a purely physical world, but which is utterly unavailable to us. A cosmic meaning would roughly involve engaging in purposeful, esteem-worthy, etc. projects in regard to extraterrestrial populations for billions of years. I have provided reason to doubt that such a meaning is much more important than meaning from a human point of view, since we would be unreasonable, in terms of the value of meaning, to sacrifice the needs of our family or other human beings in order to realize it—at least with respect to far away aliens.

First Round of Replies

Chapter 3

"Some" Meaning Without God or a Soul

Reply to Metz

Joshua W. Seachris

Contents

3.1 Introduction 140
3.2 Points of Agreement 141
3.3 God and Objective Value 143
3.4 Meaning Pluralism 2.0: Reconsidering Extreme and Moderate Supernaturalism 155
3.5 Meaning Pluralism 2.1: Passively Conditioned Meaning vs. Actively Conditioned Meaning 160
3.6 Making Meaning too Difficult? 162

> Finally, the sun set and the birds flew away. Edward hung by his velvet ears and looked up at the night sky. He saw the stars. But for the first time in his life, he looked at them and felt no comfort. Instead, he felt mocked. You are down there alone, the stars seemed to say to him. And we are up here, in our constellations, together. I have been loved, Edward told the stars. So? said the stars. What difference does that make when you are all alone now? Edward could think of no answer to that question.
> Kate DiCamillo, *The Miraculous Journey of Edward Tulane*: 119–20

> It would be wonderful to find in the laws of nature a plan prepared by a concerned creator in which human beings played some special role. I find sadness in doubting that we will. There are some among my scientific colleagues who say that the contemplation of nature gives them all the spiritual satisfaction that others have found in a belief in an interested God. Some of them may even feel that way. I do not.
> Stephen Weinberg, *Dreams of a Final Theory*: 256

3.1 Introduction

With our opening statements behind us, I am confident that Professor Metz and I have dealt another blow to the oft-repeated claim that there really is not that much one can say—philosophically and with the careful use of reason as our guide, that is—about the question of life's meaning. I count it a privilege to be a part of that progress with my colleague in this venue. We, of course, disagree about important matters. After all, we would not be participating in this project if that were not the case. And yet I do not want to begin there with my reply.

In this spirit, I open my response by reviewing substantial areas of agreement between us. This is no small matter, for these are areas of genuine progress in clarifying the sorts of ideas we have in mind when talking about life's meaning. In the philosophy classes I teach, I assign written work that follows a consistent template. I want my students to learn important skills that they can take with them in their post-philosophy class vocations and lives. I have them read influential pieces of philosophy and complete five tasks, three of which are to:

- Accurately and efficiently summarize the argument;
- Articulate a point of agreement with some aspect of the argument; and
- Articulate a point of disagreement with some aspect of the argument.

Before we do anything else, we must do everything in our power to ensure that we have interpreted and presented our interlocutor's argument(s) accurately. Downstream steps, like criticizing the argument, are inevitably misguided if we have not first represented the position correctly. Steelman another's arguments; do not strawman them. Second, it is important to find and acknowledge points of agreement before getting to the necessary philosophical task of criticism. The hope is that we all are on the same page in terms of our primary philosophical goal: *arriving at truth*. Part of the idea here is that arriving at truth often requires us to think of the philosophical enterprise corporately and collaboratively. In that case, we should be excited to find points of convergence with those with whom we disagree. Such convergence can be an important indicator that we are making progress at more closely approaching the truth. Finally, if our aim in all of this is to get closer to truth about our world, we must engage in the difficult but important task of providing resistance to claims that we think are false or implausible. One thinks here of John Stuart Mill's (1806–1873) classic point about the threefold benefit of open discourse over ideas, consisting of:

- Excahnging false beliefs for true beliefs in cases where your belief is incorrect and your "opponent's" belief is correct;
- Deepening each person's understanding of a complex truth in cases where each "opponent" has captured *part* of the *whole* truth; and
- Even in cases where your belief is true and your "opponent's" belief is false, potentially deepening each person's understanding of the truth through the process of disagreement—which, as philosophers who think about the conditions of knowledge might say, enhances the *justification* you have for your true belief (Mill 1978).

Professor Metz and I are operating on this sort of a playing field. At a time when it has become increasingly difficult to disagree about important matters without resorting to presuming the rationally and morally worst about those with whom we disagree, my hope is that we provide a model here in which strong disagreement is tempered by deep respect, and where arriving at truth is our shared goal; where we can speak our minds honestly, acknowledge that we think each other is wrong about substantive claims at the center of our belief-systems, "revel in each other's humanity" (borrowing a phrase from philosopher Cornel West), and have a beer together afterwards. That last point may be the most important, but will be hard to pull off, given that Professor Metz is in Pretoria, South Africa, and I am in northern Indiana, USA.

3.2 Points of Agreement

Before I discuss what I consider to be the most important areas of disagreement, and where I have doubts about Professor Metz's claims and arguments, I will acknowledge a few important points of agreement. These points of convergence are noteworthy, and I think they provide evidence to the reader that we have made substantive progress in answering one or more of the three questions that Professor Metz states are the focus of his opening statement:

- "What does it mean to talk of 'the meaning of life'?"
- "What would make life (perhaps mine in particular) meaningful?"
- "Is (my) life in fact meaningful?"

Our largest area of agreement is on the first question, so I will focus on that. We agree that meaning is likely a final value—that is, something that we want for its own sake and not for the sake of something else. It is not an intermediary step along the way to getting something else that we really want or want more. We want it for *itself*. Like other final ends, it makes little sense to ask: *why* do you want meaning?

We also are both pluralists about meaning: I with my Meaning Triad schema (mattering-purpose-sense-making); and he with a view that appears to expand the territory encompassed by meaning outside the boundaries of that triad. Each of us thinks that meaning is about one or more overlapping and interconnected ideas, as opposed to being about a single one; though I have been and continue to be open to the plausibility of monistic views of meaning (e.g., see Seachris 2019) where one aspect of the triad is most foundational. That said, I think the meaning pluralism views that we present in this debate are interestingly different—and in ways that may shed light on our disagreements about extreme supernaturalism (ExS) and moderate supernaturalism (MoS). I investigate this further in Section 3.4.

Additionally, we both are skeptical of ExS in its standard form and its claim that, literally, there is no meaning of or in life without God. It is a little more complicated than this, however, given what I said in Section 1.8 of my opening statement. At that juncture, I claimed that there could be no meaning without God because there would be no finite minds without an infinite Mind as their source. That said, if atheism is correct and there is no infinite Mind but only finite minds, as long as those minds possess sufficient capacities, they will be the sorts of entities to whom things matter, who can form intentions, and who can make sense of things—and in so doing, who can generate a kind of meaning. As a theist, I do not think that finite minds would exist without an infinite Mind; but I am here allowing the possibility of atheism so that we can have this discussion about the prospects for meaningful life.

Related, we both find MoS more plausible—though he, of course, finds it ultimately unpersuasive; whereas a form of MoS (or something in between MoS and ExS) is essentially what I argued for in my opening statement. There remains under-investigated conceptual territory that allows for further variations in between MoS and ExS. It would not surprise me that my view ends up being a close relative to ExS in some sense(s). I find that prospect both interesting and exciting—a feature rather than a bug of this sort of debate venue. As you read this book, you might have thought that we each had our views entirely worked out—maybe Professor Metz is closer to realizing that goal than I am; but I remain open to the possibility of refining my views in real time as I interact with his ideas that I am seeing in current form for the first time.

Finally, other points of general agreement between us include the ideas that there exists an important distinction between the meaning of life (cosmic) and meaning in life (personal); that the concept of *anti-matter*—that one can have negative meaning in life—captures something important about the nature of meaning; that certain kinds of lives are intuitively more or less meaningful when meaning *in* life is in view; and that supernaturalism (especially ExS) and nihilism share similar assumptions and intuitions about the prospects for meaningful life—especially a meaning *of* life—in a Godless universe.

As the reader will anticipate, despite areas of convergence, Professor Metz and I disagree on important matters. In the remaining sections of my first reply, I organize my doubts about his claims around four broad questions:

- What best explains the *presence* of objective value in the world?
- How does meaning pluralism complicate the distinction between ExS and MoS?
- How does meaning pluralism complicate the distinction between passively generated and actively generated meaning?
- Does Professor Metz's conception of meaningful life make the bar for meaning too high?

3.3 God and Objective Value

There is a long and venerable tradition in philosophy and theology of arguing that there is objective value in our universe; and that the best explanation for its presence (an ontological thesis, not an epistemic or moral one) is the existence of God. In this section, I offer some reasons to think God is, indeed, the best explanation for the *existence* of objective value.

3.3.1 Theism, Atheism, and the Source of Objective Value

Professor Metz and I are realists about value—both moral value and at least some important kinds of non-moral value, like meaning. We think that such value exists; that it exists independently of human minds in important respects; and that as such, human beings with our beliefs can be mistaken about such value. For example, if it is objectively morally wrong to torture infants for the sheer fun of it, then it is wrong regardless of whether someone absurdly believes it is not wrong or, worse, enjoys the activity. As with moral value, we also agree that the value of meaning is, in important senses, objective. Some activities are objectively more meaningful than others; and some activities are likely, in Professor Metz's terminology, objectively *anti-meaningful*. All things being equal, it is more meaningful (and likely *morally* better too) to invest in one's children in deep, creative, and positive ways than it is to binge-watch funny pet trick videos on YouTube, which would be objectively meaningless under most circumstances. Spending your life trying and succeeding to sow hatred, division, and discord in as many communities as possible would be objectively anti-meaningful, in addition to being objectively immoral. It would be a life that mattered greatly, but in a non-admirable, horrific way.

So, we agree that there exist objective standards by which human activity aimed at meaning and morality can be assessed. Failure to meet the relevant standards for meaning undermines the meaningfulness of one's life. A reasonable question to ask about those standards is: from *where* or from *whom* do they come? Professor Metz posits that there is good reason to doubt that God is the best explanation for "higher values such as universal morality" (Section 2.3.3.1). In what follows, I provide some reasons to doubt his doubt. I maintain that God is, indeed, the best explanation for the objectivity of values like morality and meaning, among others. I am skeptical that we can disentangle God from three important broadly moral dimensions:

> **Moral Ontology:** What is the *source* of objective value, including moral value? Where does it come from?

Moral Obligation: What grounds our *obligation* to pursue the good and the right?

Moral Accountability: By whom are we ultimately held *accountable* for our broadly moral choices, and who can ultimately *balance* the moral scales?

If there is, in fact, objective value, the best explanation for its existence is God's existence. Moral obligation will find its most natural home in the prescriptions of an ultimate Prescriber who prescribes out of an essentially good nature. And the prospects for the definitive righting of wrongs in the end wither and die without an omniscient and perfectly just Judge. In what follows in this section, I devote most of my attention to questions of moral ontology.

The kind of argument I have in mind here is what moral philosopher Mark Murphy calls an *explanandum-driven* argument. This sort of argument takes a feature of the world—in our case, objective value (though of course, there are many who deny that *objective* value exists) —and argues that this phenomenon is best or only explained by some other thing x (Murphy, 1). For example, suppose you return home to find your front door open, the lock damaged, and valuable items missing. Given these features of the situation and general background knowledge about the circumstances under which and the methods through which people enter homes, legally and illegally, you reasonably rule out legal entry and conclude that, unfortunately, you have been the victim of a crime. Similarly, suppose you—like both Professor Metz and myself—think that it is wrong to torture little children for fun: that it was wrong 500 years ago and still will be wrong 500 years from now; wrong everywhere it occurs in the world; wrong even if someone thinks it is morally permissible; and wrong even if some twisted soul delights in it. That is, in a nutshell, what it means for it to be *objectively* wrong. But *why* is it wrong? Standing in a long tradition, I submit that the existence and nature of the theistic God provide the best explanation for why it is objectively wrong. That is, the existence of God best or uniquely explains these data. In standard form, the argument is as follows:

- **Premise 1:** Meaning and morality, respectively, have objective non-moral and moral value (V), whose existence stands in need of explanation.

- **Premise 2:** God being the metaphysical ground of these phenomena or truths is the best explanation of V.
- **Conclusion:** Therefore, God likely metaphysically grounds V.

Plenty of philosophers dispute Premise 1. Of that number, many argue that value is not objective; while others argue that value is objective, but that it does not need an explanation.[1] Since Professor Metz and I agree about Premise 1, I focus my attention on giving some reasons for accepting Premise 2.

I am far from the first philosopher to find it implausible that objective value and binding, authoritative moral obligation are the sorts of things that one easily could find in an atheistic world. Such a world ultimately arises from non-mind-like and non-intentionally generated conditions. Human beings, along with our moral norms and sensibilities, arise in this unintended world—ourselves unintended by any infinite, personal Mind—through "accidental" twists and turns of an unintended evolutionary process. Our moral norms, on such an account, would be precarious; again, in the words of neuroscientist Bill Newsome, they would not be part of the "central reality of the universe and the reason the universe was built from the beginning ... [but] rather ... a kind of downstream accident that has nothing to do with what the universe is about at the deepest level" (Newsome 2010).

I and my theistic colleagues are not the only ones who find it quite unlikely that there would be objective value without God. Some of the most famous atheist philosophers of the last century-and-a-half hold this view. Both Professor Metz and I—along with you, the discerning reader—are well aware that truth is not determined by numbers; so that is not what I am up to here. Rather, I find it telling that the view that objective value requires God—because of the sort of "thing" God would be (a person; an infinite person; an infinite person with an essentially good nature; an infinite person with an essentially good nature who is responsible for the universe, etc.)—is

---

1   For example, some think that objective value is self-evident or *sui generis*—a brute fact that just is and needs no further explanation or reason for how or why it is (see Craig and Sinnott-Armstrong 2004). I myself think that this point fails to appreciate the distinction between knowing *that* something is wrong and knowing *why* something is wrong.

widely shared by theist and non-theist alike; even if Professor Metz is correct in claiming that contemporary philosophers who argue that objective value can exist without God currently outnumber those of us who think otherwise (though the math may shift if we broaden our focus to include non-contemporary philosophers). Below is a brief sampling of statements from atheists who claim that without God there is no, and likely can be no, objective value:

- **Friedrich Nietzsche (1844–1900):** Nietzsche reserved strong indictment for those who thought "morality could survive when the God who sanctions it is missing!" (Nietzsche 1968: 147).
- **Jean-Paul Sartre (1905–1980):** "[T]here can no longer be an *a priori* Good, since there is no infinite and perfect consciousness to think it ... If God does not exist, we find no values or commands to turn to which legitimize our conduct" (Sartre 1973: 22–23).
- **J. L. Mackie (1917–1981):** "There are no objective values" (Mackie 1977: 12). "[O]bjective intrinsically prescriptive features, supervening upon natural ones, constitute so odd a cluster of qualities and relations that they are most unlikely to have arisen in the ordinary course of events, without an all-powerful God to create them. If, then, there are such intrinsically prescriptive objective values, they make the existence of a god more probable than it would have been without them" (Mackie 1982: 115–116)
- **Richard Taylor (1919–2003):** "[T]he modern age, more or less repudiating the idea of divine law-giver, has nevertheless tried to retain the idea of moral right and wrong, not noticing that, in casting God aside, they have also abolished the conditions of meaningfulness for moral right and wrong as well" (Taylor 1985: 2). "[T]he concept of moral obligation is unintelligible apart from the idea of God. The words remain but their meaning is gone" (Taylor 1985: 83–84).
- **Paul Draper:** "[T]he probability that moral agents exist given naturalism [*atheism*, on the terms that Professor Metz and I have agreed upon for this exchange] is extremely low, much lower than it is given theism" (Draper 2004: 311).

It seemed to Nietzsche, Sartre, and many others, as it seems to me, that the nature of moral and non-moral value—among other things, its independence from the beliefs and desires of humanity such that we can believe falsely about such value and that there is an objective standard by which actions can be assessed; and its authoritative, binding nature that makes sense of the idea that we *ought* to pursue it—likely requires a being like God. That there are or would be objective values is far from clear, given naturalism.

Michael Ruse on the Evolution of Morality

> The position of the modern evolutionist ... is that humans have an awareness of morality ... because such an awareness is of biological worth. Morality is a biological adaptation no less than are hands and feet and teeth ...
>
> Considered as a rationally justifiable set of claims about an objective something, ethics is illusory. I appreciate that when somebody says 'Love thy neighbor as thyself,' they think they are referring above and beyond themselves.... Nevertheless, ... such reference is truly without foundation. Morality is just an aid to survival and reproduction, ... and any deeper meaning is illusory.
>
> Ruse 262: 268–69.

- Do you agree with Ruse about the source of morality? If morality is, as he says, "just an aid to survival," can it be objective in any meaningful sense?

Why think that objective value strongly points toward a being like God? I will answer this question in two brief steps:

- *Value* likely requires persons and minds; and
- *Objective* value likely requires a God-like mind.

Value is the sort of thing that is much more naturally grounded in *minds* and *consciousness*. Minds have mental states—states that can be *about* other things, including other non-mind-like entities. I can have thoughts about this book I am coauthoring with my friend; about the fire currently burning in my fireplace as I type this sentence; about the snow falling outside my window. Minds also are the sorts of entities that *judge, prescribe, evaluate,* and *value.* The existence of moral properties and normative properties more generally appears to be bound up with personhood. In which case, if no persons existed, then neither would moral and broadly normative properties. For example, we roughly understand what it means to say that a *person* is just; but what does it mean to claim that, in the absence of any persons, justice itself exists? Similarly, if no persons existed, then neither would properties like intelligence, rationality, agency, and dignity. But are finite persons enough to get us objective value, rather than some sort of subjectively construed value? It seems not.

Our own minds, on atheism, are the products of accidental processes that could have as easily gone in a different direction. Even if evolutionary pressures proved to "favor" certain proclivities about the shape of moral and non-moral values, this does not thereby make such values *objective*; nor would it ultimately ground obligation, except in the sense of: "Do this if you want life to go well for you, your community, and your species." It seems as though evolutionary processes would not give rise to anything other than *survival resulted from doing x, y, and z*. Something else is needed to provide genuine objectivity to our value ascriptions. I do not find appeals to valueless natural properties of the space-time universe or appeals to non-natural abstract objects to be persuasive. Objective, intrinsic value must be "wired in" from the get-go; and such "wiring" must come from a personal source who also possesses moral and rational properties. Non-personal, non-value stuff—like quarks and atoms—is the wrong sort of stuff to give rise to value, no matter how complex its arrangement.

However, a capital "P" *Person*—an infinite, essentially good person who exists independently of us and the universe, but who is responsible for both—is a great candidate to ground the objectivity of moral and non-moral value. Consider the following disjunction:

> **Mind or Matter:** Either mind and value emerged from matter and energy, or matter and energy emerged from mind and value.

If atheism is true, then mind, value, intelligence, and rationality emerged from non-conscious and value-less sources (cf. Goetz and Taliaferro 2008). If theism is true, finite minds—with their recognition of value, intelligence, and rationality—emerged from a conscious, value-laden source. Theists identify this source as

God.[2] With Nietzsche, Sartre, and many others, I think it is much more plausible to see objective value and obligation as grounded in mind-like, conscious, capital "P" Person stuff, rather than non-mind-like, non-conscious, and merely lower-case "p" person stuff. An infinite, independent, personal, moral Mind is the best candidate available.

Can we go a bit deeper, though? Why is an infinite moral Mind the best candidate? Consider again what it would take for values (moral and non-moral) to be objective. First, value claims (e.g., murder is wrong; assigning names to every small pebble in your gravel driveway is not that meaningful) would be the sorts of things that are true or false. Second, if something is objectively right or good or meaningful, it is right or good or meaningful at all times and places.[3] Third, such values would not be derived from our wishes and desires. For example, that murder is wrong or that friendship is good would not be reducible to the fact that we desire them. Fourth, and finally—and most relevant to what I am arguing here—is that in order for values to be objective, they must be part of the "furniture of the universe," as philosopher William J. Wainwright (1935–2020) has argued (Wainwright 2005: 49). I want to focus briefly on this fourth condition placed on objective value.

One of the twentieth century's most famous atheist philosophers, J. L. Mackie, claimed that belief in the objectivity of moral values is widespread and implicit in moral thinking and discourse (e.g., it is wrong (period) to treat people unjustly); but that such belief is actually mistaken—moral values are, in fact, *not* objective. Why did Mackie think this? An important reason is that such values would be *ontologically strange* in an atheistic universe, radically different in kind and unlike everything else in the matter-in-motion totality of what is. Facts about objective moral and non-moral values—unlike all other facts in this world—would, according to Mackie, possess prescriptive force. Such prescriptive force would require us

---

[2] On my view, God is also the source of moral obligation and other important types of obligation. Whereas value is grounded in God's character, obligation is grounded somewhere in the vicinity of God's commandments. God's commandments themselves are not arbitrary, but originate in God's essentially good nature. There are plausible ways of responding to the famous Euthyphro dilemma that Professor Metz introduces in Section 2.3.3.1 ("God's Purpose") of his opening statement (e.g., see Adams 1987 and Zagzebski 2004).

[3] That is to say, one has *prima facie* obligations to pursue the right and *prima facie* reasons to prioritize pursuing the good and the meaningful.

to abide by them (e.g., *love your neighbor*). Moral prohibition facts would have "not-to-be-doneness somehow built into" them (e.g., *do not treat people unjustly*); and something that is objectively good would have "to-be-pursuedness somehow built into it" (e.g., *pursue that which contributes to human well-being and flourishing*) (J. L. Mackie 1977, 38–41). However, according to Mackie, just how properties that connect to a thing's having objective value—for example, "not-to-be-doneness" and "to-be-pursuedness"—relate to its natural features appears to be a total mystery given atheism.

This connects moral ontology to moral obligation. If, on atheism, values like justice and love simply *are*, how does their existence result in moral obligations to pursue them for you and me? Why would I have a moral *duty* to be just or loving? As ethicist Richard Taylor notes: "A duty is something that is owed ... But something can be owed only to some person or persons. There can be no such thing as duty in isolation" (Taylor: 83). Like moral ontology, moral obligation fits more naturally within the context of persons, and *objective* moral obligations fit more naturally within the context of an infinite Person who has prescribed them. Another, more *indirect*, route from duty to God is to claim that we have duties to other contingent persons, where contingent persons, in virtue of being *contingent*, require God—a *necessary* person—for their existence. Be that as it may, moral ontology and moral obligation are unified on theism, unlike on atheism. If both atheism and moral realism were true, it would seem incredibly improbable that creatures like ourselves, with a moral dimension and whose moral thinking corresponds to some objective moral realm, resulted from the accidental processes of evolution. Far more likely seems either (1) Atheism + subjectivism/anti-realism about value or (2) Theism + objectivism/realism about value, where both the natural realm—including the origins and development of *homo sapiens*—and the moral realm are grounded in, and unified under, a divine Creator and Lawgiver.

Christian Smith on Naturalism and Morality

> Recall the features of [an atheistic] universe. There is no transcendent natural law or moral force, no divinity, no ultimate spiritual meaning or destiny that transcends human invention during the blip of cosmic time that we humans have occupied. Reality

> consists of various conglomerations of infinitesimally small particles pulled together by physical forces and processes of emergence that are in a continual state of flux ... Complex substances have slowly evolved. Life has very improbably evolved. Conscious and self-conscious human beings have even more improbably evolved.
>
> ... Eventually, sooner or later, one way or another, all life on earth will be extinguished. And energy, matter, and natural forces will simply continue to play themselves out indefinitely.
>
> In the meantime, lo and behold, one species, human beings, has by odd chance developed cognitive, emotional, and volitional capacities that result in their making valuations and judgments of a moral character ... Viruses, ticks, and foxes do not create and live in moral worlds. But human beings, it so happens, do.
>
> [So], assuming [atheism], if morality is to be acquired at all, it must be acquired from the human mind, not from a[n] [atheistic] universe. Moral "facts" and values are simply not natural givens existing "out there" for humans to recognize and embrace. They are, rather, human constructions that people must invent, believe, more or less live by, and enforce among each other.
>
> (Smith 2019: 55–57).

- Interestingly, Smith—who is not an atheist—agrees with Michael Ruse, who in the previous thought box argued that a morality (and other value) sourced in atheistic evolution would resist the description of being *objective*. Do you agree? Why or why not?

A theistic metaphysics—that is, an account of reality in which an infinite, personal, moral Mind is the source of both the space-time universe and value—can help here, in that it provides a natural home for these *ontologically strange* things we find in our universe that many of us call "objective values." For example, one way for that which is good to be objectively good is for it to resemble the capital "G" Good—that is, God—in the right way (cf. Adams 1999). Obligations, on the other hand, could be grounded differently—not in terms of resemblance to the Good, but in terms of abiding by the commands of the Good. Murder, then, would have the objective property of wrongness in that it violates God's command—a command anchored in God's character, and thus not arbitrary (contra Euthyphro's famous dilemma).

But let us return to the general point about objective value being incredibly *ontologically strange, unexpected,* and *precarious* in an atheistic universe. If atheism is true, in the words of twentieth-century British literary scholar C. S. Lewis, the narrative of the universe is ultimately a story of "atoms, and time and space and economics and politics" (Lewis 1947: 102). Atoms and time and space would be what is ontologically deep in such a world, not value and obligation (cf. Mavrodes 1986). It seems to me, though it does not to Professor Metz, that it would be *is-ness* all the way down given atheism. Things would just be. The traction of *ought-ness*—the realm of value and obligation—would be only surface level in such a world; human level at best. In a theistic world, on the other hand, the Good—a *Person*—is both the cause of what *is* and the source of what *ought* to be. Without personhood, there would be no rationality, intelligence, intentionality, and morality; and without *infinite* Personhood, there would be no *finite* personhood. In this section, I provided some reasons to think that both moral ontology and moral obligation find their most natural homes in a theistic universe. At the end of Section 3.6, I make a similar case for moral accountability.

3.3.2 Knowing that Objective Value Exists vs. Knowing that God Exists

I want to expand and amplify parts of the previous section in order to cast some doubt on Professor Metz's claim that the overwhelming majority of us are more confident of the claim, "It is wrong to torture little children for the sheer fun of it," than we are of the claim, "God exists." It may be that, at first glance, many of us are more confident of the former claim than the latter. However, upon further reflection, we can come to see that the former claim may entail—or, less strongly, provide good evidence for—the latter claim. I have in mind here the long and venerable tradition of moral arguments for God's existence. One will find some of the most influential philosophers in history offering such arguments, like Thomas Aquinas and Immanuel Kant (to learn more about the moral argument, see Baggett and Walls 2016; Evans 2018; and Lewis 2001). Take the following, deductive, version:

- **Premise 1:** There are objective moral and non-moral values and moral obligations.
- **Premise 2:** If there are objective moral and non-moral values and moral obligations, then there is a God who explains the existence and shape of these objective moral and non-moral values and moral obligations.
- **Conclusion:** Therefore, there is a God who explains the existence and shape of these objective moral and non-moral values and moral obligations.

Professor Metz claims that it is easier to be surer about the existence of objective moral and non-moral values than it is about the existence of God. In the preceding section, I gave some reasons to think that Premise 2 above is reasonable. I have enlisted the voices of atheist luminaries from the past century-and-a-half to bolster this point. If one is confident that *objective* value exists, then one can be confident that God exists. I am as confident about the inference from the existence of objective value to God as I am about the existence of objective value. Professor Metz gives a reason to doubt the existence of God by invoking the undeniable reality of horrendous pain, suffering, and evil. In order to be confident that God exists, he says that the theist must have "a terrific explanation of why God would let a three-year-old orphan suffer from terminal cancer or allow a deer to get burned alive in a forest fire" (Section 2.3.3.1). Likely millions, if not billions, of words have been written on what is commonly called the "Problem of Evil," so I risk absurdity here saying something in two sentences; but I will anyway (I referenced a few sources that provide particularly profound and penetrating treatments of the problem of evil in my opening statement; see Section 1.8.3). I call it the *Paradox of Evil*.

> **Paradox of Evil:** Our outrage, horror, and grief over evil are pointers to the theistic worldview—one where objective good and evil exist; but also one that grounds hope that good will triumph over evil. Seemingly paradoxically, the strongest argument against God's existence actually points to an independent, transcendent standard that makes sense of core moral intuitions about the good and right (and the bad and the wrong).

I think Nietzsche, Sartre, Mackie, and many others are correct that moral and non-moral values are entirely subjective if there is no God; and that moral facts and other value facts would be precariously odd in an atheistic world. They would not be nearly as metaphysically deep in such a world as they would be in a theistic world because they would be the products of mere finite minds, rather than an infinite Mind. A world consisting only of finite minds arising from non-intentional, accidental processes gets you parochial value, and at best a kind of intersubjective value grounded in and recognized by the entire human species; though even this is questionable. The deepest you can go with morality and meaning in that sort of world is a subjective variety at the level of the individual, extending sometimes to groups of people, and, in rarer instances, possibly to the entire human race. Of course, on atheism, the human race itself does not matter. That is, it does not objectively matter whether there is a human race or not.

Let us not lose sight of the forest for the trees here. The implication for which I am arguing is that if you lose God, you very likely lose *objective* value, including objective meaning. However, I do not think that losing God means that you lose *all* meaning, as I argued in my opening statement (see especially Section 1.2.5). There are other types of meaning available, which would likely fall under the heading of "subjectivist" meaning. These would be the varieties that we might place in the category of meaningful *to me*, even if we would not put them in the category of meaningful *full stop*. Perhaps an eccentric hobby is a candidate for this kind of meaning. With this distinction, it appears as though I have reintroduced a form of ExS through the back door. It is to this point that I now turn.

3.4 Meaning Pluralism 2.0: Reconsidering Extreme and Moderate Supernaturalism

If objective moral and non-moral value requires God, then it follows that ExS is true, at least in one important sense—God is necessary for *objective* meaning. In this section, I want to explore various ways in which both extreme and moderate supernaturalism capture something important about God's multi-faceted relationship to meaningful life. Professor Metz has done a service for the field in introducing the important distinction between ExS and MoS (see especially Metz 2019); but I think this distinction requires further elucidation. As it stands, it is too simplistic. It does not capture the full sweep of conceptual space of meaning's relationship to finite minds and an infinite Mind. To foreshadow, *real* meaning is not synonymous with *objective* meaning. On my view, sufficiently sophisticated finite minds—with their cares and concerns, intentions, purposes, and sense-making faculties—generate a real type of meaning. But that is not the only sort of meaning possible.

Professor Metz and I both are pluralists about meaning, which is the view that meaning is about a cluster of overlapping and interlocking ideas, and not simply a single idea. On my view, most (if not all) of those ideas directly or indirectly connect to the Meaning Triad—mattering, purpose, and sense-making. On his view, meaning extends beyond the confines of the triad. He may be right about that; but I suspect that even those ways in which he thinks meaning extends beyond the parameters of the triad are still at least indirectly connected to, or implicit within, the triad. After all, in developing the triad, I was careful to attune to the semantic range of the term "meaning"—that is, to its range of denotative and connotative meanings. And the *meanings* of "meaning"—its *semantic range*—are closely aligned with the triad of mattering, purpose, and sense-making.

How does this relate to the distinction between ExS and MoS? Remember, in general, that ExS claims that God is *necessary* for meaningful life; whereas MoS claims that God *enhances* meaningful life. On the latter view, God's existence would *add to* meaning that is already available in a Godless universe—perhaps by providing for *more*, or *greater*, or *deeper*, or *amplified*, or *ultimate* meaning. This binary taxonomy of meaning seems to obscure some important ways in which versions of both types of supernaturalism can be true.

I offered reasons in Sections 3.1 and 3.2 to think that God is likely required for objective value. If that is true, then there can be no *objective* meaning in a Godless universe—in which case a version of ExS would hold at the level of objective meaning. But objective meaning thus defined is not the only sort of meaning. As I argued in my opening statement, finite minds (for our purposes here, I have finite *human* minds in view) with sufficient mental capacities—capacities making possible the formation of cares and concerns, intentions, purposes, and sense-making—generate meaning, *real* meaning. Remember, according to the Meaning Triad, meaning centers on mattering, purpose, and sense-making, on my view. When conditions are present that generate mattering, purpose, and sense-making, meaning itself emerges. If Sarah enjoys the smell of coffee and the sound of birdsong on a bright spring morning, and these things matter to her, then she "encounters" meaning. If Owen envisions a desirable goal—like taking first place in his next wrestling tournament—and aims to achieve that goal, then he encounters meaning. Owen would experience some meaning in working toward the goal and additional meaning in accomplishing that goal. When Eugene reflects upon a season of his life (his service in World War 2, for example), or upon the entire arc of his life, and arrives at a sense that the various parts of his life fit together into a satisfying story, he experiences meaning. One can imagine subjective versions of these scenarios where the meaning experienced is of the subjective sort—where it is meaningful because it matters to Sarah, Owen, and Eugene—even if the conditions generating such meaning are not objective features of reality.

Indeed, it is in this way that I think certain forms of subjectivism about meaningful life are correct, though ultimately incomplete. Roughly, according to a common form of subjectivism, a person's life is meaningful to the extent that it exemplifies properties like fulfillment, satisfaction, and the like. A slight variation is the view that meaningful life is relativized to what matters to the individual person, relativized to the kinds of purposes that the individual person wants to pursue, and relativized to how one narrates and feels about the story arc of one's individual life; all without any sort of connection to objective standards—standards against which ascriptions of mattering, decisions, resultant activities, and life story arcs are measured. With subjectivism, mattering, purpose, and sense-making begin and end with the individual. And yet what we have here is clearly meaning, not something else. Insofar as the—finite—mind in which mattering, purpose, and sense-making originate is real, so too is the meaning that this mind generates and experiences. God, conceived of as an infinite Mind, is not necessary for this type of meaning—except in the sense that perhaps *nothing else* would exist if a necessary being like God did not exist first. Meaning, grounded in the capacities of finite subjectivity, is still meaning by virtue of the fact that finite consciousness has cares, concerns, and intentions, and exercises its sense-making faculties.

God, therefore, would not be necessary for this kind of subjectivist meaning; and thus ExS would be false at this level. And yet ExS could be true at the level of objective value and meaning—the kind of meaning that I have argued is connected with an infinite, personal, essentially good Mind. As I argued previously, I think God is necessary for *that* kind of meaning, and so think that a version of ExS is true. Is there any sense, then, in which MoS is also true at some other level or focal point? Well, one might think that there can be real meaning without God—subjectivist meaning; but that God gets us *more kinds* of meaning, which rather straightforwardly fits the definition of MoS. The *more* meaning that God gets us is *objective* meaning. So, it looks like the view I have in mind here is a kind of hybrid between ExS and MoS. It is not clear to me that God so much enhances the meaning connected with finite minds, unless one views the difference between subjective meaning and objective meaning as one of *enhancement*—a characterization to which I am open but not committed at this point.

Another idea worth exploring is that the kinds of meaning available in a theistic universe, in addition to objective varieties, would be those that have a cosmic reach—allowing, for example, the human race to matter *sub specie aeternitatis* (see Section 1.3). Perhaps we do not need God to matter ... *to ourselves, family*, and *friends*; and so ExS is not true at that level. However, mattering to God would be a new kind of mattering that emerges in a theistic universe. I would argue that it also would be a kind of mattering worth wanting. There might be multiple ways in which we matter to God. One way is that God cares about our wellbeing—which itself may indicate that moral value presupposes some notion of non-moral value like wellbeing, and where acting morally is ultimately *good* for us. Again, is it more appropriate to think of this through the lens of ExS or MoS? I am not quite sure at this point. What I think I am confident of is that the distinction between the two supernaturalist views is more complex than at first glance.

God, Religion, and Meaning

I am not alone in my claims that God and meaning are intricately intertwined. Some of the most formidable intellects who themselves did not believe in God or who were not religious in the ordinary sense make similar claims:

- A purely "'scientific' interpretation of life ... would understand nothing, really nothing, of what is the 'music' in it" (Nietzsche 1974: 336).

- "The idea of life having a meaning stands or falls with the religious system" (Freud 2005: 76).
- "To know an answer to the question, 'What is the meaning of life?' means to be religious" (Einstein 1954: 11).
- "To believe in God means to see that life has a meaning" (Wittgenstein 1979: 74eL 8.7.16).

Do you think that Nietzsche, Freud, Einstein, and Wittgenstein are on to something here? Are God and meaningful life so closely intertwined?

When considering whether God is best thought of as necessary for meaning or as enhancing meaning, we should extend our focus beyond the distinctions between subjective and objective and terrestrial and cosmic versions of the elements of the Meaning Triad to include ideas indirectly connected to or implicit within the triad. For example, the kind of objective mattering humans would have in a theistic universe also would be an objective mattering that *lasts* forever. And if it is objectively valuable that we matter to God, it additionally would be a good thing for us to know and experience this reality forever. Such mattering would not disappear from reality. That which matters would continue to matter indefinitely. The existence of the theistic God also would ground the prospects for ultimate justice, where the worst wrongs are righted and the gravest ills are healed by a perfect Being. This would be a way in which the "story" of the cosmos could be said to *make sense*. After all, many are inclined to call a universe where ultimate justice is not realized a kind of absurdity or tragedy. In this way, God could be thought of as enhancing the imperfect human attempts at justice (MoS), or as being necessary for *perfect* justice (ExS). Either way, God rescues the cosmic narrative from the charge of absurdity, broadly construed as a kind of *existential absurdity* (see Section 1.6).

Finally, many of us find within ourselves a strong desire to be a part of something larger. This is sometimes described as an *urge to transcend oneself* (see Cottingham 2022). One's sense of meaning is often heightened when participating in something that began long before us, stretches wide beyond us, and remains long after us. We seek to be part of projects, movements, causes, and communities that help us transcend our limits. One idea here is that participating in those "spaces" that better aid us in transcending limitations does a better job of quenching our thirst for meaning than participating in those that are self-focused and parochial. Extending our focus to family, community, culture, and even the entire human race is one way of doing this. Still, the reach of such transcending is fairly narrow. A theistic universe would allow for entirely new and higher levels of expression and fulfillment of our urge to transcend. Again, in the words of sociologist Peter Berger, whom I quoted previously, we are seeking to locate our lives "within a sacred and cosmic *frame of reference*" (Berger, 27). A frame of reference that is both cosmic and *sacred* gives our lives—including their joys and pains, struggles and triumphs—a deeper traction which transcends the vantage point of the human eye.

3.5 Meaning Pluralism 2.1: Passively Conditioned Meaning vs. Actively Conditioned Meaning

Professor Metz makes an illuminating distinction between *passive* and *active* conditions that confer meaning on a person's life (see Section 2.3.4). This tracks the distinction I introduced in Section 1.9 between intrinsic and extrinsic meaning; and it sheds further light on the vast territory associated with life's meaning. Roughly, a life could acquire some meaning, but not very much that is relevant for assessing meaningfulness, by virtue of being intentionally created or cared about by someone else. This is an example of passively conditioned meaning—one had to do *nothing* to acquire it. According to Professor Metz, what is more important is that one engage in the right sorts of activity in order to secure meaningful life. This is an example of actively conditioned meaning—one has to do *something* to acquire it. I think that passively conditioned meaning is more important for meaning than Professor Metz has recognized.

The distinction between passively and actively conditioned meaning probably intersects, even if not perfectly, with the distinction between the meaning *of* life and meaning *in* life. If, for example, the meaning *of* life is something like the grand cosmic story that narrates why we are here, what matters, why we suffer, what we should do while we are here, and where we are going, then this is more of a passive idea. There is a kind of meaning that human life has simply in virtue of *what sort of thing it is and what sort of place it occupies within* this grand narrative. We do not have to do anything to acquire this kind of meaning. For example, if God created us in His own image, then we would matter, full stop. Our lives would have meaning *by virtue of being created by God*. This clearly would be a natural sense of meaning that our lives could have; and, I would argue, also a very important sense worth wanting. Such "passive" meaning would not be trivial; rather, it would be *meaningful*. Being created and cared for by an infinite, necessarily existent, and essentially good Mind who cares about our wellbeing would be a *big* deal. A *really* big deal. What matters would matter forever; and what matters mattering forever would be better than what matters mattering only for a short time. And because of God's care and concern for His creatures' wellbeing, God would bring ultimate justice and healing to a broken world.

Actively conditioned meaning, on the other hand, seems to more closely track the idea of meaning *in* life, where acquiring meaning revolves around *doing stuff*. We actively engage our minds and bodies to bring about states of affairs—for example, building deep relationships, accomplishing laudable goals, acquiring knowledge—that confer meaning on our lives. Taking both sets of conditions in hand, one's life could be meaningful in virtue of what that life is and the dignity it possesses—a passive condition—and yet fail to exemplify actively conditioned meaning. A couch potato who spends inordinate amounts of time playing video games, binge-watching shows on Hulu, Amazon Prime, and Netflix, and thinking little of other people misses out on important avenues of meaning—even if his life is passively meaningful in virtue of being a human being.

It seems to me that passively and actively conditioned meaning cannot so easily be separated. For example, if humanity owes its existence to the theistic God, then presumably God has endowed us with passive meaning in virtue of being made in His image; and also has provided norms consistent with His essentially good nature that we should actively follow in order to lead meaningful lives given the kinds of creatures we are. Being made in God's image is no guarantee that one's life is meaningful in every relevant sense that it could be meaningful, and maybe not even in the most important senses. That said, the proper route to achieving actively conditioned meaning—at least of the *objective* sort—would be informed by the account of why and how our lives have passively conditioned meaning.

We see then another potential form that ExS and MoS can take: God is required (ExS) for certain conceptions of passively conditioned meaning—for example, the passive meaning that would result from being made in the image of God. On the other hand, one might view this in terms of MoS, where being made in the image of God better secures this type of passive meaning than, for example, grounding human dignity in our rational capacities alone.

This also opens up a discussion over which varieties of meaning we value the most. Put another way: which ones are the most *meaningful* to us? Passively conditioned or actively conditioned varieties? Subjective meaning or objective meaning? Capital-letter versions of the parts of the Meaning Triad or lower-case versions? Meaning *sub specie aeternitatis* or *sub specie humanitatis*? These are important questions that will need answering in order to fully assess the relationship between God and meaningful life.

3.6 Making Meaning too Difficult?

Professor Metz and I agree that there can be some meaning that comes from passive conditions. I think that meaning deriving from passive conditions—especially if those conditions are theistic in origin—*means* more for considerations of overall meaning than he does. Both he and I also think that the meaning in one's life can be assessed in terms of active conditions—particularly, to what extent those active conditions are met. In that sense, I largely agree with the following claim he makes in his opening statement:

> I do not think that all lives are meaningful … [For example,] someone who has been a serial killer since his teenage years and a three-year-old orphan who gets cancer, suffers horribly for a year, and dies [do not lead meaningful lives]. I might want to grant that there is some meaning in even these lives, but I do not believe there is enough for them to be characterized as meaningful on the whole.
>
> (Section 2.5).

Both he and I think that such lives have passively conditioned meaning, and perhaps even some small amount of actively conditioned meaning; but he thinks that this will not be enough to count them as meaningful "on the whole." I largely agree with him here. That said, I think it is worth investigating this territory further. I do not consider what follows so much a point of disagreement, but rather an invitation for Professor Metz to further clarify what he thinks it takes to make life meaningful "on the whole."

Early in his opening statement, he offers the following account of meaningful life:

> I maintain that most of us are considering whether there is something more valuable than our own pleasure and desire satisfaction; or whether we are connected with something greater than ourselves; or whether there is something that merits pride about our lives; or whether our lives constitute a good life-story. (Section 2.1).

In that same section, he further claims that obtaining meaningfulness is about "exercising intelligence"; utilizing "higher faculties beyond your animal nature of pleasure and desire"; "connecting you to something greater than yourself"; "[making] a difference"; and "[acting] out of love." The more such conditions are met, presumably, the more meaningful one's life is. To sum it up, he says, "a life is more meaningful the more it exercises intelligence in positive, intense, and sophisticated ways that involve advancement."

The exercise of human intelligence, rationality, and creativity factors heavily in his account of meaningful life. At one level, this resonates deeply with me. A life sufficiently exercising these capacities is, all things being equal, more meaningful than a pleasant life consisting of pulling small paint chips from the walls of one's home, repainting the walls, and doing it all over again. Still, I have some concerns. I worry that a theory that so heavily prioritizes the exercise of reason and rationality potentially narrows the routes to meaningful life such that those among us who have one or another form of mental disability—especially some manifestations of autism spectrum disorder (ASD)—fail to have actively conditioned meaningful lives.[4] *Prima facie*, such an implication would seem to be problematic.

---

4 I am aware of the fact that there are numerous views about the correct way of describing this. For example, one increasingly encounters terms like "neuroatypicality" and "neurodiversity" to describe some individuals and groups, especially within the autistic community. Space here does not permit entering this debate. Even within the autistic community, there are vigorous debates about how best to think of ASD, with some within the community thinking of it in terms of a problem or abnormality to be fixed and others viewing it through the lens of neurodiversity—and, of course, many with views somewhere in between. Autobiographically, my thoughts in this section are informed and inspired by my close and sustained interactions with a beloved person with ASD who is very close to me.

It is not uncommon for some persons with autism to exhibit a narrow, hyper-focus on activities that others of us would deem to be so trivial as not to matter. Though one would be hard pressed to find detailed lists of activities that have so-called *objective* worth or value, it is doubtful that such activities as those I have in mind would find their way onto such lists. Not only would such activities not find their way on these lists; it would be tempting to conclude that devoting such an inordinate amount of attention to them ends up mattering *negatively*, since one is not attending to that which *really*—objectively—matters.

I am genuinely curious what space Professor Metz's conception of meaningful life makes for such individuals. Let me reiterate: I am not raising this question primarily as an objection to his theory, but as a question to which both of us (and the entire field working on life's meaning) should devote more thought and energy. I do worry about any theory of meaningful life that makes it difficult for someone living with ASD, and whose ASD manifests in certain ways, to lead a meaningful life. Some persons with ASD clearly check off the important actively conditioned meaningfulness boxes in his theory, no doubt. But others do not. The person who is obsessed with pulling things apart, spending time looking at and playing with pipes, and watching YouTube videos about magnetic slime does not appear to have much of a meaningful life, on his view.

I have similar questions about young children, on Professor Metz's view. Does his theory of meaningful life make space for children to lead meaningful lives? If not, that seems *prima facie* problematic. Though I agree with him that a "three-year-old orphan who gets cancer, suffers horribly for a year, and dies" lives a tragic life that lacks substantial (actively generated) meaning—after all, that we think of such lives as tragic is largely because they lack important dimensions of value that we think good lives possess—I worry about a view that makes *most* children's lives lack meaning because they do not "[exercise] intelligence in positive, intense, and sophisticated ways that involve advancement," in his words.

I imagine that Professor Metz has several potential replies here. He could claim that children do, in fact, exercise their intelligence thusly; but that they do so in child-centric ways—building with Lego, cultivating emotional and social intelligence through interactive free play with others, and so on. He might also reply that even if the activities of children, like playing with Lego, are not themselves exercises of this type of intelligence, they are instrumentally valuable because they are part of cultivating the very capacities that *adults* can use to exercise the kind of intelligence required for meaningful life. He could also claim that those with ASD who are fixated on seemingly trivial pursuits exercise their intelligence in some types of ASD-centric ways. I worry, however, that this sort of reply may not be available to him in this case—especially since common counterexamples to subjectivism (e.g., memorizing phonebooks and counting blades of grass) seem to rule out such activities as appropriately generating meaning. I think it is a mark in favour of theories of meaning if they allow for most children's lives and the lives of many with ASD, like my loved one, to count as meaningful. Though, I admit, it perhaps will be difficult to discern the threshold for when one's life becomes so tragic and impoverished that very little actively conditioned meaning is available—*at least in this life*.

That last phrase, "*at least in this life*," brings to mind Professor Metz's tragic case of the three-year-old orphan who dies of cancer after a brutal and short life. Thinking about this case reveals an important way in which God intersects with meaning. If the death of that child is the absolute end of his story, then this is unspeakably tragic. That child did not have the opportunity to acquire much meaning in life, except for some strands of meaning that come from passive conditions and maybe satisfying a few active conditions here and there. If atheism is true and this life is all we have, then that three-year-old's prospects for meaningful life go to the grave along with him. On the other hand, if there is an infinite, necessarily existent, essentially good person responsible for our universe, this child's story is not over. This view, of course, must wrestle with the profoundly problematic problem of evil that Professor Metz and I both acknowledged in our opening statements. It is a formidable challenge, to put it lightly, to conceive of ways in which the horrendous suffering of this little child is consistent with the theistic God. And yet the God whose existence seems in doubt:

- Grounds the value and normative intuitions through which we cry out, "No!" and "Evil!" and "Terrible!" and "Injustice!";
- Entered this world, according to Christian theism, in the person of Jesus of Nazareth, lived a perfect life, suffered and died *unjustly*, rose again on the third day, ascended to heaven, and is coming again to judge the living and the dead and reign forever (a rough retelling of the Apostles' Creed); and

- Anchors the very prospect of hope that this little one, whose life on Earth causes us to shudder, will receive perfect meaning, among other values, in another chapter of the narrative of reality.

I began Section 3.1 by claiming that God provides a more natural home for three moral (and normative more broadly) dimensions: moral ontology, moral obligation, and moral accountability. On theism, God unifies all three dimensions. God is the source of objective value. God's prescriptions obligate (or perhaps God's good and beautiful nature motivates) us to align our lives with this objective value. And God can hold moral agents ultimately accountable with perfect justice, and bring everlasting flourishing to our broken world.

Returning to the epigraph at the beginning of my reply to Professor Metz, there is real meaning available in a Godless universe: the sort of meaning that finite minds—with their cares, concerns, intentions, purposes, and sense-making faculties—can generate. I doubt, however, that there can be *objective* meaning in such a world; and I am unable to see how the sorts of meaning available in a Godless world are sufficiently robust to block the pessimistic outlook often associated with atheism. Whether this makes me an ExS, an MoS, or something in between, I am not sure. What I do think is that an atheistic world in which we love and are loved only to someday find ourselves "alone"—and I have in mind here a metaphorical, but nonetheless deep kind of aloneness ushered in by death in an atheistic universe, like in the case of the little porcelain rabbit, Edward Tulane—is a lamentable world indeed.

Chapter 4

Considering the Benefits of God

Reply to Seachris

Thaddeus Metz

Contents

4.1 Introduction 167
4.2 What Does "Life's Meaning" Mean? 168
4.3 What Would Make Life Meaningful? 170
4.4 Is Life Meaningful? 180

4.1 Introduction

I have now read Professor Seachris' opening statement with interest, and am eager to continue the conversation with him here. I do so in the light of the three major questions about life's meaning that I had sought to answer in mine: what we mean by "life's meaning" (Section 4.2); what, if anything, makes life meaningful (Section 4.3); and whether our lives are indeed meaningful (Section 4.4).

On all three counts, there is a lot of overlap between my answers and those of Professor Seachris. We both are pluralists about what talk of "life's meaning" means; and we believe that it is neutral between religious and non-religious theories. We both deny that God and a soul are necessary for life to have some meaning in it. Instead, I maintain that engagement with the good (beneficent relationships), the true (intellectual reflection), and the beautiful (creativity) is sufficient, whereas Professor Seachris might believe that, but at least clearly believes that a subjective meaning is available in an atheist world. We both also reject nihilism: the view that no one's life is meaningful. Despite the differences between Professor Seachris' Christian theist background and my secular one, there is a substantial overlap in our philosophical judgment. Hey, maybe we're right!

There are, however, some places where he and I do have differing views, and I naturally focus on those areas in what follows. Most of these points of contention concern what I had labelled "moderate supernaturalism": the view that, although our lives can be meaningful without God and a soul, they would have a greater meaning if and only if these existed and we engaged with them in the right ways. I use the most space below to provide reason to doubt Professor Seachris' arguments for this view.

4.2 What Does "Life's Meaning" Mean?

Recall the difference between a monist and pluralist approach to understanding what we essentially have in mind when thinking about life's meaning. The former is the view that we all have just one property in mind, whereas the latter is that we have more than one property in mind, and indeed perhaps several properties. Professor Seachris and I are pluralists.

The difference between us concerns the extent to which his "triad" captures thought about meaning. Professor Seachris maintains that when we enquire into life's meaning, we are "centrally" addressing three features: namely, mattering, fulfilling a purpose, and making sense. Although he does not quite say that these are the only three properties, my concern is that his heavy focus on them might lead us to forget about other ways in which a life can conceivably be meaningful. In this section, I work to remind the reader of what else "life's meaning" plausibly could involve, by the definition of terms.

Recall what mattering, fulfilling a purpose, and making sense amount to for Professor Seachris. Mattering, insofar as it concerns meaning in life, consists of having "significant positive impact" (Section 1.2.1). Fulfilling a purpose would involve leading "lives that are heading somewhere rather than nowhere in particular," where we "do not want to be alienated from the purposes that guide our lives" (Section 1.2.2). Making sense is constituted by "*fitting* something within a larger context or whole," or "intelligibility within a wider frame" (Section 1.2.3). Professor Seachris' analysis is much more eloquent and compelling than these soundbites; but they should be enough for the reader to attend to the key ideas.

Now, I accept that part of what we have in mind when thinking about life's meaning are these three conditions; but I here contend that one should be careful not to suppose they are exhaustive of what we have in mind. There are additional ways in which there could, in principle, be meaning in life that are not easily shoehorned into one of Professor Seachris' three categories.

Consider, for instance, taking a walk in a forest and more generally being open to nature's bounty; really paying attention to and empathizing with another living creature; listening closely to a powerful piece of music; being loved by another person; living among old, hand-worked crafts and one-off architectural constructions; seeing one's family members flourish (but not because you did anything); avoiding causing harm to others; taking care not to degrade one's soul; hearing the voice of God inside oneself. Some of these were part of the "rich life" I described previously (Section 2.3.1). These ways of living do not necessarily involve influencing others in positive ways, with a lot of them instead focused on the individual. In addition, they do not seem to consist of exercising agency in pursuit of specific ends; note that some instead are a matter of observing constraints—that is, *not doing certain things*—when pursuing ends. Finally, they rarely amount to understanding how a part fits into a whole or an otherwise larger scheme, which is what Professor Seachris means by "coherence." However, they are *prima facie* candidates for what would confer meaning on a life, despite not being easily captured by the triad.

Similar remarks go for a possible world in which all the good people are fittingly rewarded and all the bad people are punished appropriately. Penalties do not seem well described as "good impacts on those around us" (Section 1.2.1); we cannot achieve the aim of perfectly rewarding the good; and it is not clear what wider context is involved when the guilty are punished—or at least it is doubtful that we would find that state of affairs meaningful only because it makes our lives more intelligible.

Professor Seachris might respond that all of the above are conditions that could "matter to" a person. However, that would be much too broad to capture the sense of "life's meaning," for then anything at all could conceivably count, including a life spent in an Experience Machine or even the life of Sisyphus brainwashed into thinking that what he is doing matters.

The point I want to make is not that the above would in fact be sources of meaning. Rather, my claim is that it would not be logically contradictory for someone to hold that they are sources of meaning, whereas it is difficult to make sense of that claim by mere appeal to the triad of significance, purpose, and intelligibility. When we are thinking about life's meaning, we plausibly have more in mind than the triad, as useful and revealing as that schema is.

4.3 What Would Make Life Meaningful?

Professor Seachris might well accept that there is conceivably more to meaning than the triad suggests but point out—plausibly—that there is no reason to doubt that the triad is crucial to understanding meaningfulness. For all I have said, he is correct that a lot of what we have in mind when considering life's meaning is significance, purpose, and intelligibility; and he maintains in his contribution that at least these would be enhanced by the existence of God and a soul.

Professor Seachris advances several reasons in support of moderate supernaturalism: the view that "the prospects for meaning ultimately are better if God exists" (Section 1.2.2). I addressed some of them in my opening statement. For instance, Professor Seachris points out that if God does not exist, then we are "simply accidental collocations of atoms" (Section 1.6) that were not created for a reason, and also that there is no Creator out there who cares about all of us. Recall that I granted those points, but suggested they are not weighty (Section 2.3.4). When considering the meaningfulness of Einstein's life, no one is really interested in how he was created, where similar remarks apply to the species; and then, it seems more meaningful for a life—whether individual or collective—to care about others than to be cared for by others. In the following, I instead spend the most time addressing rationales from Professor Seachris for thinking that a greater meaning could come only with God and a soul that I did not take up in my opening statement, or about which I have more to say. I count three big ones.

4.3.1 *Just Deserts (Redux)*

In my opening statement, I addressed an argument for extreme supernaturalism according to which life is meaningless if justice cannot be perfectly done (Section 2.3.3.3). If the morally upright cannot be rewarded, the innocent cannot be compensated for their wrongful suffering, and the wicked cannot be punished, then to some it seems as though life is utterly in vain. Two points I made in reply were that some meaning could come from striving to impart that kind of justice, even if it would never be perfectly realized, and that some meaning in life has nothing to do with justice at all. However, even if I am correct about those points, Professor Seachris could sensibly advance a more moderate claim: our lives would be much more meaningful if what he often calls "ultimate justice" were served.

On this score, Professor Seachris articulates a poignant example concerning a young human who has been wrongfully killed. He suggests that in a world without God and a soul, "there is no ultimate justice for the little child murdered, whose last moments of conscious existence were sheer terror" (Section 1.8.3). In addition, there is also no justice for the child's parents:

> When you bury a child, is that it? In unfathomable pain, have you said goodbye to him for the final time? When grief is so acute that you feel as if you will explode, is there anyone to whom this matters; who can bring everlasting *shalom*—deep peace and harmony—to the cosmic order?
> (Section 1.8.1).

The answer to the last question is "no," if there is no God and a soul, so the argument goes.

For all Professor Seachris has said, God and a soul would be sufficient for ultimate justice to be done, where ultimate justice would enhance meaning in our lives in one respect. However, granting this point does not yet give Professor Seachris the conclusion he presumably wants, which is instead that God and a soul would be necessary for ultimate justice to be served. The claim he seeks to defend is that theism, rather than atheism, would make much more meaning available to life—hence the title of Section 1.8, "Why God Is Better News for Meaning." My point is that although theism might be better than *this* atheist world, there could be some *other* atheist world that is better than this one and no worse than the theist one, when it comes to ultimate justice.

Recall that in my opening statement, I described a possible world without God and a soul in which it appears ultimate justice could indeed be done (Section 2.3.3.3). I invited the reader to imagine that all her mental states over the course of her life were uploaded into a computer and then transferred to a new body, which would last a few more hundred years. Some Christians believe that Jesus will return to Earth, at which point those whose bodies have died will receive new bodies and the upright will enjoy felicity. My suggestion is that, in principle, we could obtain new bodies without Jesus and without a soul; for it appears we are identical to our minds, which do not have to be housed in a spiritual substance in order for them to continue beyond the death of our current body and then receive their just deserts for a temporary period.

One might be inclined to think that, even if people's selves could survive without souls, at least God must exist in order to judge them accurately. However, that also does not seem true. Consider the concept of *karma*, accepted by many people in South and East Asia, according to which an impersonal force regulates the distribution of benefits and burdens in proportion to one's deeds. I am not saying that *karma* is real; instead, my point is that *karma*—or something like it—is conceivable, which shows that justice could be done in the absence of God *qua* personal judge. Downloading one's mind into another body plus something like *karma* would facilitate justice to no less a degree than surviving the death of one's body with a soul plus God.

In addition, there is a more speculative and tentative reason for thinking that if we want ultimate justice, we should not want God and a soul, and should instead prefer the download + *karma* option! Giving people what they deserve would ideally involve them undergoing different fates, according to the choices they have made. It is a matter of reaping what you sow. The innocent deserve compensation to make up for any harm done to them; the upright deserve reward proportionate to their goodness; and the wicked deserve punishment proportionate to their badness. Now, if God and a soul exist, then it appears impossible for people to receive what they deserve in a straightforward sense. On the one hand, if the wicked are sent to Hell, that would in fact be an injustice, since nothing one can be or do during one's 80 or so years on Earth is proportionate to *eternal* damnation. People plausibly deserve punishment, but no one deserves an infinity of it. On the other hand, if the souls of the wicked are sent to Heaven, then everyone's life would turn out the same; all would have an infinity of bliss, which is also arguably an injustice.

This reasoning calls to mind certain passages from the Christian Bible, where what is prized is clearly not people receiving their just deserts, either from others or from God. Consider: "That you may be sons of your Father in heaven; for He makes His sun rise on the evil and on the good, and sends rain on the just and on the unjust" (Matthew 5:45); and:

> But love your enemies, do good to them, and lend to them, expecting nothing in return. Then your reward will be great, and you will be sons of the Most High; for He is kind to the ungrateful and wicked.
>
> (Luke 6:35).

Perhaps what theism would offer is a greater meaning by virtue of enabling not ultimate justice, but a different sort of value—everlasting flourishing.

4.3.2 Everlasting Flourishing

Some parts of Professor Seachris' opening statement defend moderate supernaturalism by arguing that God and a soul would uniquely offer a greater meaning by virtue of enabling flourishing to continue forever. Professor Seachris remarks that a "specific way of thinking about the purpose of life on Christian theism is in terms of perfect happiness" (Section 1.8.2); and he then surveys a number of theologians who maintain that infinite happiness is our ultimate end. "We want the most important things in life to last indefinitely" (Section 1.7), which it appears they would not if atheism were true. Whereas in a theist world, we can expect to wind up in Heaven (or at least some of us can), in a world without God and a soul, "death has the final word, and happiness and love are eventually consigned to everlasting oblivion" (Section 1.7.2).

In my opening statement, I argued that the prospect of Heaven is not enough to support moderate supernaturalism, since along with that prospect would come that of Hell (Section 2.4.2). It is not clear that one should wish for a world with Heaven and Hell, since one could end up in the latter. However, let us suppose that the best understanding of God is that neither a loving God nor a just God would condemn anyone to eternal damnation. Professor Seachris might sensibly contend that universal salvation would be on the cards if theism were true, with the thought of everyone enjoying eternal flourishing being a supremely meaningful state of affairs.

I have three criticisms of this rationale for moderate supernaturalism. One is that eternal happiness would not in fact be meaningful (even if eternal love would be) (Section 4.3.2.1). A second is that, if eternal happiness would in fact be meaningful, or at least everlasting love would be, then it would be possible without a spiritual realm (Section 4.3.2.2). A third is that an appeal to any eternal state—whether happiness, love, or ensouled communion with God—is "too big" to capture the moderate supernaturalist intuition that a meaningful life, such as Gandhi's, is possible without God and a soul (Section 4.3.2.3).

4.3.2.1 Happiness vs. Meaningfulness

I accept that everlasting happiness would be *desirable* to some real degree. There might be debate about whether it would have to come at a price—for example, it might be that living forever would mean that we forget much of our lives and that they become repetitive over time, somewhat like an Alzheimer's patient. However, even supposing that a non-forgetful and non-repetitive state of happiness would be possible for us, it is hard for me to see why that would be *meaningful*. After all, in the early part of his opening statement, Professor Seachris contrasted the values of meaningfulness and happiness. He developed the meaning triad to make sense of the idea that we want more than morality and happiness: "Meaning is a value that most of us want our lives to possess; though it appears relevantly distinct from other values we want in our lives, like moral goodness and happiness" (Section 1.2).

In my opening statement, remember that I also worked to show that meaningfulness is distinct from happiness. Recall, for instance, the Experience Machine thought experiment—which shows, I believe, not merely that talk of "life's meaning" is not equivalent to happiness, but also that happiness is far from sufficient for any meaning. A life spent in the Experience Machine would be terrifically happy, for all that is on offer in a physical world; but most would deem it to be utterly meaningless.

I therefore cannot see how appealing to everlasting happiness could support moderate supernaturalism: the claim that God and a soul would make a much greater meaning possible than what would be available in a world without them. They are two separate goods, such that addition of happiness in itself makes no contribution to meaningfulness, as the Experience Machine thought experiment demonstrates.

Professor Seachris might reply that an eternal life in Heaven would be a special kind of happiness; and he mentions Thomas Aquinas' (1225–1274) suggestion that "man's ultimate felicity consists only in the contemplation of God" (Section 1.8.2). But let us be careful here. Contemplating God's nature is, I accept, a good candidate for meaningfulness, but not happiness—at least not the way most modern Western people think of it. Normally we conceive of happiness in terms of pleasant experiences, satisfied desires, or positive emotions such as gladness, and not in terms of contemplation—that is, thinking. If contemplating God is not one and the same thing as (i.e., is not identical to) pleasure, satisfaction, or gladness—which it does not seem to be—then it is not happiness.

I am open to the idea that contemplating God would in fact be a source of meaning if God existed, even if (or precisely because!) it would not consist of happiness; and I see no reason to question the suggestion that love is too. So, for all I have said so far, Professor Seachris still has a promising point: eternal contemplation of God and eternal love of God and others would alone make possible a greater meaning than can be found in any atheist world. Let me address that next.

4.3.2.2 Everlasting Flourishing Without God and a Soul

Suppose, though, that I am wrong, and that happiness—whether in terms of experiences, desires, or emotions—can in fact constitute meaningfulness under certain conditions. My second criticism of the claim that an atheist world necessarily means that "death has the final word, and happiness and love are eventually consigned to everlasting oblivion" draws on the above distinction between *this* atheist world and some *other* possible one. To defend moderate supernaturalism, Professor Seachris needs to show that everlasting flourishing could exist *only* in a world with God and a soul. It will not suffice for him to show that a theist world would be better than this one; for all I would need to do, by parity of reasoning, is to show that some atheist world would be better than this one. This world clearly sucks in a lot of ways, and would not be tough to beat! The interesting philosophical debate, therefore, is about whether a theist world is essential to obtain a greater meaning than is possible in any atheist world.

I do not believe Professor Seachris has shown that yet. After all, think about an ever-expanding spatiotemporal universe in which we continue to download our minds successively into new bodies which, due to some super-duper technology, feel little or no pain, frustration, or negative emotions, but instead the opposite mental states to an intense degree. Imagine, furthermore, that we continue to love one another while forever embodied in a spatiotemporal universe. That sort of purely physical world is just as possible as one with God and a soul, which entails that, if both everlasting happiness and love are greatly meaningful, theism gains no advantage over atheism.

However, Professor Seachris has another card up his sleeve: namely, the idea of forever contemplating and more generally communing with God. Surely *that* is impossible in a world without God. Yup, that is true. And I note that, for a number of philosophers of religion, the closest one could come to God is by shedding one's physical form and having one's pure soul relate to God. This point further suggests that only theism could offer a greater meaning. However, I too have another card up my sleeve.

4.3.2.3 Eternity as Immoderate

At this stage, I reiterate the objection I made in my previous chapter to the idea of a moderate supernaturalism that appeals to eternal significance; it was roughly the claim that the latter is "too big" to support the former (Section 2.4.3). According to moderate supernaturalism, a life can be meaningful in a world without God and a soul. Professor Seachris wants to acknowledge that, for he claims that theism would be merely *better* for meaning, not *essential* for it. However, if what would make theism better is an "eternal," "everlasting," "indefinite," or "infinite open-ended" state that lasts "forever" (all terms from Professor Seachris' opening statement)—whether it is happiness, love, or communion with God—then it becomes extremely hard to make sense of the intuition that a life of about 80 years could be meaningful by comparison. Einstein's earthly life would amount to nothing when juxtaposed with an infinitude of flourishing.

Professor Seachris might reply that he can easily account for the judgment that a life would not be utterly meaningless in a purely physical world. So long as you engage with the good, the true, and the beautiful, then your life can to some extent matter, fulfill a worthwhile purpose, and be intelligible. However, the intuition that needs to be captured, I submit, is not merely that there would be *some meaning* in a world without God and a soul, but in addition, that there would be enough meaning to describe some lives as *"meaningful"*—that is, full of meaning. Given that it is plausible to identify a large portion of meaning-talk in terms of what is admirable or, in Professor Seachris' terms, "praise- or esteemworthy" (Section 1.2.1), most have the intuition that Einstein's earthly life was meaningful—that is, merited reactions of admiration and praise. However, his life would *not* merit those reactions *compared to a life with an eternity of love and communion with God (and maybe happiness)*. And so, an appeal to everlasting flourishing undercuts the ability of Professor Seachris to account for the meaningfulness of Einstein's earthly life, even if he can admittedly show this life was not utterly empty of meaning.

Consider an analogy.¹ Imagine two humans, one of whom is taller than the other. Now put them both next to the Eiffel Tower and ask whether either one is tall compared to it. Surely not. However, now imagine that the Eiffel Tower is infinitely high! It is then utterly unreasonable to suggest that one of us would be tall by comparison to it. Analogous remarks go for meaning, I submit.

4.3.3 Deep Desires, Longings, and Hopes

A distinguishable strand of thought in Professor Seachris' opening statement is the recurrent appeal to "depth"—specifically in regard to what we would like out of life. He speaks of "our deepest desires (which) remain unfulfilled amidst cosmic silence"; "deep longings for love to continue forever and for ultimate justice to be served"; and "deep hopes for *ultimate* justice and a *lasting* place for love and felicity" (Section 1.6). The suggestion is that it is part of human nature to have these desires, longings, and hopes. That is why Professor Seachris mentions them as integral to "the human search for meaning" (Section 1.6), such that all our lives would be absurd and tragic in a world where they are unmet—which, according to him, would be any world without God and a soul.

Now, I have already suggested in effect that some of these desires are not in fact that deep. In particular, in the same way few of us care at all about how Einstein originated when considering the meaning in his life, and we instead attend to what he did with his life, few of us care much about how human life as such originated, and instead we are much more concerned about whether and how we as a species might develop.

Similarly, although some might want to be cared for by God in the way a parent cares for a child, some of us would find it much more significant to be one who cares intensely for others. Still further, a number of us adults might prefer not to be in something akin to a parent/child relationship with anyone—not even God (e.g., Kahane 2011). If God exists, then we would have to "bend the knee," as my independent-minded teenage son, Mika'il Metz,

---

1 From Antti Kauppinen in conversation.

once pointed out (drawing on an image from *Game of Thrones*) in respect to whether a world with God would be desirable.

This point, that Professor Seachris is incorrectly presuming all human beings share his strong wants, can be pressed further. Hindus typically do not believe in a personal God, and instead think of ultimate value in terms of an unconscious force from which everything in the universe sprang, and that continues to permeate and unite all that exists. For them, any talk of "God" refers to something that is not aware of itself, and hence that cannot care about us in the way that Professor Seachris himself would like. When he speaks of "our" deepest desires that remain unfulfilled in the face of cosmic silence, that does not include many who subscribe to Hinduism.

Finally, it is simply not true that all human beings—or even a clear majority—have had deep longings or hopes for either ultimate justice or eternal bliss. For a first example, consider indigenous sub-Saharan Africans, whose religion does postulate an afterlife, but not one that either lasts forever or metes out just deserts. Instead, the standard belief is that, upon the death of one's body, one's imperceptible self continues to reside on Earth for about four or five generations, during which time one continues to watch over one's family (Metz and Molefe 2021: 402–406). There is no thought of punishment for all the wicked, redemption for all the innocent, or reward for all the upright; and there is also no expectation of (or apparent hope for) immortality in the sense of eternal flourishing.

For yet another example, consider Confucianism in East Asia, which has been in existence for some 3,000 years. Many Confucians believe that there might well be life after death; but very few pretend to have any idea about what it might involve, such that they instead focus squarely on relationships in this earthly life:

> (T)he whole Confucian corpus, however rich and diverse, has only a few things to say about a spiritual essence that continues in an afterlife. A key reason is that the good life is thought to lie in the here and now; it does not get better after we die.
> (Bell and Metz 2011: 82).

The prospect of one's soul communing with God forever simply does not feature in this worldview. Not at all.

Now, Hinduism, Traditional African Religion, and Confucianism have been held by literally several billions of people over the centuries. Many billions in South Asia (especially India), sub-Saharan

Africa, and East Asia (especially China) have not in fact deeply desired, longed, or hoped for the existence of God and a soul—or even for states for which Professor Seachris believes these spiritual conditions are essential. Furthermore, it is, I submit, implausible to suggest that adherents to these non-Western philosophies all lacked the concepts of a caring Creator, ultimate justice, or everlasting flourishing, such that they would have immediately come to share Professor Seachris' strong wants upon becoming aware of them.

I conclude that it is a mistake to suppose that "the human search for meaning" essentially involves wanting the world to be the way that Professor Seachris would like it to be. Our psychologies have been much more variable than I am afraid he supposes, such that talk of "human cares and concerns" involves making an unwarranted generalization. I personally share Professor Seachris' desires, longings, and hopes to a much greater degree than people from these non-Western traditions! However, some of his argumentation for moderate supernaturalism involves supposing that it is part of human nature to have these orientations. It is not. When Professor Seachris speaks of the "discrepancy .... between central longings of the human heart and a world devoid of God and an afterlife" (1.7), it is not the human heart as such that has these longings, but rather his heart, along with many in the West.

To his credit, Professor Seachris at other times acknowledges the contingency of the strong wants that he is invoking. At one point he says, "I cannot speak for all, since not everyone claims to have a desire to live forever in loving relationship within a community, but many do. This is a deeply engrained longing that many of us have" (1.8.3).

The trouble is that acknowledging the variability of human psychologies in this way undercuts Professor Seachris' defense of moderate supernaturalism. In the first instance, he was advancing the idea that any human person's life would have a greater meaning in a world upon relating to God in the right way—say, by fulfilling God's purpose and having a soul that entered Heaven. However, if only some of us have the relevant desires, longings, and hopes, then it is apparently only the lives with them that would have a greater meaning from their satisfaction. By appealing to subjective factors, Professor Seachris' view becomes relativist in a way that is in tension with other claims of his and that in any event, I submit, is implausible for those drawn to the thought that the heart of meaning in life is the good, the true, and the beautiful (Section 2.3.1).

I believe Professor Seachris should be striving to show that we all should crave eternal flourishing because it would be meaningful, as opposed to arguing that eternal flourishing would be meaningful because we (or many of us in the West) crave it.

4.4 Is Life Meaningful?

Professor Seachris does not often directly address this question—at least not when it comes to the respects in which he thinks spiritual conditions would make life meaningful. Setting aside God and a soul, his language suggests that many of our lives in fact have meaning in them from a human point of view. For instance, he says that:

> our lives can have a personal, local, terrestrial kind of mattering. This is noteworthy. It is good news. Our lives are not totally insignificant. Our lives matter; they are important; they are special; and they are objects of care and concern ... to us and those around us.
>
> (Section 1.8.1).

He and I agree on that.

When it comes to whether our lives have the sort of meaning that Professor Seachris thinks is particularly choice-worthy, he has not quite said. "Admittedly, God being *better* news for meaning does not make such news *accurate* news. That question, however, is not the topic of this debate" (Section 1.8.3). If God and a soul are crucial for a greater meaning, then we cannot know whether our lives have that sort of meaning unless we do some metaphysics and consider whether they exist. In one way, Professor Seachris is correct that metaphysical questions are not what he and I are debating; but in another way, they are relevant since one central question about life's meaning is whether our lives are in fact meaningful, where answering that unquestionably requires doing some metaphysics. We have to ascertain whether the conditions that would make our life meaningful, or meaningful in a particular way, exist.

The point I want to make in this final section of my reply is that it is Professor Seachris' view that portends nihilism and the pessimistic view that our lives are tragic. The more one craves everlasting flourishing, the more one must be disappointed if it is not forthcoming for us. And I am afraid that it is hard to find evidence that everlasting flourishing is on the cards. The scientific method is humanity's most successful epistemic endeavor in regard to apprehending the nature of reality, and using it provides little to no reason to believe that any sort of non-physical agency exists—whether God or a soul. Readers might suggest that the scientific method is appropriate only for enquiring into physical things, whereas philosophy would be more apt to ascertain whether a spiritual realm exists. However, even if that were so, the philosophical evidence appears weak; and, in fact, only a small minority of contemporary Anglo-American philosophers are theists.[2]

Of course, just because a majority of people believe something does not make it true—at least not when it comes the non/existence of God and a soul. However, when a large majority of experts converge on a view, that is strong evidence it is correct. After all, why do you believe that the Earth is round and that water is H_2O? Presumably because most of those who have enquired into the nature of these things with care have arrived at that judgment and not, say, because you figured it out for yourself.

While Professor Seachris suggests that "a theistic account of reality tends toward the *comic*, whereas atheism tends toward the *tragic*" (Section 1.8), I submit that there is an important sense in which the opposite is true. If the crucial sort of meaning depends on the existence of God and a soul, and if they do not exist for all we can tell, it is then that our lives are tragic. If, however, a satisfactory sort of meaning is possible in a purely physical world that we have no reason to doubt is real, then our lives are comic, in the sense of inviting laughter and satisfaction. Not everyone's life in this world will turn out to be meaningful, on balance. However, my hunch is that enough of a rich life is within the grasp of a very large majority of readers of this conversation between me and Professor Seachris.

---

2 Specifically, less than 15% according to one major survey; see https://philpapers.org/surveys/results.pl.

Second Round of Replies

Chapter 5

God Is Still Better News for Meaning

Response to Metz's Reply

Joshua W. Seachris

Contents

5.1 Introduction	185	Supernaturalism: The Inescapability of the Cosmic Frame	199
5.2 The Meaning Triad and the Meaning of Life's Meaning	186	5.5 Existential Desires: Deep and Universal vs. Shallow and Parochial	203
5.3 God Is Still Better News for Meaning	188		
5.4 On the Supposed Immodesty of Moderate		5.6 Is Life Meaningful?	206

> Almighty and everlasting God, whose will it is to restore all things in thy well-beloved Son, the King of kings and Lord of lords: Mercifully grant that all the peoples of the earth, though now divided and in bondage to sin, may be made free and brought together under his most gracious rule, who liveth and reigneth with thee and the Holy Ghost, one God, now and for ever. *Amen.*
> ("For the Reign of Christ" prayer in the 1662 *Book of Common Prayer*).

> What no eye has seen, nor ear heard, nor the heart of man imagined, what God has prepared for those who love him …
> (1 Corinthians 2:9; ESV).

5.1 Introduction

Areas of agreement and disagreement between us have emerged with greater clarity as Professor Metz and I now have provided our opening statements and initial responses. Space is limited for our final replies to each other, meaning that neither of us will be able to

DOI: 10.4324/9781003436386-8

respond in detail to everything of interest. Consider that situation an invitation for you, the reader, to continue investigating the many issues raised in this debate—including and especially those that we have left to the side for one reason or another.

One of our primary goals in this format is to give you a clear, wide-ranging, intellectually stimulating, thematically unified, rationally grounded, civilly argued debate about what it takes for life to be meaningful. In my final response to Professor Metz's claims and criticisms, I hope to interact with his worries in a way that naturally connects with, amplifies, and builds upon ideas from my first two sections. In responding to his doubts about my position, I want to do so in a way that ties up loose ends and leaves the reader with a sense of closure, even though many of you will disagree with at least some of my claims and conclusions in this debate.

5.2 The Meaning Triad and the Meaning of Life's Meaning

In his reply to my opening statement, Professor Metz expresses doubt that the Meaning Triad—mattering, purpose, and sense-making—fully captures the various aspects of meaning. He says:

> Now, I accept that *part* of what we have in mind when thinking about life's meaning are these three conditions; but I here contend that one should be careful not to suppose they are *exhaustive* of what we have in mind. There are additional ways in which there could, in principle, be meaning in life that is not easily shoehorned into one of Professor Seachris' three categories.
> (Section 4.2, emphasis added).

Let me begin by making a concession: he may be right about this. I am open to that possibility. The group of philosophers working on life's meaning is still relatively small, and the body of work produced by them remains relatively young. Conceptualizing the *meaning* of "meaning" remains an important and underdeveloped task. So, it is not at all implausible to think that the Meaning Triad fails to capture everything important to meaning. That said, this is a debate; so I want to go to bat just a bit more for the Triad as containing most, if not all, of what is important to meaning. Why think this?

In developing the Triad, I was sensitive to the semantic range—the range of meanings that a word has—of *meaning*. That semantic range most closely tracks the ideas of mattering, purpose, and sense-making. There is a reason we use *meaning* to pick out the kind of value that we are after in seeking a meaningful life. Of course, there are probably additional values that we want in life. But what separates *meaning* from such values is that it is focused on the Triad of mattering, purpose, and sense-making. Desirable features of life that reside outside of the Triad are no less desirable, but simply are a different *kind* of value. I remain skeptical of trying to conflate them, conceptually at least, with meaning. Put simply, I take the semantic range of the word "meaning" to be doing a fair amount of heavy lifting in how I think of meaningful life. The range of denotations and connotations is important. Any activity or condition that does not closely link to an aspect of that semantic range, regardless of how valuable or desirable it is, should probably be called something else and not "meaning."

Professor Metz lists a number of candidates for adding meaning in life—candidates that he claims do not naturally fit into my threefold characterization. Below is a sampling of such activities:

- Taking a walk in a forest;
- Being open to nature's bounty;
- Paying attention and empathizing with another living creature;
- Listening closely to a powerful piece of music;
- Being loved by another person; and
- Living among old, hand-worked crafts (Section 4.2).

I agree with Professor Metz. Such activities undoubtedly add meaning to life. I am skeptical, however, that such activities move us beyond the immediate scope of the Meaning Triad. He worries that if I say that such activities are meaningful because they *matter to the individual*, then this allows nearly anything to count as meaningful, which would be much too permissive. Surely, we would not allow compulsive paper-wadding or pencil-sharpening to count as meaningful, even if they mattered to a person—right?

Well, not so fast. According to subjectivists about meaning, such activities would enhance the meaningfulness of one's life if such activities mattered to the one pursuing them. What matters is that it is an issue of *mattering*. The Triad is largely neutral between subjectivist and objectivist theories of meaningful life. It says nothing about whether mattering should be construed objectively, subjectively, or in some hybrid sense. Both Professor Metz and I find objectivist views to be more plausible. As someone who favors such views, I would claim that the list of activities he offers does, in fact, provide conditions that contribute to a meaningful life precisely because they are objectively valuable. They *actually* matter. And in terms of another side of the Triad, sense-making, I would say that a life where such activity is "properly" distributed is one that *makes sense*—especially in that it fits together with what is true about the world, and true about the shape that human life should take against the backdrop of what is true about the world.[1]

5.3 God Is Still Better News for Meaning

I framed my opening statement in terms of God being *better* news for meaning—even if not absolutely essential news, given that I think a type of subjectivist meaning would be available in a Godless universe where certain kinds of finite minds exist. Professor Metz, in his response to my opening statement, offered his reasons for thinking that God is not really better news for meaning, and may actually be worse news for meaning in some ways.

5.3.1 God and a Good Ending: Ultimate Justice

Professor Metz gives reasons to think that while God might be better news for ultimate justice when compared to *this* atheist world, one can conceive of possible atheist worlds where such news would be no worse than the sort of theistic world I have in mind in this debate. Let us consider the *soul* part of the equation first. He asks us to envision a world where all of your mental states over the

---

1   With the sense-making and mattering sides of the Meaning Triad in view, meaning might be a kind of *meta-value*—a value that picks out that which is important in and to life. A meaningful life might be a life that contains a sufficient number and a sufficiently *arranged* number of "parts" that matter. Meaning is not the same thing as subjective wellbeing; nor is it the same as a morally good life—though both subjective wellbeing and moral goodness are values that most of us desire and most of us think it is rational to desire. In that way, they would *contribute* to a meaningful life. A meaningful life will have these values (and much more, including activities from Professor Metz's list above) because they *matter*; they are important. This brief foray into the idea that meaning may be a kind of meta-value is, of course, quite tentative; and I encourage readers to investigate it further to see if we can get additional mileage out of it or, alternatively, put it to rest as little more than a dead end (cf. the end of Section 1.2.3).

course of your life are uploaded onto a computer and then downloaded into a new body which will exist at least long enough for wrongs to be righted and so on (Section 4.3.1). The details do not seem important at first glance. The basic idea is that there are atheistic possibilities for securing a *sufficiently long* existence in order to enact ultimate justice—the sort of justice that does not occur in *this* life for most, if not all of us.

It will come as no surprise that I am doubtful about this. A big part of my doubt stems from my skepticism of what appears to be a functionalist view of the self. At the risk of oversimplification, functional definitions of this or that prioritize what something *does* over what something *is*. For example, functionally, a mousetrap is something that traps (or kills) mice. There are many variations of such devices. Indeed, some of them work much better than others! A device need not be made of wood and wire to be a mousetrap. It could be made entirely of plastic. Or consider a heart. A heart is something that pumps blood. You might have a blood pumper consisting of flesh (and blood); or you may have one made of special plastics and high-tech metals. Maybe self and mind are similar. Roughly, on a functionalist view of the mind, *I* (Josh Seachris) am some sort of abstract set of mental states. If that is the case, those mental states presumably could be uploaded, downloaded, sideloaded, or whatever the case might be to computers or different substrates. Though I lack the space to argue against such functionalism here, I do want to point out that this is only one among several competing views about mind, identity, and personhood. It happens to be one that I do not presently hold. On my view, there can be one and only one *me*, and simply uploading my mental states into a potentially infinite number of "bodies" does not allow for *my* continued existence. Rather, it would mean that there are a potentially infinite number of Josh-like entities who share mental states that I myself had.

For readers who have studied philosophy of mind, you will notice that I sound like a dualist here. That is because I am something of a dualist, and I make no apologies about that. I do not think that strong forms of dualism, including some types of substance dualism, have been shown to be untenable, either by physicalist theories of the mind or by the advent and advances of contemporary neuroscience, impressive as it is (for two recent defenses of strong forms of dualism, see Swinburne 2019; and Cottingham 2020). Add to substance dualism views like those of Aristotle and Aquinas, and there are a range of theories of mind that provide formidable alternatives to functionalism.

But back to my point. If ultimate justice requires that the *actual* person who deserves recompense exist, then I am doubtful that a functionalist view like that of Professor Metz gets us the actual person rather than some sort of simulacrum. The one who suffered and the one who committed injustice still need to be around in order for ultimate justice to be served (by the way, are not we all both "sufferers *and* sinners"?). I worry that this sort of functionalism will make it difficult for *us* to still be around. That is the soul part of the ultimate justice equation. What about the *God* part?

Professor Metz argues that there are non-theistic alternatives to grounding ultimate justice that are possible in atheistic universes—one such example being the concept of *karma*, "according to which an impersonal force regulates the distribution of benefits and burdens in proportion to one's deeds" (Section 4.3.1). About *karma*, he says that it "is conceivable, which shows that justice could be done in the absence of God *qua* personal judge" (Section 4.3.1). I have a hard time conceiving of what it would mean for an *impersonal* force to *regulate* a distribution of anything, let alone benefits and burdens. Regulating or dispensing distributions is starting to sound very much like something only a person can do, even if through implementing a *downstream impersonal process*.

That said, let us assume that *karma* is (1) possible and (2) possible in an atheistic universe. There is still the question of which scenario more plausibly and naturally secures the prospect of ultimate justice. It seems to me that a perfect judge—where a judge is a person, and a perfect judge is a perfect person of the sort I have described at various places in this debate—is the best and most likely route for securing ultimate justice. Professor Metz thinks the sort of perfect judge I have in mind would be *sufficient* for the realization of ultimate justice but not *necessary*. If his *karma* proposal is right, then, yes, the theistic God would not be necessary. But I worry that thinking of this solely in terms of necessary and sufficient conditions clouds possibly important considerations—for example, between different ways of conceiving ultimate justice, where ultimate justice looks different via *karma* than it does via a personal, perfect judge.

A more interesting point, I think, is pausing to consider the kinds of atheistic worlds that Professor Metz is having us envision in his examples. I suspect that he would concede that they are distant possible atheist worlds in comparison to the one that he thinks we all *actually* live in. Indeed, introducing elements like *karma* moves them toward worlds that have transcendent, quasi-transcendent, or at least non-physical elements—unless he can find a place for *karma* in the physical space-time universe without any extra metaphysical baggage. A universe with *karma* has, at minimum, a quasi-religious flavor to it. We are in the realm of logical possibilities—which is important for conceptual analysis and getting clear on necessary and sufficient conditions—but I wonder if it is more appropriate here to operate in the realm of *plausibilities*. Let us compare the worlds that we both *actually* think exist. Professor Metz thinks we live in an atheistic world without God and souls, and where the *actual* prospects for ultimate justice do not exist. I, on the other hand, think we live in a theistic world with God and souls, and where the *actual* prospects for ultimate justice do exist. The world that I think we actually live in is much better news for ultimate justice than the world that he thinks we actually live in.

5.3.2 God and a Bad Ending (for Some): Eternal Separation

That there is a "place" or state of (potentially) never-ending separation from God is a common doctrine across, especially, theistic religions. It should come as little to no surprise that, as a Christian theist, I take seriously the tradition which says that those who willfully, consistently, and finally reject God's offer of loving communion through the person of Jesus of Nazareth will find themselves somehow, and in some way, apart from God. A deeply lamentable reality awaits those who fully and finally decide to call *all* of the shots, down to every jot and tittle, about the manner and means of human flourishing. I think Professor Metz is right to conclude that this would be very bad news for those who find themselves in such a predicament.

However, not only does he think that it would be bad news; he thinks it would be *unjust* news. Why? He claims that acts done over a finite lifetime would not *deserve* infinite, never-ending discipline or punishment. He worries about what appears to be an extreme asymmetry. After all, good human parents do not give ten-year timeouts to their nine-year old who throws a fit and says he hates them. Professor Metz's worry is a common one, shared by atheist and many a theist alike. Let us define this view as follows:

> **Unjust Hell:** Being separated forever from the loving presence of God because of finite wrongs done over the course of a finite lifetime would be unjust.

One general strategy for responding to "Unjust Hell" is to do something similar to what Professor Metz himself does often in this debate: investigate possible worlds, in this case *theistic* possible worlds. For example, some theists hold the view that those who reject God's offer of communion are not separated from God for an *everlasting* duration, but receive just discipline for a finite duration and then are annihilated. In this way, they would not suffer infinite discipline for finite actions, but finite discipline for finite actions. Still, to many, extinguishing living beings seems like a non-starter to address the "Unjust Hell" worry.

Another view under this general strategy is that people suffer finite discipline, which itself leads to profound moral and relational transformation, the completion of which results in encountering the presence of God along with all those who desire such presence. In such a case, even though the person ends up in Heaven, it is not quite right to say that this happens *no matter how they lived on Earth*, given that the person would come to lament the shape of one's pre-death life through this transformation (cf. St. Luke 16:19–31 for a cautionary tale). I am sympathetic to these sorts of strategies, but currently do not favor them; so I would rather tell you what I actually think.

The "Unjust Hell" problem is a tough one, but I do not think it is as intractable as it might first appear. I think it is a misunderstanding of Christian theism to see the ultimate human problem in relation to God and our fellow humans as one of our *actions* alone. God does not ultimately discipline, punish, or condemn us because of our actions *alone*, but because of a prior *orientation* out of which those actions flow. Our hearts and lives are either increasingly oriented toward God or they are not. It is out of our heart that we speak and act (cf. Matt. 15:18). In the Christian Scriptures, the *heart* refers to the center of one's being to include will and emotions. It is the deep and ultimate wellspring of who we are and what we do. On such a view, being separated in the end from God ultimately will not be merely because of the things that we do (sins of commission) or do not do (sins of omission) with our finite lives on this Earth, but because of the primary orientation of our hearts either toward or away from God. Why is this move away from actions alone and toward including *orientation* relevant?

The thought here is that our primary orientations, our character, and the like can become habituated and, eventually, settled. These especially include our inclinations, dispositions, emotions, and desires, among others. Eventually, we can become so settled in who we are that we might not actually *want* God—the ultimate True, Good, and Beautiful—anymore. On such a view, hell is a "place," in the words of C. S. Lewis, where the doors are "locked from the inside" (Lewis 1996: 114; Lewis's entire chapter "Hell" in that work is quite fascinating). To put it bluntly, those who find themselves in this predicament close the door on God willfully, continually, and finally. The one who does so has decided over and over again to pursue human flourishing on his own terms, and in so doing, is excluding himself from fulfilling the purpose for which he was created—communion with infinite beauty and goodness, resulting in perfect blessedness. Hell, at minimum, is not experiencing the purpose for which humans were created. Beyond that, I care to speculate or say very little. That may not be the view of hell that one often encounters in various pop venues, ranging from the religious to the secular. It may seem tame in comparison; but it remains a hard, sobering word nonetheless. To not experience the full flourishing for which we were created is described by the Christian Scriptures as "outer darkness," and where there is "weeping and gnashing of teeth" (Matt. 8:11; ESV). It is to miss out on a reality about which St. Paul, in his second letter to the Corinthian Church, remarks: "For this light momentary affliction is preparing for us *an eternal weight of glory beyond all comparison*" (2 Cor. 4:17; ESV, emphasis added). But back to the idea of Hell's doors being locked *from the inside*. The point is that those experiencing such a state actually, in some meaningful sense, *want* and *choose* to be there.

What if one were to abandon any notion of everlasting separation from God and affirm a doctrine like universalism: the idea that everyone eventually enjoys everlasting communion with God? Professor Metz thinks this, too, would be unjust; for then, everyone's life—no matter how moral or immoral—will turn out the same in the end. Both the psychopathic serial killer and his victims will find themselves in God's presence in the final chapter. How can that be fair? The theist appears to be faced with a serious dilemma. On the one hand, some ending up in an everlasting Hell seems unjust; and on the other, everyone ending up in Heaven also seems unjust. In addition to "Unjust Hell," then, let us define the latter view as follows:

Unjust Heaven: Everyone ending up in heaven, *regardless* of how they lived their earthly lives, would be unjust.

Whether or not it would be unjust for everyone ultimately to end up in Heaven would depend on important points along their *route of arrival*. If everyone ends up in Heaven, and if everyone who ends up there has been morally and relationally transformed in ways that (1) acknowledge the full force of their brokenness and how that brokenness has affected others and (2) have led to a complete change in orientation to one of loving God and loving people, then I do not see a problem. Everyone in Heaven would *want* to be there, and *wanting* to be there would be conditioned on (1) and (2) (for two sophisticated theological discussions of universalism, see Bentley Hart 2019; and Von Balthasar 2014). Quite apart from issues of *justice*, would everlasting and perfect happiness even be meaningful?

5.3.3 God and a Good Ending: Everlasting Flourishing

Professor Metz and I both agree that everlasting happiness would be desirable. However, he is suspicious that everlasting happiness would be meaningful. I might be too; but that depends on the relationship between *everlasting* happiness and *perfect* happiness, where, at minimum, perfect happiness is happiness that lasts forever and is obtained via the right means. At places in my opening statement, I leaned toward the view that perfect happiness is the purpose for which we were created. Indeed, significant streams within the Christian theistic tradition affirm something like this. However, in the introduction to my opening statement, I claimed that meaning "appears relevantly distinct from other values we want in our lives like moral goodness and happiness, even if it overlaps with them." Professor Metz points out that there appears to be a tension here in my view.

Let us remind ourselves that this is a debate. I do not know about you, but I walk away from most debates frustrated, having seen neither side concede any ground. This makes me worry that people are not actually being rational, but are stubbornly entrenched in their views, clinging to them for irrational reasons. The person who produces the best *ad hoc* justification for her positions, or the person who is the most rhetorically savvy "wins." Professor Metz and I both are fully aware of such dangers. There is a lot of investment in the views that each of us currently hold. Would it not be refreshing to our readers to see real-time concessions? I feel the force of Professor Metz's worry: do I think that happiness and meaning are two different kinds of value, or do I conflate them? At places, I seem to do both. I say meaning is different from happiness; and later, I say that perfect happiness may in fact be the meaning of life, if by "meaning of life" we interpret it as that *for* which humans have been created. How can that be?

One straightforward response is simply that it cannot. I contradicted myself—end of story. That is possible. I imagine that I have contradicted myself often; and I suspect that currently within the vast web of beliefs that make up my worldview, I have some incompatible sets of beliefs. Maybe this is one such incompatible set. If that is the case, I will need to abandon one of them to resolve the contradiction. I am not ready to go this route yet. Is this a case of me stubbornly trying to dig myself out of this hole with sophistry and slick rhetoric? I do not think so. Rather, I am trying to do what we philosophers do—continue to investigate, conceptualize, and reconceptualize until we have left no philosophical stone unturned. If the contradiction "survives" this process, then we must abandon one of the contradictory claims.

So here it goes. It does seem to me that happiness and meaning are not the same thing. That is what I was trying to communicate in the claim early in my opening statement: "[Meaning] appears relevantly distinct from other values we want in our lives, like moral goodness and happiness, even if it overlaps with them." Meaning is the sort of thing captured by the elements of the Meaning Triad—mattering, purpose, and sense-making. In this way, meaning is not *conceptually* identical to happiness. According to the Triad, a meaningful life will be about doing stuff that matters. Recall my definition of "meaningful life" that you have encountered a number of times already in this debate:

> **Meaningful Life:** One's life is meaningful to the degree that it is oriented around that which matters (mattering that is of positive rather than negative value), which in turn fuels the purposive activity one pursues to give one's life direction, and, therefore allows one's life to make sense and exhibit proper fit with reality—a fitting place within the whole of what is true, good, and beautiful. Someone who lives such a life will tend to be happier, more fulfilled, satisfied, and engaged.

Whatever a meaningful life is, it will have as its focus these three dimensions. Now notice that I include happiness in this definition, but only as a *corollary* of leading a meaningful life. This means that one could lead a meaningful life but fail to be happy *in this life*. The "in this life" qualifier seems important.

Other ideas that likely matter to settling this include: (1) the *level* at which happiness enters into the meaning equation, and (2) the *type* of happiness in view. Regarding (1), it would be a contradiction for me to say that meaning *means* the same thing as happiness. I am not saying that. Rather, I am saying that meaning *means* mattering, purpose, and sense-making; and the level at which happiness enters the picture is at the level of *being one of the purposes, if not the purpose* for which we have been created. In this way, happiness is one of those potential features of human existence that *matters*. Happiness is meaningful because happiness matters. On Christian theism, our happiness matters both *to us* and *to God*, who created us. There are other things that matter too, though. And yet I entertained the idea in my opening statement that happiness matters *most*. This is where the qualifier "perfect" may be helpful. It is not just *happiness* that is the end toward which we aim—it is a *perfect* kind; and a perfect kind will not only be infinite in duration, but will be the kind that is held in balance with other values in life like morality, loving relationships, and—yes—bending the knee to God to seek such perfect happiness on God's terms, the one who created us for this end. The happy serial killer cannot lead a meaningful life nor the person who sharpens pencils for eternity. Any happiness experienced by such persons will not be *perfect*.

5.3.4 God and Greater Atelic Meaning

In his reply to my opening statement, Professor Metz claims that meaning can take on forms that are not easily captured by my Meaning Triad. I responded to that claim in Section 5.2. Here, I want to add that not everything that matters in life will or even should be in the form of attaining forward-looking, future-oriented goals. In addition to such goals, our lives should have what philosopher Kieran Setiya calls "atelic ends' (see Setiya 2017). Roughly, atelic ends—unlike telic ones—have their goal or aim or fulfillment contained within them. They are the sort of thing that can be *stopped*, but never *completed*. For example, walking in order *to get somewhere*, like to home from work, is a telic activity; whereas walking for the sheer enjoyment of walking in nature is an atelic activity. Once you have arrived home, you have accomplished the goal of walking to get home. However, you cannot really finish walking for the sheer enjoyment of walking. You might stop doing it periodically; but you cannot really *complete* it, because it is not the sort of orientation toward an activity or experience that allows for completion. Other examples of atelic activity include enjoying a pleasing meal (eating food for something more than simply staying alive); enjoying the staggering beauty of nature; and enjoying deep companionship with others, to include companionship with God. I submit that such atelic activities matter to our lives, deeply and *objectively*.

Too Much Telic Activity?

Goal-pursuit is an important aspect of life. It is also important for *meaningful* life. A life with no goals and heading nowhere (related to P-meaning in the Meaning Triad) seems impoverished from the standpoint of meaning. Imagine the following dialog:

Andre: "Why did you get out of bed this morning?"
Amara: "Because I wanted to go to class."
Andre: "Why did you want to go to class?"
Amara: "Because I want to get a good grade."
Andre: "Why do you want to get good grades?"
Amara: "Because I want to graduate with a high GPA."
Andre: "Why do you want to graduate with a high GPA?"
Amara: "Because I want to get a good job."
Andre: "Why do you want to get a good job?"
Amara: "Because I want to provide a quality standard of living for myself and loved ones."

You see where this is headed, right? We engage in such activities because we perceive them as heading somewhere valuable. Eventually, we give an answer to which no further "why" question can be asked.

Much of our lives are structured by the purposes toward which we aim. We engage in activity in order to *get somewhere* in the future about which we can say that we arrived.

Something worth reflecting on further is whether we can have *too much* preoccupation with accomplishing these sorts of goals in life. In terms of the distinction between *telic* and *atelic* ends in this section, the idea is that a meaningful life will exhibit a balance between the two. For more on these issues see (Goetz and Seachris 2020: Appendix 1).

The point I want to make here is that *greater* atelic meaning is available in a universe with God, souls, and afterlife. For example, the atelic activity of enjoying the sublimity of nature acquires the extra interpretive layer of being enjoyment of the creation of a good and powerful Creator. Gratitude at the beauty of our world and for our existence within it is transformed into a deeper and more genuine emotion, since gratitude directed toward persons seems more apt than gratitude directed toward impersonal or random states of affairs. Indeed, with God in the picture, the awe and gratitude we experience during our leisurely walk in nature make more sense; they are more fitting.

Atelic activities often, though not always, involve companionship with others—a companionship which is focused not on what others can do for us, but rather on reveling in them simply as other persons. The value of, and pleasures in, human relationships are real, powerful, and varied. Even relationships between finite creatures exhibit deep open-endedness and boundlessness. The depths of another person, along with the accompanying joy and wonder of experiencing those depths through a relationship, may be inexhaustible. It would be better, then, for such relationships to continue indefinitely. Now imagine such companionship with an infinite person, God. If God is of infinite value—where such value is tied to God's nature as necessarily existent, essentially good, and sublimely beautiful, etc.—then atelically relating to an infinite God would be the absolute pinnacle of atelic experience: an inexhaustibly good and positive experience that never ends. Each of these various new layers of atelic experience uniquely available in a theistic universe is powerfully captured in the Eastern Orthodox Christian Hymn of Praise, *Akathist [hymn] of Thanksgiving: "Glory to God for All Things!"*[2]

> Glory to Thee for calling me into being; glory to Thee, showing me the beauty of the universe.
> Glory to Thee, spreading out before me heaven and earth, like the pages in a book of eternal wisdom.
> Glory to Thee for each different taste of berry and fruit; glory to Thee for the sparkling silver of early morning dew.

---

2   Interestingly, this *Akathist* was found among the effects of Protopresbyter Gregory Petrov upon his death in a prison camp, of all places, in 1940. I thank my brother, Corey Seachris, for introducing this hymn to me.

Glory to Thee for the inventiveness of the human mind.
Glory to Thee, bringing from the depth of the earth an endless variety of colors, tastes and scents.
Glory to Thee for our unquenchable thirst for communion with God.
Glory to Thee for Thine eternity in this fleeting world; glory to Thee for Thy mercies, seen and unseen.
Glory to Thee for the hope of the unutterable, imperishable beauty of immortality.
Glory to Thee for the pledge of our reawakening on that glorious last day, that day which has no evening.
Glory to Thee, Father all-holy, promising us a share in Thy kingdom.
Glory to Thee, Redeemer Son, who hast shown us the path to salvation.
Glory to Thee, Holy Spirit, life-giving Sun of the world to come.
Glory to Thee for all things, Holy and most merciful Trinity.
Glory to Thee, O God, from age to age!
(excerpts from Mikitish and Majkrzak: 189–203).

5.4 On the Supposed Immodesty of Moderate Supernaturalism: The Inescapability of the Cosmic Frame

The appeal to a moderate form of supernaturalism is supposed to account for fairly common intuitions (1) that a person can lead a meaningful life—at some level and in some sense—even if God and soul do not exist; but (2) that God would enhance the prospects for meaningful life. Professor Metz doubts that the move to a moderate form of supernaturalism will actually help. He worries that this common move to make theism *better but not absolutely essential* news for meaning—especially the infinite, everlasting context it provides for human life in the presence of God—actually makes any finite life in comparison look quite insignificant and, therefore, meaningless. One way of thinking about this worry is that moderate supernaturalism collapses into something similar to extreme supernaturalism—if not in letter, then in spirit.

In order to reply to this particular form of the worry, let us focus our attention on the issue of *frame of reference*. Recall a point I made in Section 1.2.3 of my opening statement. There I claimed that meaning is often associated with the activity of *locating* something within a larger context or frame of reference. "Things" often mean what they do within this larger frame—words within sentences paragraphs, and novels; musical notes within measures, movements, and symphonies. Meaning can and often does *shift* when something is set within a larger context. An expanding context might include temporal dynamics too. The significance of the past and present shifts through a dynamic relationship with later events (see Section 1.7.1). So, how does this address Professor Metz's worry?

Assessments of whether our lives are meaningful or full of meaning will be intertwined with the frame of reference we use in assessing them. Such frames will have not only spatial and temporal elements, but also normative ones. For example, if the frame of reference is one that includes objective value, then—regardless of whether that frame is large or small, short or long—such lives that appropriately interact with objective value will have the property of meaningfulness. In my first reply to Professor Metz's opening statement, I offered reasons to think that frames of reference which include objective value also include God. But for the sake of argument, let us say that a frame of reference can have objective value without God. Let us also say that this frame of reference does not include souls or afterlife. Following Professor Metz, let us consider Einstein's life within that frame of reference. It would be meaningful because Einstein would have been appropriately linked to objective value, even if only for several decades. I am happy to conclude that his life would be meaningful under those circumstances—if such circumstances were possible. However, because I do not think it likely that objective value would exist without God existing, I do not think such circumstances would exist. But let us keep playing along. If Einstein's finite life could be accurately described as being meaningful or full of meaning, then how is that consistent with the assessment that his life on theism would be *so much better*? Would not his finite life, in comparison, have a level of meaning next to nothing? This, I think, is where the frame of reference point is helpful.

Within the human, terrestrial frame of reference, Einstein's life would be meaningful. From the perspective of the average longevity of human life, from the perspective of the average scope of human activity and its impacts, and from the perspective of human accomplishment, he led a very meaningful life. But that is not the only frame of reference within which to consider Einstein's life. We could switch to a frame that includes God and afterlife, for example; and against this backdrop, much about Einstein's current life would pale in comparison. I agree with Professor Metz about this, though I do not see the problem. Relative to the human timeframe, and relative to many human cares and concerns, Einstein's life looms quite large, which tracks important aspects of meaning. Against the backdrop of infinitely expanding time, however, it does not. His life takes up less and less of the endlessly expanding timeline of reality.

Let us add the layer of objective value to the mix. If engagement with objective value is crucial for leading a meaningful life, then engaging with objective value *forever* would be much better than engaging with objective value for, say, 75 years, and then ceasing to exist. In this case, engaging with objective value forever would make engaging with objective value for 75 years seem like next to nothing; hence Professor Metz's worry. But there remains a way of retaining the intuition that 75 years of engaging with value would be (quite) meaningful, because it would be meaningful from a more localized frame of reference. If the frame of reference has objective (or subjective) value within it, then one can have real meaning regardless of how large and old that frame is. But there would be other senses (remember, meaning is about quite a lot!) in which a larger, older frame within which we do not have a *lasting* place would be bad news for meaning. For example, the significance—on some senses of "significance"—of one's activities and life would wane when placed in increasingly larger contexts. Or, if there is such a thing as objective value, then one's engagement with something intrinsically valuable would come to an end after a very short time. Interaction with objective value—in the form of creative accomplishments, understanding reality, and loving relationships—is valuable regardless of how long it lasts. That said, it would be much better if it lasted indefinitely. For those who think that eventually we would get bored after billions and billions of years of interaction with objectively valuable states of affairs, I too have thought about this worry quite a lot, both professionally and personally, and I ultimately do not find it compelling (for arguments for and against this view, see, for example, Fischer 2020).

Is this situation like Professor Metz's Eiffel Tower example (Section 4.3.2.3)? If two humans, one shorter and one taller, stand next to the Eiffel Tower, both will be very short indeed. Is moderate supernaturalism like the Eiffel Tower situation, such that no human life, without God, soul, and afterlife, can be called *meaningful* without some major caveats? Again, I think it comes back to frame of reference. When compared to one another, one person *is* taller, full stop. When compared to the Eiffel Tower, both are short. When it comes to meaning, there are very real senses in which human lives can be genuinely spoken of as being meaningful from the *sub specie humanitatis* perspective, even if there are other senses in which their meaning is threatened *sub specie aeternitatis* (see Section 1.2.1). One can account for both intuitions: that life can be meaningful in important senses without God, soul, and afterlife; and, in other senses, that life's meaning would be better—a *lot* better—with God, soul, and life everlasting.

That said, I am inclined to agree with Professor Metz that, when compared with a never-ending interaction with objective value, a limited encounter with objective value, while good, would pale in comparison. What is true at the cosmic level is important. What is true about and within that larger frame matters for assessments of life's meaningfulness. Certain types of meaningfulness are available in narrower frames, yes; but what is true of wider frames—including the widest—will inevitably be relevant for assessments of life's meaningfulness at other levels. The widest frame very well might be what is *most* relevant for assessments of life's meaningfulness at layers that matter the most. Consider the following example from philosopher John Hick (1922–2012):

> I am in a strange building, and walking by mistake into a large room I find that a militant secret society is meeting there. Many of the members are armed, and as they take me for a fellow member I think it expedient to acquiesce in the role. Plans are being discussed for the violent overthrow of the constitution. The whole situation is alarming in the extreme. Its meaning for me is such that I am extremely apprehensive. Then I suddenly become aware in the dim light above us of a gallery in which there are silently operating cameras, and I realize that I have walked by accident onto the set of a film. This realization consists in a changed awareness of my immediate situation. Until now I had automatically experienced it as "real life" and as demanding considerable circumspection on my part. Now I experience it as having a quite different significance. But at ground level there is no change in the course of events; the meeting of the secret society proceeds just as before. However,

my new awareness of the more comprehensive situation alters my experience of the more immediate one. It now has a new meaning for me such that I am in a very different dispositional state in relation to it

(Hick 2004: 56).

Setting something within a wider context or adding new elements to the existing context results in shifting meaning. It also seems to me that it is not obvious that the narrow context of looking at life from the average human lifespan or through a terrestrial scope of human affairs on Earth *ought to be privileged* over the cosmic one. Hence, I think an atheistic *sub specie aeternitatis* perspective invites deep worries.

5.5 Existential Desires: Deep and Universal vs. Shallow and Parochial

Professor Metz has concerns about some of my more anthropological claims that most humans find within themselves existential longings for, among other things, answers to questions about why we are here; a lasting place for genuine love and relationships; ultimate justice to be served; and the satisfaction of our deepest hopes and longings. He thinks that my claims are both too strong and too Western.

To Professor Metz's claim that forward-looking assessments of life are more commonly in focus and more relevant for meaning than backward-looking assessments of life, I would simply say that insofar as I am interested in the meaning of my life (and life and the universe in general), I am very much concerned—and I think the reader *should* be too—about where we came from and how we got here; in other words, with *why* we exist. This "why" question admits of at least two interpretations:

> **Efficient Causal Interpretation:** We are here because particular sperm fertilized particular eggs, and so on and so forth.
> **Final Causal Interpretation:** We, and the universe, are here ultimately because God wanted us to be here.

If someone asks me why the water in my electric kettle is boiling, I could give an efficient, mechanistic causal explanation invoking mean kinetic energy; or I could also simply say: "I want some coffee." Whereas Professor Metz claims that "few of us care much about how human life as such originated" (Section 4.3.3), it seems to me that the circumstances in which life originated—whether accidently or intentionally—matter quite a lot for important senses in which life is or is not meaningful. Is there merely an efficient causal story of our origins, or an additional final causal layer to that story? Of course, it is an empirical question as to just how many people *believe* that backward concern for human origins is important.

Professor Metz claims also that human longings for lasting loving relationships, infinite flourishing, and ultimate justice are much more parochial than I make them out to be. He offers reasons to think that there are many people, especially in non-Western cultures, who do not have such desires—at least in their theistically expressed forms. For example, he notes that Hindus do not believe in a personal God in the same way that theists do; and, alternatively, think of ultimate value as an unconscious force (Section 4.3.3). I am not sure what it would mean for ultimate value to be an unconscious force. But more to the point, I understand a text like the *Bhagavad Gita* to actually presuppose that most of us begin with desires for pleasure (or happiness, or fulfillment, or flourishing), and then to encourage us to renounce such desires that we actually *have*. In this way, it is not clear to me that some Hindus, for example, fail to have a desire for some sort of deep happiness, as opposed to being instructed to renounce or manage a desire they actually have. For what it is worth, the Christian Scriptures advocate a kind of renunciation as well: dying to self and choosing to pursue flourishing on *God's terms*.

I know much, much less about cultural and religious practices in sub-Saharan Africa than Professor Metz, so I will take him at his word. That said, I find it interesting that indigenous sub-Saharan Africans believe in something soul-like—a belief they share with most of the world, both currently and across time. If the self does persist after death, what are we to make of the idea that it watches over the remaining loved ones? What is its concern with watching over its family? Their happiness? Their flourishing?

As for the Confucian tradition, Professor Metz claims that it has little to say about the "spiritual essence that continues in an afterlife" (Section 4.3.3). I agree. I would simply respond that, similarly, the Hebrew Bible says very little about the afterlife. Most of its focus is on the story of the nation of Israel on Earth as part of God's redemptive plan. I think it would be wrong to conclude from this lack of information that there was no concern about what happened after death. Neither it nor the Christian Scriptures are philosophical texts on the nature of the afterlife or the meaning of life. Even the Christian Scriptures, to include the New Testament, include scant information about the *nature* of the new Heaven and new Earth.

> ### Theistic Longings or Human Longings?
>
> While the Asia-Pacific region continues to be home to the vast majority of all Buddhists (roughly 1 billion), it also is home to over 1 billion Muslims and Christians, both groups of whom are theists. These trends are projected to continue at least until 2050. There are complex theories to explain these demographics and trends. One idea to consider is how such numbers might (or might not) shed light on the disagreement between Professor Metz and me regarding the scope of the sorts of desires under consideration here.
>
> - Are these so-called "theistic" and "Western" desires perhaps more universal?
>
> (cf. pewforum.org/2015/04/02/asia-pacific)

Emerging from the details about what this or that group believes regarding such issues, the general point I am trying to make here is that more space is needed to properly answer the question of just how deep and widespread the desires are for human flourishing to continue on after this life; for deeply loving relationships to persist (possibly indefinitely); and for ultimate justice to be done and everlasting peace to be experienced. I made some sweeping claims in my opening statement, and Professor Metz has given some reasons to call them into doubt. Still, I find myself in agreement with philosopher Alasdair MacIntyre, who said:

> Finite beings who possess the power of understanding, if they know that God exists, know that he is the most adequate object of their love, and that the *deepest desire* of every such being, whether they acknowledge it or not, is to be at one with God.
> (MacIntyre 2009: 5–6).

Long before MacIntyre, St. Augustine, the North African Bishop of Hippo, claimed that "our hearts are restless, until they can find rest in you [God]" (Augustine, 1). *Homo sapiens* are also *homo religiosus*.

In this brief section, I have tried to provide some additional reasons for the following response to Professor Metz's claims:

> **Inter-Cultural Variability Skepticism:** It may not be the case that there is as much inter-cultural variability with these desires, even if there exists diversity in how such desires are expressed and managed.

Let me end this section with a concession. Professor Metz is correct. I do incline toward saying that humans *qua* humans (and not, for example, *Western* humans or humans with *theistic* sensibilities) have these deep longings for wanting reality to be a certain way—a certain way "conveniently" captured by theism. Despite my misgivings above about his claim, I take his worries seriously. Have I absolutized and universalized mere "local" longings? Perhaps; and I am willing to keep the dialog going on that topic after the close of this book. But let me close this section with a question:

> If, philosophically, one acknowledges that something is intrinsically, objectively good—for example, genuine, loving relationships, full human flourishing, and ultimate justice—how could one *not* be concerned with its continuance and fulfillment?

5.6 Is Life Meaningful?

In my opening statement, and in my subsequent responses to Professor Metz's statements, my views about whether life is, in fact, meaningful have remained fairly implicit. Space is short, so let me close by saying that, yes, I think life is meaningful—in some senses that require nothing from us; and in other senses where what we do factors significantly into our life's meaningfulness. I think there is objective value in our world. I think God exists in Trinity—Father, Son, and Holy Spirit. I think something soul-like exists. These are *present* realities. I also think everlasting life continuing in a new Heaven and a new Earth looms on the horizon (cf. Rev. 21ff). Perfectly loving relationships, full human flourishing, ultimate justice and everlasting peace are *yet-to-come* realities. All of these features are good news—good news for:

- Passively conditioned meaning;
- Actively conditioned meaning;

- Meaning *subs specie humanitatis*; and
- Meaning *sub specie aeternitatis*.

We are created in God's image—the *imago dei*; and as such, each of us has profound and inherent dignity—a kind of mattering that we have in virtue of what *we are* (passively conditioned meaning). Human psychology includes subjective states like fulfillment and satisfaction. Whether or not we consider them to be constitutive of meaning (as subjectivists about meaning do) or partly constitutive of meaning (as hybridists about meaning do), many of us think it is valuable to experience such states. God provides the conditions for experiencing them in part in this life, and perfectly in the life to come. We live in a world filled with objective value because we live in *God's* universe. Being able to sufficiently connect to some of this objective value is independent of whether or not one believes in the source of this objective value; it is available to all (which will result in some actively conditioned meaning for all who "access" this objective value). However, a life with the fullest sort of actively conditioned meaning—at least if Christian theism is true—will be a life not simply *lived in* God's universe, but *lived in full recognition of and proper orientation within* God's universe. It will be a life properly oriented toward God in all relevant ways, to include knowing God and properly relating to God—for example, in worship. Professor Metz says that if God exists, then we "would have to 'bend the knee'" (Section 4.3.3). Yes, we would; and we do. Ultimately, we did not create this life; we do not sustain it; and we do not get to fully define it and what constitutes human flourishing. Living in God's universe also provides a meaning *to* life—or, put differently, *the* meaning *of* life, cosmically speaking. Human life means something—not only *sub specie humanitatis*, from the perspective of human cares and concerns; it also means something *sub specie aeternitatis*. Theism not only gets us more layers of meaning; it gets us better and deeper layers of meaning.

How does theism relate to the formal definition of "meaningful life" that I have stated at various places throughout this debate? Consider again that definition:

> **Meaningful Life:** One's life is meaningful to the degree that it is oriented around that which matters (mattering that is of positive rather than negative value); which in turn fuels the purposive activity one pursues to give one's life direction,

and therefore allows one's life to make sense and exhibit proper fit with reality—a fitting place within the whole of what is true, good, and beautiful. Someone who lives such a life will tend to be happier, more fulfilled, satisfied, and engaged.

This definition focuses primarily on the shape of actively conditioned meaning. What would a particularly Christian theistic version of this look like? A meaningful life would be oriented around God and what God prescribes as the route to true and full human flourishing, first and foremost by relating to God on His terms. On Christian theism, relating to God on His terms involves relating properly to Jesus, the incarnate second person of the Holy Trinity. Jesus himself says in St. John that he has come to give abundant life (St. Jn. 10:10). About the route to such life, St. John is quite clear: "For God so loved the world, that he gave his only son, that whoever believes in him should not perish but have eternal life" (Jn. 3:16; ESV).

The primary calls on our lives are to repent, believe the Gospel (cf. 1 Cor. 15:1–11), and love God and our neighbor (Mark 12:30–31). In Section 5.3.2, I spoke of the need for a heart that is properly oriented toward God. Our heart's fundamental orientation provides the wellspring of human action. Repentance and faith fuel a proper orientation that nurtures genuine love of God and neighbor.

In addition to relating to God on God's own terms, full human flourishing on Christian theism includes cultivating deep and lasting human relationships, developing our creative potential, stewarding the Earth, marveling at the created universe, finding deep joy in these activities, regularly resting from our strivings (*sabbath*), and so on. All of these pursuits matter, and take concrete form in the purposes to which we devote ourselves, and which are embodied in our callings and vocations; and in time spent in rest and leisure. Much of the precise form of all of this is left up to you and me.

When one's life is infused with such elements, it will be a life of gravitas (*mattering*-meaning). Those elements will give rise to purposes that motivate us to action; that give our lives directionality; and that infuse our moments with a kind of meaning (*purpose*-meaning). A life thusly lived is one that makes sense: it fits together properly with what is true, good, and beautiful about the reality in which we find ourselves (*sense-making*-meaning). For those who do not sufficiently orient their lives in accordance with the truth about reality, their lives lack important kinds of actively conditioned meaning. They are not as meaningful as they could be. None of us orients our life perfectly in accordance with the truth about reality, though. Moreover, each of us, to a greater or lesser extent, encounters heartbreak, tragedy, and less-than-full human flourishing in other ways in this life—all of which potentially mitigate meaning to some extent (though cf. Frankl 2006). Despite these sometimes soul-crushing, lamentable realities, real and deep meaning are available now. But they are not the last word. Perfect and everlasting meaning awaits us in a better "chapter" still to come—one grounded in the fully consummated reign of Christ (cf. "For the Reign of Christ," 1662 *Book of Common Prayer* in the epigraph at the beginning of my final response):

> What no eye has seen, nor ear heard, nor the heart of man imagined, what God has prepared for those who love him ...
> (1 Cor. 2:9; ESV).

> So we do not lose heart. Though our outer self is wasting away, our inner self is being renewed day by day. For this light momentary affliction is preparing for us an eternal weight of glory beyond all comparison, as we look not to the things that are seen but to the things that are unseen. For the things that are seen are transient, but the things that are unseen are eternal.
> (2 Cor. 4:16–18; ESV).

Chapter 6

Types of Meaning and the Natural as Their Source
Response to Seachris' Reply

Thaddeus Metz

Contents

6.1 Introduction 210
6.2 Whose Lives Have Meaning and How Much? 211
6.3 The Sources of Objective Value 214
6.4 Which Source Would Be Better? 219
6.5 Which Source Exists? 221
6.6 Concluding Remarks 223

6.1 Introduction

Recall the three questions that lie at the heart of philosophical reflection on life's meaning, or at least have structured much of my own thinking about how to engage with Professor Seachris: (1) "What do we mean when speaking about 'life's meaning?'"; (2) "What would make our lives meaningful?"; and (3) "Are any of our lives meaningful?"

There is little disagreement between Professor Seachris and me about (1). We both are pluralists about the sense of the phrase "life's meaning" and cognate terms, holding that these words connote a cluster of overlapping and otherwise related ideas. Professor Seachris and I both argue against a monism according to which meaning-talk is about a single idea. There remain quibbles between us about precisely which ideas are included; but they are not worth emphasizing here in a final statement, as little of our debate in respect to the other questions depends on it.

In terms of (3), we both answer affirmatively that some—even many—human lives have some meaning in them, and further, are meaningful (i.e., are full of meaning) on balance. Professor Seachris and I both argue against a nihilism according to which no one's or virtually no one's life is meaningful. Although Professor Seachris and I agree that many lives have meaning in them, we disagree about exactly *which* lives have meaning in them and *to what extent*. My approach, centered on the active exercise of intelligence, seems to put meaning out of reach for a number of human beings, which grounds an objection from Professor Seachris that I address first below (Section 6.2).

Where Professor Seachris and I continue to disagree most sharply, however, concerns question (2): what it is that constitutes meaning in a life. In a nutshell, in his third chapter, Professor Seachris clearly holds that there are two kinds of meaning in life—subjective and objective and that God's existence is necessary for the latter sort. I, in contrast, believe that subjective conditions are insufficient for meaning in life and that objective conditions do not require God. These are not quibbles.

Now, I already provided reason to doubt subjectivism as a source of any meaning in my opening statement (Section 2.3.2); also, in the abovementioned chapter, Professor Seachris uses much space to defend the idea that objective meaning could not exist without God. I therefore devote most of this chapter to providing reason to doubt that God's existence is necessary for objective meaning in our lives. I first indicate how objective meaning could conceivably exist in the absence of God (Section 6.3); after that I argue that it would be a sufficiently attractive sort of grounding (Section 6.4), and that there is strong reason to think it is the only grounding we in fact have (Section 6.5). I briefly conclude by noting some issues that merit further consideration beyond the scope of this book (6.6).

6.2 Whose Lives Have Meaning and How Much?

Toward the end of his third chapter, Professor Seachris expresses the concern that my view of meaning in life makes it too difficult to achieve or, as is sometimes put, is "elitist." I do suspect he is more liberal about how many lives are meaningful and how much meaning is in them compared to me. That is because Professor Seachris accepts subjectivism as a kind of meaning, and hence appears committed to thinking that meaning is present in just about any life that is not comatose or otherwise unconscious; in contrast, I hold that certain objective conditions are essential to the final value of meaning in life. Objectivism naturally invites the charge of elitism, to which I respond in this section.

Professor Seachris claims in his third chapter that simply enjoying the smell of coffee, achieving any goal one happens to prize, or deeming parts of one's life to cohere is enough to count as meaning-conferring (Section 3.4). In contrast, I think that enjoying the smell of coffee is better understood to be an instance of happiness, not meaningfulness (cf. Section 2.2.2); in addition, for meaning to accrue, the relevant goal cannot be, say, to count how many blades of grass there are in a lawn, and the relevant coherence cannot be a matter of finding an instance of blade of grass counting to fit with many other instances of blade of grass counting in one's life. I have argued that meaningful activities—that is, the kinds of things that merit substantial pride or admiration, or that involve higher purposes—instead normally involve the exercise of our intelligence in certain positive, effortful, and developmental ways. This objectivist view admittedly entails that fewer people have meaningful lives—or at least not as much meaning in them—relative to what subjectivism entails. After all, objectivism, but not subjectivism, rules out: blade-of-grass counters; couch potatoes; and those who chip paint, paint over the missing piece, rechip the same spot, repaint the same spot, rechip, repaint, and so on *ad infinitum*.

Note that deeming a life to be relatively lacking in objective meaning is consistent with acknowledging that a human being might count as "important" in several other ways. To judge that someone's life is meaningless or lacks the meaning that many others have should clearly not be taken to imply that they do not matter from a moral point of view, or that we have no duty to act in their interests. In fact, often exactly the opposite is true: if someone's life is missing some meaning that it could have, this means we have extra moral reason to go out of our way to help them! If a being has a life that could go better or worse—and especially if we are responsible for having created that being, which is unable to help itself—then there is moral reason for us to help it (e.g., for us to enable an infant to mature into an adult). Furthermore, if a being can do things such as make choices that express a self and cooperate with others (or if it has a divine spark lacking in the rest of the mineral, vegetable, and animal kingdoms), then it has a dignity and merits our respect, too. Still further, a being might be worthy of our love, apart from any moral considerations. There can therefore be a variety of reasons to care for and more generally support a being that has little in its life to admire, or that is unable to realize much of the good, the true, or the beautiful.

It would be insensitive and even callous to *say* to someone—or to someone who cares about him—that his life is "meaningless" or even "not yet meaningful," just as it would be to call someone "ugly." What that point most clearly suggests is that one should not speak or otherwise express certain things. However, it could still be in fact true that the individual is lacking substantial meaning in life that is exhibited by many others (or, well, is in fact ugly), even if he has other things going for him, such as the ability to be happy or an inherent dignity.

Here is a thought experiment in support of my objectivist perspective. Consider why you would not want, upon waking up tomorrow morning, to have lost the following: 40 IQ points; or the ability to empathize with others; or the capacity to see beauty in people, paintings, or landscapes (or—gulp—all three). Is not a major part of the reason that you suspect your life would become less meaningful in certain weighty respects and specifically in relation to the inability to exercise intelligence of various kinds—namely, intellectual, emotional-social, and esthetic?

Note that, with all these impairments, it could still be you who survives them and that you could also still be loved, whether by your parents or by God (if God exists, of course). Being loved might well count as a source of meaning. I am open to that, even though it might be an exception to the rule that the exercise of intelligence is what confers meaning on life (note that it might not be an exception if one were loved, for example, because of the character one had actively formed—as opposed to merely one's looks that one had passively received from one's gorgeous mom and handsome dad). However, my question to the reader is whether that would really be enough. Would you not want to retain all your rational faculties? If so, is that not because you would want to make your life substantially more meaningful than it could be without them?

If you would not want to lose your rational faculties overnight, and if considerations of meaning largely explain why not, then two things probably follow. First, you likely think, upon reflection, that it is much more meaningful to be a person who loves than it is to be loved (consider again the actions of Jesus reportedly leading up to and including crucifixion). Second, you likely doubt that subjective conditions confer much, if any, meaning—since, after all, you could still enjoy the smell of coffee being 40 IQ points lighter and being utterly unable to imagine what it is like to be another person or to appreciate beautiful patterns. Both judgments support a kind of objectivism about meaning in life, and specifically one that prizes "activeness"—for example, in the form of exercising emotional intelligence and interacting with others on that basis.

Fortunately, most human beings have their wits about them and elect to exercise them, too—which I submit means that the charge of elitism is inapplicable. A very large majority of human beings can do objectively meaningful things, such as learn, love other people, and appreciate (and, often enough, make) beautiful patterns; and indeed, very many of them in fact do to some degree or other. Furthermore, a very large majority of fetuses, infants, and toddlers will develop those capacities, if treated in supportive ways. Hence, the way I understand what substantially makes life meaningful is available to all but a small minority of humans. It is true that some humans are incapable of exhibiting such a value, but—as I have pointed out—their lives might be important in other ways, while I submit that those who could exhibit such a value but are chronic couch potatoes are reasonably excluded from the description of "living meaningfully" when philosophizing.

6.3 The Sources of Objective Value

Professor Seachris is not a pure subjectivist, for he, too, believes in objective conditions as a key source of meaning. What we most markedly disagree about is what would make such an objective value possible. Where could objective value come from? Professor Seachris argues that only God could make it possible, invoking what I have labelled the "Divine Command Theory" (Section 2.3.3.1). In one straightforward sense, this approach means that his view counts as an "extreme" supernaturalism, for entailing that no objective meaning is possible without God. Most philosophers these days are more "moderate," for holding that more than merely a subjective meaning can be present in a world where God is absent. For example, even many religiously inclined philosophers accept that Gandhi's life was meaningful to some degree, supposing he lived in an atheist world. I now provide more grounds to support their judgment. Here I explain how objective meaning is conceivable without God, while in the following sections, I provide some reason to accept this account, which is a form of realism (see Section 2.3.3.1).

Let us pause to say more than I have so far about what makes a value objective as opposed to subjective. One key idea is that an objective value is mind-independent, in the sense that whether it is valuable is not determined merely by some human beings believing that it is or taking an interest in it. A second, related idea is that it is possible for an individual one of us, and even a group, to be mistaken about whether it is valuable.

To illustrate, consider that whether carrots taste good is not objective and is instead subjective. Whether carrots taste good is determined merely by the fact that one of us finds it so, such that it is not possible for that individual to be mistaken about whether he or she does find them to taste good or does not (supposing that the person has, of course, tried them out). Another way to put this point is that it is "relative" whether carrots taste good—that is, relative to the subject who tastes them. It is "true for some" human beings that carrots taste good, while that is not true for others. The claims that it is rude to belch at the table and that it is appropriate to drive on the left are also subjective in these ways; they are true relative to certain human persons, but not others.

In contrast, whether water is H_2O is objective. The fact that it is H_2O is not determined merely by some of us thinking it is, for it was really H_2O even before *anyone* was aware of chemistry. It is indeed possible for an individual and group to be mistaken about the nature of water, for if you or your society think water is instead something other than H_2O, you are incorrect. The truth of water being H_2O is not relative to a subset of human persons; it is instead a mind-independent fact that many (but not all) human beings have learned. It is universally the case, or "true for everyone," that water is H_2O—even if some people are not aware of that truth and do not believe it; there is a fact of the matter about water being H_2O, regardless of what anyone thinks about it. Similar remarks apply to claims that the Earth is round and there are no unicorns in my basement.

Professor Seachris and I both think that meaning in life is more like water being H_2O than carrots tasting good—or at least that one major part of life's meaning is water-like. We differ on whether there is a subjective dimension to meaning, but we do at least concur that there is a large objective dimension. The objective approach is the best way we know to avoid absurdities such as that a life full of counting blades of grass or drinking daquiris while watching sitcoms alone could be *maximally* meaningful.

Now, how could it be the case that meaning is objective? More generally, how could something be valuable if it is not merely a matter of what some humans value? How could it be possible for us to be mistaken about what is good and what is not?

For many centuries in the West, God was the main explanation of how objective values are possible. If it were a perfect being who valued certain things, this would explain how it could be that something's being valuable is not determined by our beliefs or interests, and also how we could be mistaken about what is good. It would be "true for everyone" that certain things are good as opposed to bad, since God's nature or will would make it so—even if some of us have incorrect beliefs about them due to a failure to apprehend God sufficiently well. When it comes to meaning in particular, God having assigned human beings purposes would make that value objective—that is, something that is good independent of our beliefs about it, and about which we can be mistaken (but about which we can learn, too). These purposes assigned to us would be, in Professor Seachris' terms, "prescriptions of an ultimate Prescriber who prescribes out of an essentially good nature" (Section 3.3.1).

The Divine Command Theory of objective values such as morality and meaning is powerful, and Professor Seachris is not alone in accepting it—even if it is not as popular among professional Western philosophers as it was during the medieval and early modern eras. In this chapter, I do not really try to provide enough argumentation to *convince* you that there is an explanation of how objective values are possible that is better than the supernaturalist one. Instead, what I do in this brief, final response is to sketch what a naturalist explanation of objective value might look like as a viable alternative, and provide some reason to take it seriously.

To see how objective values might be possible without a God determining what is good and how we are to act, return to the case of water. How is it possible that water's being H_2O is objective—that is, a fact that obtains independent of our thinking of it (about which we can be mistaken), and that is true for everyone, even if only some are aware of it?

Since the 1980s, many philosophers of science and related thinkers have come to believe it is possible because of what is known as the "**causal theory of reference**."[1] To keep things simple, the core idea is that human beings became aware of this stuff that is present

---

1 The following is a crude summary of the sophisticated views of Hilary Putnam (1975). For a more thorough application of them to moral values, see Brink 1989; and for some application of them to the value of meaning in life, see Metz 2013: 91–96, 171–172.

in lakes and rivers and that falls from clouds, and once dubbed it with a term such as "water," with later humans using "water" to pick out the nature of the stuff initially dubbed with the term. When the earlier humans first called something "water," they associated certain "surface properties" with the term, such as being a colorless, odorless liquid that we must drink to remain alive; but in so doing, they completely left open the "deep properties" or essence of the thing responsible for the surface properties. Over time, with the development of the scientific method—including the undertaking of various experiments and debates among chemists—many human beings discovered that water's deep property is the chemical composition H_2O. That feature, we have learned, is essential to water, and explains many of the surface features associated with the term "water."

Some value naturalists or value realists maintain that a similar kind of process has taken place in respect of not merely descriptive terms such as "water," "gold," and "beech tree," but also many evaluative and prescriptive terms. Consider the word "illness." It was useful for human beings to call certain conditions of the human body (or mind) that are thought to merit avoidance "illness," "injury," "disease," or the like. Picking out those clusters of features would have been particularly important when it came to survival, reproduction, and flourishing. It does not follow, though, that human beings have known much about what disease or injury essentially is—that is, its "deep" properties. Indeed, it is only recently that we seem to have learned much at all about how the human body (or mind) works and what interferes with its proper functioning. We have known the "surface" properties of disease, such as seeing skin discoloration or broken bones, since we first called something "illness" or the like. However, we have not similarly known things such as how that discoloration relates to a malfunctioning liver or how bones really work, and what is going on when there is a malfunction in either. It has taken an awful lot of empirical inquiry to ascertain how organs, bones, and other body parts operate, making that an objective matter about which especially biologists and physicians have learned.

Parallel remarks apply to the term "health," which is plausibly something that has non-instrumental value and merits going out of one's way to exhibit. Value naturalists often hold that there are objective facts about whether our bodies (or minds) are healthy, by virtue of us having used the word "health" to refer to certain states of ourselves about which we initially knew very little, but about which we have learned over time through empirical enquiry (see the discussion in Lutz and Lenman 2018).

Notice that, by this analysis, God would not have to exist for something to count objectively as healthy or not. Even in a world without God, some conditions could really be ones of health and others ones of illness, by virtue of us having referred to certain states of the human body (or mind) but not initially known much, if anything, about their essence. Now, if it is conceivable that there can be an objective fact of the matter about which states of the body (or mind) are healthy (good) or diseased (bad) without an appeal to God, it is likewise conceivable that there can be an objective fact of the matter about which conditions of a life are meaningful or meaningless without an appeal to God.

To fill out the parallel, consider that at some stage in human history, people called certain states, relationships, and activities "meaningful," with an awareness of surface properties such as what merits pride or admiration and what involves a connection with something greater than (some part of) oneself. However, upon dubbing these conditions "meaningful," the earlier humans did not specify the deep properties of the behavior that account for the surface properties. These we have had to discover over time, through philosophical, psychological, literary, and religious reflection. In my contribution to this book, I have in effect argued that these deep properties of meaning in life are largely constituted by (in catchwords) "the good" (beneficent relationships), "the true" (intellectual reflection), and "the beautiful" (creativity), where these, in turn, all share the feature of intelligence exercised in certain positive, robust, and progressive ways. What H_2O is to water is what rationality (employed in a particular manner) is to life's meaningfulness. Or so I propose.

In sum, it is the way linguistic reference operates that can make naturalist sense of how objective values such as health and meaning are possible. Human beings use terms to refer to certain deep or essential features of things about which they know little upon so referring, but about which they tend to learn over time with evidence and argument. In the way that God is not necessary for water objectively to be H_2O and for cirrhosis of the liver objectively to be an illness that you should avoid, so God is not necessary for it to be objectively true that helping other innocent people is meaningful while living in an Experience Machine would not be.

So, there are now two explanations on the table of how something could objectively be meaningful. On the one hand, there is a supernaturalist account, according to which God assigns human beings a purpose that is fixed by God's nature; on the other, there is a naturalist account, according to which human beings have referred to certain features of life as "meaningful," but have not known all or even many of the deep features that ground judgments of what merits pride or admiration. Our next question is how to pick between these accounts.

6.4 Which Source Would Be Better?

In his third chapter, Professor Seachris provides some reason to think that the supernaturalist account of objectivity in the form of the Divine Command Theory is more attractive than any naturalist account could be. I see two major reasons given, to which I respond in this section.

First, Professor Seachris imagines that, according to the naturalist, the process of natural selection is what would be largely responsible for our being inclined to think of certain things as valuable or not. Of this kind of process, Professor Seachris says:

> Even if evolutionary pressures proved to "favor" certain proclivities about the shape of moral and non-moral values, this does not thereby make such values *objective*; nor would it ultimately ground obligation, except in the sense of: "Do this if you want life to go well for you, your community, and your species." It seems as though evolutionary processes would not give rise to anything other than *survival resulted from doing x, y, and z*. Something else is needed to provide genuine objectivity to our value ascriptions.
>
> (Section 3.3.1).

To illustrate Professor Seachris' point, note that a belief in the sanctity, dignity, or otherwise superlative value of human life would have been useful to promote survival and reproduction on our part. If we had lacked such a belief, we probably would have done much less to protect humans from death or to procreate. That fact, according to him, is not enough to make it objectively true that we have such a value. More is required.

I agree that more is required, but deny that it is God. I submit that it is instead how our value language functions. If human beings used the word "dignity" to pick out whatever on Earth merits the most respect and care, and if it turned out that being a human person (or perhaps human beings more generally) is what makes the best sense of judgments of what merits those reactions, then it would be objectively true in a straightforward sense that human persons have dignity. Indeed, many of us appear to have learned over the past few centuries that it is being a human person—and not being a member of a particular race, gender, religion, nationality, or clan—that is what has dignity (see Gilbert 1990). That learning process, I suggest, is not qualitatively different from having learned that water is H_2O or that cirrhosis of the liver is an illness.

At this point, Professor Seachris would surely invoke his second reason for favoring a supernaturalist account of objective value: namely, that "in order for values to be objective, they must be part of the 'furniture of the universe'" (Section 3.3.1)—something that only God could ground. Describing an atheist world, Professor Seachris remarks of morality and other values:

> Human beings along with our moral norms and sensibilities arise in this unintended world, ourselves unintended by any infinite, personal Mind, through "accidental" twists and turns of an unintended evolutionary process. Our moral norms, on such an account, would be precarious; again, in the words of neuroscientist Bill Newsome, they would not be part of the "central reality of the universe and the reason the universe was built from the beginning".
>
> (Section 3.3.1).

That, I accept, is true. If there is no God, then moral and other values such as health and meaning were not reasons why the universe was created. In addition, if there is no God, then these values would not be necessary in the sense of obtaining in all possible worlds (or even being invariably true for all beings throughout this universe).

My reply, though, is to point out that Professor Seachris' notion of objectivity is much stronger and rarified than the concept we normally use. My stock example of an objective truth has been that water is H_2O. I explained how it is possible that water being H_2O is true for all human persons, and is a fact about which we could be mistaken, even if God does not exist. And then I drew an analogy between the objectivity of the nature of water and the objectivity of the nature of values such as health and meaningfulness.

Note that there are possible worlds in which there is no water. There are also possible worlds in which humans do not exist and have not called anything "water," even though water exists. And—even in our world, where there are both humans and water—there might be intelligent aliens in another galaxy who have something that is like water but is not H_2O, or who might have water but do not use the chemical scheme H_2O to apprehend it. Now, so what? None of these considerations undermines the straightforward sense in which it is objectively true that water is H_2O. When we think about objectivity, we normally do so from within a human frame of reference. We are interested in what is independent of our human minds and what we can know (or fail to know) with reference to them. We are not characteristically interested in which conceptual scheme has to be used by literally all intelligent enquirers, let alone why the universe was created in the first place.

In short, Professor Seachris' notion of objectivity is indeed best supported by invoking God; but his notion of objectivity is far removed from what we usually have in mind or what is intuitively sufficient in respect of values. The latter point is clear when it comes to health: something need not be part of the "furniture of the universe" in order to count as healthy for human beings. Similar remarks go for beauty. For something to count as beautiful for us, it need not also be beautiful to intelligent aliens in another galaxy or to God; and it certainly need not be a reason why the universe was created. Vincent van Gogh (1853–1890) created paintings that are indeed beautiful, simply considering things from a contingent, human point of view. What goes for health and beauty plausibly goes for meaning, too.

6.5 Which Source Exists?

So far, I have articulated one way that a naturalist could make sense of objective value, and have also argued that this kind of objectivity is familiar and intuitively satisfactory when considering what we characteristically value in life. I have not yet addressed the question of which sort of objectivity is true, which I consider in this section.

Of course, it might be that neither account of objectivity is true; perhaps all values are merely subjective. Supposing, though, that there are some objective values (which Professor Seachris and I both accept), and that meaningfulness in particular is objective (which we also accept), the question becomes: what is the better explanation of why? Is there objective meaning because a perfect spiritual being exists and has assigned us all some purposes; or instead, does it exist because human beings in a merely physical universe have called certain ways of living "meaningful," but have thereby left open the nature of those states, relationships, and activities—about which we have arguably learned that they substantially involve the exercise of intelligence in certain ways?

Here is a big reason to favor the naturalist explanation over the supernaturalist one: there is little evidence that God exists. Recall the point made from my opening statement about what is often called "the problem of evil" (Section 2.3.3.1). The problem is that there is horrendous suffering in this world—not merely on the part of innocent human beings, but also animals—which seems incompatible with the existence of an all-knowing, all-powerful, and morally perfect being. I still fail to see a plausible explanation from Professor Seachris (or anyone, really) of why God, so conceived, would let a three-year-old orphan suffer from terminal cancer or allow a deer to get burned alive in a forest fire. If such wretched pain is incompatible with God, but if there are objective values, then the naturalist explanation of where they come from is a strong contender.

In fact, recall that I argued in Chapter 2 that there is a kind of incoherence in believing that God could ground objective values such as morality or meaning in life (Section 2.3.3.1). On the one hand, many of those who enquire into the philosophy of life's meaning know that it is not merely subjective; objective considerations—such as whether people have advanced justice, or promoted knowledge, or exhibited creativity—confer meaning on their lives. On the other hand, we do not know whether God exists, even if we have faith that God does. If we know that objective meaning exists, but accept that we do not know that God exists, then it would be incoherent to claim to know that God grounds objective meaning.

Professor Seachris replies to this argument by saying that, since God is necessary for objective meaning, which indeed exists, we can infer that God exists, too (Section 3.3.2). However, I do not think this reply can fairly be invoked to support an account of objective meaning at the present stage of the debate. Here is why not (drawing on some discussion toward the end of Section 2.3.3.1). The question at hand is whether to believe that objectivity is constituted by God's will, or by (roughly) human reference to something mind-independent. I argue that the latter, naturalist explanation of where objectivity comes from is more plausible, since there is no conclusive evidence that God exists. For Professor Seachris to say that we know that God exists because we know that objectivity is constituted by God's will begs the question—that is, supposes to be true what is calling for argumentation. We are looking for a reason to believe that objectivity is constituted by God's will, and so that claim cannot be used as a premise to support a different conclusion about whether God exists (which, in turn, provides reason to believe that objectivity is constituted by God's will). Instead, Professor Seachris needs to provide some other, independent reason for believing that God exists, has assigned us purposes, and has thereby constituted an objective meaning for us—all in the face of the problem of evil. Prof, what about that deer?

6.6 Concluding Remarks

The debate between myself and Professor Seachris has become rather technical here at the end! The logic of the debate about the value of meaning in life has driven us to consider complicated issues in metaphysics, epistemology, and language—including: what objectivity is; what would make it possible; whether there is evidence that God does or does not exist; how we refer to things in the world; and how we come to learn about the essences of natural objects. We have also raised metaphysical topics such as free will, personal identity, and human nature, where some of our disagreements about life's meaning have invoked contested views about them. Our views of life's meaning are ultimately dependent on complex webs of belief about a large array of other philosophical matters.

Sorry about that. You might have been hoping to arrive at a firm conclusion about life's meaning by the end of this debate, without having to think carefully about other parts of philosophy. I am afraid I do not think that can be done. Philosophical enquiry into life's meaning is deep, in the sense that it addresses issues that are foundational to human existence and hence are bound up with other foundational matters about, say, what exists, what we can know, and how language works.

It takes time to develop a comprehensive **worldview**—one in which views of meaning in life cohere with plausible philosophical views about other things. Developing a worldview is well worth doing—indeed, I close by pointing out that it would be a meaningful enterprise. It would involve the effortful exercise of intellectual intelligence that is positively contoured toward the fundamental nature of human existence and, in the ideal case, comes to reveal something new about it to other interlocutors. Perhaps sensing how that would be a meaningful project, you are a bit less overwhelmed by the thought of having to do a lot more philosophy in order to arrive at well-founded views of life's meaning, and instead are keen to do more reading and thinking in the field. If you do, I hope that you encounter more debates like this one.

Further Readings

General level

- Baggini, Julian. 2004. *What's It All About?: Philosophy and the Meaning of Life*. Oxford: Oxford University Press. (A highly readable treatment of many of the most important questions connected to life's meaning that breaks down the grand question, "What is the meaning of life?" into what the author considers more manageable questions. He proposes naturalistic answers to those questions.)
- Belliotti, Raymond. 2001. *What Is the Meaning of Human Life?* Amsterdam: Rodopi. (A critical engagement with classic figures such as Tolstoy, Schopenhauer, and Camus.)
- Benatar, David, ed. 2016. *Life, Death, and Meaning: Key Philosophical Readings on the Big Questions*, 3rd edn. Lanham, MD: Rowman & Littlefield. (An anthology of readings for students, with sections titled "The Meaning of Life," "Death," and "Immortality.")
- Benatar, David. 2017. *The Human Predicament*. New York: Oxford University Press. (Argues that although life has meaning from a human point of view, it is meaningless from a cosmic perspective and could not be otherwise, which provides reason not to procreate but usually not any reason to commit suicide.)
- Camus, Albert. 2018. *The Myth of Sisyphus*. New York: Knopf Doubleday Publishing Group. (A classic treatment of nihilism and the nature of absurdity, specifically as it relates to the place of humans in a silent, uncaring cosmos. Camus advocates a kind of defiance in the face of this situation.)
- Cholbi, Michael, and Timmerman, Travis, eds. 2021. *Exploring the Philosophy of Death and Dying: Classical and Contemporary*

Perspectives. New York: Routledge. (A fresh anthology of some of the most important classic and contemporary readings on death, including what death is; whether and how it is bad for the one who dies; and whether immortality would be better or worse news for us.)
- Cottingham, John. 2003. *On the Meaning of Life*. London: Routledge. (Written for a generally educated audience, this eloquent book argues that a purely physical world is not enough for a meaningful life; we must believe in God if we are to live meaningfully.)
- Fischer, John Martin. 2020. *Death, Immortality, and Meaning in Life*. New York: Oxford University Press. (Investigates important questions at the intersection of the meaning of life and the meaning of death. Argues that death can be bad for the person who dies and also that immortality need not be irredeemably boring and could exhibit a kind of meaningful narrative.)
- Frankl, Viktor. 2006. *Man's Search for Meaning*. Boston, MA: Beacon Press. (A classic work on the hopeful prospects for leading a meaningful life, even amid life's most difficult circumstances.)
- Goetz, Stewart, and Seachris, Joshua. 2020. *What Is This Thing Called the Meaning of Life?* London: Routledge. (An accessible introductory overview of contemporary philosophical reflection on life's meaning composed for students.)
- Gold, Paul. 2022. *A Good and True Story*. Ada, MI: Brazos Press. (An accessible investigation and defence of a Christian theistic narrative of the universe that intersects closely with many topics addressed in this debate.)
- Kessler, David. 2019. *Finding Meaning: The Sixth Stage of Grief*. New York: Scribner. (A powerful journey beyond Elisabeth Kübler-Ross's classic five stages of grief to include "meaning" as the sixth stage. Filled with riveting personal narratives.)
- Klemke, E. D., and Cahn, Steven, eds. 2018. *The Meaning of Life: A Reader*, 4th Ed. New York: Oxford University Press. (One of the most popular anthologies of classic and contemporary philosophical essays on life's meaning, it includes 25 essays with section headings such as "The Theistic Answer," "The Nontheistic Answer," and "The End of Life.")
- Landau, Iddo. 2017. *Finding Meaning in an Imperfect World*. New York: Oxford University Press. (Criticizes both the

supernaturalist view that meaning requires God or a soul and the nihilist view that it requires having some major impact on the world that we cannot make; instead provides guidance about how to obtain an earthly meaning. Can also be read as defending a middle way between pessimistic atheism or outright nihilism and views that require some form of cosmic meaning in order to block such pessimistic conclusions.)
- Leach, Stephen, and Tartagilia, James, eds. 2018. *The Meaning of Life and the Great Philosophers*. London: Routledge. (A collection of short, contemporary articles on what important historic figures had to say about life's meaning and ideas in the neighborhood.)
- Lewis, C. S. 1986. "On Living in an Atomic Age." In *Present Concerns*. Edited by Walter Hooper, 73–80. San Diego, CA: Harcourt. (An important piece by one of the twentieth century's most influential Christian writers which argues that humans having longings that both point to a supernatural realm and which only a supernatural realm can fully satisfy.)
- May, Todd. 2015. *A Significant Life: Human Meaning in a Silent Universe*. Chicago, IL: University of Chicago Press. (Supports the view that we can know that a meaningful life is possible, principally through the development of certain virtues, even if there is no foundational or cosmic justification for this belief.)
- Messerly, John. 2013. *The Meaning of Life: Religious, Philosophical, Transhumanist, and Scientific Perspectives*. Seattle, WA: Darwin & Hume Publishers. (A critical overview of the ideas of more than 50 philosophers and related thinkers on life's meaning.)
- Metz, Thaddeus. 2019. *God, Soul and the Meaning of Life*. Cambridge, UK: Cambridge University Press. (A useful, brief primer on the range of theories and viewpoints about how spiritual conditions as conceived in the Abrahamic faiths and meaning might be related.)
- Morris, Thomas. 2002. *Making Sense of It All: Pascal and the Meaning of Life*. Grand Rapids, MI: William B. Eerdmans Publishing Company. (A highly readable discussion of the human condition, and how/why faith in God is the most appropriate rational and practical response to that condition.)
- Pascal, Blaise. 1995. *Pensées*. Translated by A. J. Krailsheimer. New York: Penguin Books. (A historic classical series of short

statements and reflections on important aspects of the human condition.)
- Robinson, Marilynne. 2020. *Gilead*. New York: Farrar, Straus and Giroux. (An award-winning novel that captures the wonder and profundity of the human condition through the words of a dying minister and father writing down his musings for his young son to eventually read.)
- Seachris, Joshua, ed. 2013. *Exploring the Meaning of Life: An Anthology and Guide*. Malden: Wiley-Blackwell. (A collection of nearly three dozen philosophical essays on life's meaning, mainly from the analytic tradition, most of which are contemporary, albeit peppered with a few classic sources. Includes helpful section introductions from prominent philosophers working on the topic.)
- Taylor, Richard. 2000. "The Meaning of Life." Reprinted in *The Meaning of Life*, 2nd Edition. Edited by Elmer Daniel Klemke, pp. 167–175. Oxford: Oxford University Press. (An early and noteworthy essay defending subjectivism that first appeared in 1970. Taylor claims that a meaningful life is entirely a matter of how we feel about our lives. Assessing whether or not our lives are meaningful requires an inward turn to an ideal state of desiring to do what we are doing.)
- Thomson, Garrett. 2003. *On the Meaning of Life*. South Melbourne: Wadsworth. (Composed principally for undergraduate students; chapter titles include "The Infinite," "Is There a Plan?" "The Invention of Meaning," and "Beyond the Self.")
- Tolstoy, Leo. 2006. "A Confession." In *Spiritual Writings*. Edited by Charles E. Moore, 46–59. Maryknoll, NY: Orbis Books. (A classic autobiographical reflection by the famous Russian novelist where he wrestles with worries about life's meaning in the light of death's inevitable march.)
- Wolf, Susan. 2010. *Meaning in Life and Why It Matters*. Princeton, NJ: Princeton University Press. (The definitive exposition and defense of the most popular version of naturalism: namely, the view that meaning in life consists of being subjectively attracted to what objectively merits such attraction. Originally given as a set of lectures.)
- Wolterstorff, Nicholas. 1987. *Lament for a Son*. Grand Rapids, MI: Eerdmans. (A deeply moving autobiographical account of a philosopher wrestling with the tragic death of his son.)

Advanced level

- Baggett, David and Walls, Jerry. 2016. *God & Cosmos: Moral Truth and Human Meaning*. New York: Oxford University Press. (A sophisticated discussion of naturalistic ethics and its perceived shortcomings. It includes an extensive survey of a broad array of secular ethical theories, followed by arguments for why classical theism offers more resources for making sense of moral realities; and it concludes with an abductive—inference to the best explanation—moral argument for God's existence.)
- Ballard, Brian. 2017. "The Rationality of Faith and the Benefits of Religion." *International Journal of Philosophy of Religion* 81: 213–227. (Argues that the practical benefits of religion can be more than just practical; they actually can enhance the *epistemic rationality* of faith.)
- Bennett-Hunter, Guy. 2014. *Ineffability and Religious Experience*. Oxford: Routledge. (Argues that, for human life to be meaningful, it must obtain its meaning from what is beyond the human and is ineffable, which amounts to a certain conception of God.)
- Calhoun, Chesire. 2018. *Doing Valuable Time: The Present, the Future, and Meaningful Living*. New York: Oxford University Press. (A powerful and sophisticated form of subjectivism, according to which a person's life is meaningful to the extent that she acts in accordance with her own judgment that she has good reason to value something highly for its own sake.)
- Caruso, Gregg and Flanagan, Owen, eds. 2018. *Neuroexistentialism: Meaning, Morals, and Purpose in an Age of Neuroscience*. New York: Oxford University Press. (A collection of 18 essays addressing the impact of neuroscientific investigations on conceptions of the self, free will, morality, and meaning in life.)
- Cottingham, John. 2005. *The Spiritual Dimension: Religion, Philosophy and Human Value*. Cambridge, UK: Cambridge University Press. (A key work on the topic which argues that only God—or a spiritual dimension—can provide the necessary conditions for truly meaningful life. Argues specifically that only God could be the source of objective or universal norms pertaining to logic, morality, art, and the like.)

- Goetz, Stewart. 2012. *The Purpose of Life: A Theistic Perspective*. London. Continuum. (Argues that a natural way to understand the question, "What is the meaning of life?" is as one asking about the purpose of life. The answer it proposes to the latter question is that the purpose of life is to be perfectly happy; and it further argues that theism provides the best resources for securing the perfect happiness of humans.)
- Kahane, Guy. 2013. "Our Cosmic Insignificance." *Noûs* 47: 745–772. (A unique article that defends a view not widely held: that human life can be significant, cosmically speaking, even if—and perhaps precisely because—there is no God and we are alone in the universe as conscious beings.)
- Kraay, Klaas, ed. 2018. *Does God Matter? Essays on the Axiological Consequences of Theism*. New York: Routledge. (An important collection of discussions on "pro-theism" and "anti-theism"—the view that God would either enhance or detract from the value, and specifically meaning, in our lives.)
- Mawson, T.J. 2016. *God and the Meanings of Life: What God Could and Couldn't Do to Make Our Lives More Meaningful*. London: Bloomsbury Publishing. (Maintains that there is a wide array of different types of enquiry into life's meaning—that is, that the question, "What is the meaning of life?" is actually an amalgam of many questions. Argues that, for the most important sorts of these questions, compelling answers will appeal to God.)
- Metz, Thaddeus. 2013. *Meaning in Life: An Analytic Study*. Oxford: Oxford University Press. (Using a critical discussion of rival contemporary views as a springboard, defends the naturalist view that meaning in life comes from fully exercising one's rational nature in certain ways, which does not require God or a soul.)
- Metz, Thaddeus. 2007. "New Developments in the Meaning of Life." *Philosophy Compass* 2: 196–217. (An important survey article on the most important aspects for understanding the philosophical discussion of life's meaning within the analytic tradition as of the mid-2000s. Useful for anyone wanting to understand the topic.)
- Nagel, Thomas. 1971. "The Absurd." *Journal of Philosophy* 68: 716–727. (A classic article articulating why and how human life is absurd.)
- Nozick, Robert. 1981. *Philosophical Explanations*. Cambridge, MA: Harvard University Press, chap. 6. (An early and influential

treatment of a variety of facets of enquiry into life's meaning, it defends the view that a life is more meaningful, the more it connects with value beyond it.)
- Seachris, Joshua and Goetz, Stewart, eds. 2016. *God and Meaning: New Essays*. New York: Bloomsbury Academic. (All contributions to this collection are by prominent Christian philosophers defending a supernaturalist approach to meaning in life and the meaning of life, defending the claim that God either is necessary for meaning or would enhance it. Includes two essays by Biblical scholars who investigate the intersection between the Old Testament book of *Ecclesiastes* and contemporary philosophical reflection on life's meaning.)
- Stump, Eleonore. 2010. *Wandering in Darkness: Narrative and the Problem of Evil*. Oxford: Oxford University Press. (A long, scholarly, but rewarding academic treatment of the problem of evil from a leading philosopher of religion. Provides substantial interaction with Thomas Aquinas, relevant biblical texts, and narrative theory.)
- Weinberg, Rivka. 2021. "Ultimate Meaning: We Don't Have It, We Can't Get It, and We Should Be Very, Very Sad." *Journal of Controversial Ideas* 1: 1–22. (A very recent defense of a kind of pessimistic atheism which argues that it is deeply lamentable that life lacks "ultimate meaning"—that is, meaning for the life as a whole.)
- Wielenberg, Erik. 2005. *Value and Virtue in a Godless Universe*. Cambridge, UK: Cambridge University Press. (A thoughtful defense of naturalism that raises several important challenges to the view that God is central to life's meaning.)
- Williams, Clifford. 2020. *Religion and the Meaning of Life: An Existential Approach*. Cambridge, UK: Cambridge University Press. (An important recent contribution that offers a multifaceted argument for the importance of religion in framing and answering the question of life's meaning. Nicely bridges the gap between the best of current analytic philosophy on the topic and the driving human emotions from which the question of life's meaning arises.)

Glossary

Actual/Real: Of this world.

Anti-Matter/Anti-Meaning: Conditions that are not merely the absence of meaning, but that reduce the amount of meaning in a life.

Argument: A series of propositions in which some claims, called "premises," provide evidence that another claim—a conclusion—is true.

Analytic Philosophy: The dominant method and style of philosophy in the Western, Anglophone world beginning in the early twentieth century and continuing today. Analytic philosophy prizes argumentative clarity and precision through rigorous conceptual analysis. Central figures in the rise of analytic philosophy were Bertrand Russell, Ludwig Wittgenstein, and G. E. Moore. Precursors of analytic philosophy can be traced back further, though, to the scholastic philosophy of the medieval period all the way back to antiquity, insofar as many philosophers throughout history also have prized clarity and precision.

Atheism: The view that the evidence shows that no spiritual beings as characteristically conceived in the Abrahamic faiths exist. The view that, instead, the space-time universe is all that exists; that there is no God or gods, no angels or demons, no souls; and that human beings are exclusively material beings who cease to exist at death. Carl Sagan once gave this succinct statement of atheism: "The universe is all there is, was, or ever will be." Atheism often includes a metaphysical component—everything is composed of natural entities; and an epistemological or *methodological* component—the appropriate methods of explanation or justification are those of science.

Bearer: Which sort of thing can exemplify a property such as meaningfulness.

Causal Theory of Reference: The view that what a term picks out in the world is fixed not by what its current speaker has in mind, but instead by the essence of a thing initially dubbed with the term.

Contributory Condition: A property or thing that enhances, but is not necessary for, something else.

Counterexample: An apparent exception to a proposed general rule; a case that a theory cannot easily entail or well explain.

Divine Command Theory: A meta-ethical theory of the source of moral rules, according to which right acts are permitted by God's commands and wrong acts are those forbidden by them.

Eliminitivism: A kind of materialism (where materialism is roughly the view that matter and its properties are all that exists) which claims that our ordinary, common-sense understanding of our minds is fundamentally mistaken. Some or all of the mental states that common sense would have us believe exist—like beliefs, intentions to do this or that, hopes, etc.—actually do not exist. Because they do not exist, they should play no role in a complete, *scientific* account of the mind and its properties.

Existentialism (Existentialist; Existential): Existentialism was largely a twentieth-century philosophical movement (primarily originating on the European continent) concerned with existence and the way humans live in the world. For existentialists, the human condition is a central philosophical problem because the human being, as a thinking, feeling, acting, living subject, is central. Generally speaking, existentialists think that we exist first, and then are faced with the lifelong task of molding our own essence or nature (*existence precedes essence*). In this way, existentialism is a philosophy that prioritizes developing the self and finding meaning through free will, choice, and personal responsibility. Existentialism is one of the most well-known philosophical movements outside of the discipline of philosophy, especially with such representatives as Jean-Paul Sartre and Albert Camus, whose work (especially their novels) appeals to a wider audience. The adjective "existential" here refers to a salient aspect of the human condition—for example, that we all face the reality of pain, suffering, and death.

Extreme Supernaturalism: The theory that life is meaningless if God and a soul do not exist; God and a soul are necessary conditions for life's meaning.

Euthyphro Problem: An argument for the view that God is not the source of moral (and other objective) values, which takes the form of a dilemma: either an act is right simply because God commands it, in which case it would be possible for patently immoral acts such as slavery to be right; or God commands an act because it is right, in which case what makes something right is not the fact God commands it.

Final Value: See Intrinsic Value.

God: The supreme being as characteristically conceived in the Abrahamic faiths of Judaism, Christianity, and Islam; a spiritual person who is all-knowing, all-powerful, and all-good, and who is the ground of the physical universe.

Happiness (Subjective Wellbeing): Features such as pleasurable experience, satisfied desires, or positive emotions.

Human Predicament (or Human Condition): The general state, predicament, or condition in which human beings find themselves in virtue of existing in the universe. This includes the characteristics and situations which compose human existence from cradle to grave, including birth, growth, emotionality, aspiration, suffering, and death. Experiencing this condition causes us to ask existentially weighty questions about our origins, purpose, value, suffering, death, and destiny. Often, the idea of the human condition carries negative connotations as it focuses on the epistemic (limitations of knowledge) and practical (limitations of control) struggles that we face. That we ask questions about life's meaning is both part of the human condition and a response to the human condition.

Hybrid Atheism (Hybridism): The combination of subjective and objective conditions as both necessary for meaning in life. An Optimistic Atheistic view according to which life is meaningful to the extent that one is fulfilled or satisfied in engaging in objectively worthwhile activity and/or being causally responsible for good effects of that activity. Put simply, one must be satisfied by doing the right stuff in order to have a meaningful life. Neither the miserable person responsible for good effects of activity nor the fulfilled person satisfied in worthless projects leads a meaningful life according to this view.

Hypothetical: Not real; merely possible.

Instrumental Value: Something that derives its value from its causal relationship to some other value. A $100 bill would be an example of something that is instrumentally valuable.

Intrinsic (Final) Value: Something that does not derive its value merely from its relationship to some other value. Happiness is

an example of something that is intrinsically valuable, as it is good for its own sake.
Intuition: A judgment about a particular scenario that is meant to be relatively uncontroversial.
Logically Contradictory: Inconsistent by definition; conceptually impossible.
Logically Possible: Not excluded by definition of terms; conceivable.
Logotherapy: A meaning-centered method of psychoanalytic therapy devised by Holocaust survivor and psychoanalyst Viktor Frankl, in which he claimed (and counseled from the view) that striving to find meaning in our lives is the primary motivational force animating human activity.
Meaning in Life: A value involving such things as meriting esteem or admiration, fulfilling a purpose, making a positive difference, and having a good life-story that could be exhibited in the life of *a particular human person*.
Meaning of Life: A value involving such things as meriting esteem or admiration, fulfilling a purpose making a positive difference, and having a good life-story that could be exhibited in the life of *the human species as a whole*.
Meaningful: A life full of the sort of value involving such things as meriting esteem or admiration, making a positive difference, achieving important purposes, and having a good life-story.
Meta-ethics: The branch of philosophy that studies the metaphysics, epistemology, and language of value judgments.
Metanarrative: An all-inclusive story-like or narrative-like setting, context, framework, or explanation that helps us understand and fit together answers to questions about origins, purpose, value, suffering, death, and destiny. Though you can narrate your weekend, such narration would not be a *meta*narrative. A metanarrative is much larger in scope. See **Worldview** (for our purposes in this book, we treat metanarratives and worldviews as more or less synonymous).
Moderate Supernaturalism: The theory that God and a soul are not necessary for a meaningful life but would be contributory conditions for it—that is, would enhance meaning.
Monism: The view that a certain subject matter is reducible to a single property.
Naturalism: The theory that physical properties and substances are central to what would make life meaningful. The view that

neither God nor any spiritual condition more broadly is necessary for meaning.

Necessary Condition: A property or thing that is required in order for something else to obtain.

Nihilism (Pessimism): The view that there is no objective value either in general or perhaps of a certain kind such as meaning in life. Nihilism is often associated with extreme pessimism and radical skepticism. In one of its existential forms, life is thought to be without objective meaning, purpose, or intrinsic value. In this way, one might be nihilistic about any kind of deep, cosmic meaning, but optimistic (not nihilistic) about terrestrial forms of subjective meaning. For example, there may be no overarching purpose *of* life, but one can still pursue one's own, self-chosen purposes *in* life. Another name for many of forms of nihilism might be "Pessimistic Atheism" in contrast to Optimistic Atheism.

Normative (Normativity): Having to do with evaluation, standards of evaluation, value, prescription, and ought. Often contrasted with mere description or descriptive facts. "The Earth *is* flat" is a descriptive claim. "We *ought* to be good stewards of the Earth" is a normative claim.

Objective: Mind-independent; facts that obtain not merely because they are the object of a human person's mental states.

Objectivist naturalism (Objectivism): An Optimistic Atheistic view according to which life is meaningful to the extent that one engages in objectively worthwhile activity and/or is causally responsible for good regardless of whether or not one is fulfilled or satisfied in doing so.

Optimistic Atheism: The view that consists of the following two claims: (1) God does not exist, but (2) meaningful life is possible in a world without God.

Pessimistic Atheism: See Nihilism.

Physical: The subatomic and spatiotemporal world as known particularly well by the scientific method.

Pluralism: The view that a certain subject matter cannot be reduced to a single property.

Point of View of Humanity (*Sub Specie Humanitatis*): What would positively affect human lives.

Point of View of the Universe (*Sub Specie Aeternitatis*): What would positively affect those throughout the cosmos.

Problem of Evil: An argument for the view that God does not exist, according to which the amount and distribution of pain, suffering, and other harms in this world are incompatible with the existence of an all-knowing, all-powerful, and all-good person.

Realism (Realist): Very generally, the view that reality and many of its properties exist external to and independent of the mind. A moral realist, for example, thinks that a moral principle like "It is wrong to murder" exists independent of human beliefs, desires, and emotions. The moral realist would say that the expression "It is wrong to murder" expresses a moral fact similarly to how the expression "The Earth is spherical" expresses a physical fact independent of what people believe about the shape of the Earth.

Rightness: Actions that are morally permissible or required.

Soul: What enables an afterlife as characteristically conceived in the Abrahamic faiths; a spiritual substance that contains our mental states and will persist forever.

Spiritual: An agency, whether God or a soul, that is not determined by the physical.

Subjective: Mind-dependent; facts that obtain merely because they are the object of a human person's mental states.

Subjectivist Naturalism (Subjectivism): An Optimistic Atheistic view according to which life is meaningful to the extent that one is fulfilled or satisfied. Meaning, then, is merely a matter of having positive affective states that fit a certain psychological profile.

Supernaturalism: In general, the view that spiritual conditions (e.g., proper relationship to God) are necessary for meaning, or at least a certain kind of it. More specifically, the view that God is necessary and sufficient for meaningful life, likely on metaphysical (God must exist), epistemic (one must, in some sense, believe in God), and axiological/relational (one must be in a trusting relationship with God as expressed, for example, in worship, devotion, and the right kind of life lived in relation to others) levels. Other, more moderate forms of supernaturalism hold that God, though not *necessary* for meaningful life, would *enhance* the meaningfulness of life. It is worth noting that there can be subjectivist, objectivist, and hybrid forms of supernaturalism that connect supernaturalist meaning to either subjective fulfillment (in God), proper engagement with objective value (objective value grounded in God and/or with God Himself), or a combination of the two.

Teleology: From the Greek word *telos*, meaning purpose, end, or goal. Teleological explanations often appeal to the purposes, aims, and goals of agents who have intentions. Such explanations are contrasted with (mechanistic) causal explanations that appeal to matter and motion, and which do not make use of ideas like reasons, desires, and goals, all of which seem to require agents.

The Good, the True, and the Beautiful: Three exemplars of meaning, particularly for those in the Western tradition: namely, beneficent relationships, intellectual reflection, and creativity.

Theism: The view that there is an all-powerful, all-knowing, morally perfect, necessarily existent, personal being who created the universe and sustains it in existence. Christianity, Islam, and Judaism are three examples of theistic religions. Often includes the view that such a being has created souls.

Theory: A principle meant to provide a basic and comprehensive account of a subject matter.

Transcendence: The characteristic or property of being beyond or outside. In theism, God is ascribed with transcendence because God is not identical with (and is thus beyond) the cosmos.

Value: The worth of something, the basic forms of which are good and evil. There is nonmoral value, some forms of which might be either qualitative in nature (e.g., the goodness of pleasure and the evilness of pain), esthetic in nature (e.g., the goodness of beauty and the evilness of ugliness), etc. There is also moral value, in the forms of virtue and vice.

Worldview: An all-inclusive, sense-making framework that helps us understand and fit together answers to questions about origins, purpose, value, suffering, death, and destiny. A worldview can be thought of as a kind of map. It helps us to see facts in relationship to one another, and it aids us in navigating life. See **Metanarrative** (we treat metanarratives and worldviews as more or less synonymous).

References

The 1662 Book of Common Prayer. 2021. Edited by Samuel L. Bray and Drew Nathaniel Keane. Downers Grove, IL: InterVarsity Press, Academic.

Adams, Marilyn McCord. 1993. "The Problem of Hell: A Problem of Evil for Christians." In Stump, Eleonore, ed. *Reasoned Faith*, 301–327. Ithaca, NY: Cornell University Press.

———. 2000. *Horrendous Evils and the Goodness of God.* (Cornell Studies in the Philosophy of Religion). Ithaca, NY: Cornell University Press.

Adams, Robert M. 1987. *The Virtue of Faith and Other Essays in Philosophical Theology.* New York: Oxford University Press.

———. 1999. *Finite and Infinite Goods.* New York: Oxford University Press.

Anselm, St. 1998. *Anselm of Canterbury: The Major Works.* Davies, Brian and Evans, G. R., eds. Oxford: Oxford University Press.

Aquinas, St. Thomas. 1975. *Summa Contra Gentiles: Book Three.* Translated by Vernon J. Bourke. Notre Dame, IN: University of Notre Dame Press.

Audi, Robert. 2005. "Intrinsic Value and Meaningful Life." *Philosophical Papers* 34: 331–355.

Augustine, St. 1963. *The Confessions of St. Augustine.* Warner, Rex, trans. New York: Mentor.

———. 2008. "The Happy Life." In Cahn, Steven M. and Vitrano, Christine, eds. *Happiness: Classic and Contemporary Readings in Philosophy*, 51–60. Oxford: Oxford University Press.

Baggett, David, and Walls, Jerry. 2016. *God & Cosmos: Moral Truth and Human Meaning.* New York: Oxford University Press.

Baier, Kurt. 2000. "The Meaning of Life." In *The Meaning of Life*, 2nd Edition. Klemke, Elmer Daniel, ed. 101–132. New York: Oxford University Press.

Barrow, John. 2005. *The Infinite Book.* London: Jonathan Cape.

Bell, Daniel A., and Metz, Thaddeus. 2011. "Confucianism and *Ubuntu*: Reflections on a Dialogue Between Chinese and African Traditions." *Journal of Chinese Philosophy* 38 (supp. 1): 78–95.

Benatar, David. 2006. *Better Never to Have Been: The Harm of Coming into Existence*. New York: Oxford University Press.

———. 2017. *The Human Predicament*. New York: Oxford University Press.

———. 2021. "The Meaning of Life." In Oppenheimer, Mark and Werbeloff, Jason, eds. *Conversations about the Meaning of Life*, 1–37. Johannesburg: Obsidian Worlds Publishing.

Berger, Peter. 1967. *The Sacred Canopy*. New York: Doubleday.

———. 1970. *A Rumor of Angels: Modern Society and the Rediscovery of the Supernatural*. New York: Anchor Books.

Boethius. 1973. *The Consolation of Philosophy*. Tester, S. J., trans. Cambridge, MA: Harvard University Press.

Bowler, Kate. 2021. *No Cure for Being Human (and Other Truths I Need to Hear)*. New York: Penguin Random House.

Boyle, P.A., Buchman, A.S., and Bennett, D.A. 2010. "Purpose in Life Is Associated with a Reduced Risk of Incident Disability Among Community-Dwelling Older Persons." *American Journal of Geriatric Psychiatry* 18: 1093–1102.

Brink, David. 1989. *Moral Realism and the Foundations of Ethics*. Cambridge, UK: Cambridge University Press.

Bronk, K.C., Hill, P.L., Lapsley, D.K., Talib, T.L., and Finch, H. 2009. "Purpose, Hope, and Life Satisfaction in Three Age Groups." *The Journal of Positive Psychology* 4: 500–510.

Buckareff, Andrei and Plug, Allen. 2017. "Divine Love and Hell." In Nagasawa, Yujin and Matheson, Benjamin, eds. *The Palgrave Handbook of the Afterlife*, 197–214. London: Palgrave Macmillan.

Calvin, John. 2008. *The Institutes of the Christian Religion*. Beveridge, Henry, trans. Peabody, MA: Hendrickson.

Campbell, Stephen and Nyholm, Sven. 2015. "Anti-Meaning and Why It Matters." *Journal of the American Philosophical Association* 1: 694–711.

Camus, Albert. 1955. *The Myth of Sisyphus*. O'Brian, Justin, trans. London: H. Hamilton. Originally published in 1942.

Cottingham, John. 2003. *On the Meaning of Life*. London: Routledge.

———. 2005. *The Spiritual Dimension: Religion, Philosophy and Human Value*. Cambridge, UK: Cambridge University Press.

———. 2016. "Meaningfulness, Eternity, and Theism." In Seachris, Joshua and Goetz, Stewart, eds. *God and Meaning*, 123–136. New York: Bloomsbury Academic.

———. 2020. *In Search of the Soul: A Philosophical Essay*. Princeton, NJ: Princeton University Press.

———. 2022. "The Meaning of Life and Transcendence." In Landau, Iddo, ed. *The Oxford Handbook of Meaning in Life*, 205–215. Oxford: Oxford University Press.

Craig, William Lane. 2009a. "The Kurtz/Craig Debate." In Garcia, Robert and King, Nathan, eds. *Is Goodness without God Good Enough?*, 23–46. Lanham, MD: Rowman and Littlefield.

———. 2009b. "This Most Gruesome of Guests." In Garcia, Robert and King, Nathan, eds. *Is Goodness without God Good Enough?*, 167–188. Lanham, MD: Rowman and Littlefield.

———. 2013. "The Absurdity of Life Without God." In Seachris, Joshua, ed. *Exploring the Meaning of Life: An Anthology and Guide*, 153–172. Malden, MA: Wiley-Blackwell. Originally published in 1994.

Craig, William Lane, Sinnott-Armstrong, Walter. 2004. *God? A Debate Between a Christian and an Atheist*. New York: Oxford University Press.

Danto, Arthur C. 1968. *Analytical Philosophy of History*. Cambridge: Cambridge University Press.

Dennett, Daniel. 1984. *Elbow Room: The Varieties of Free Will Worth Wanting*. Cambridge, MA: The MIT Press.

———. 2003. *Freedom Evolves*. New York: Viking Penguin.

DiCamillo, Kate. 2006. *The Miraculous Journey of Edward Tulane*. Somervile, MA: Candlwick Press.

Draper, Paul. 2004. "Cosmic Fine-Tuning and Terrestrial Suffering: Parallel Problems for Naturalism and Theism." *American Philosophical Quarterly* 41: 311–321.

Einstein, Albert. 1954. *Ideas and Opinions by Albert Einstein*. New York: Dell.

Evans, C. Stephen. 2018. "Moral Arguments for the Existence of God." *Stanford Encyclopedia of Philosophy* (https://plato.stanford.edu/entries/moral-arguments-god/).

Fischer, John Martin. 2020. *Death, Immortality, and Meaning*. New York: Oxford University Press.

Frankfurt, Harry. 1969. "Alternate Possibilities and Moral Responsibility." *The Journal of Philosophy* 66: 829–839.

Frankl, Viktor. 2006. *Man's Search for Meaning*. Boston, MA: Beacon Press.

Freud, Sigmund. 2005. *Civilization and Its Discontents*. New York: W. W. Norton & Co.

Friend, David, and the Editors of Life. 1991. *The Meaning of Life: Reflections in Words and Pictures on Why We Are Here*. Boston, MA: Little, Brown and Company.

Gilbert, Alan. 1990. *Democratic Individuality*. Cambridge, UK: Cambridge University Press.

Gilovich, Thomas. 1991. *How We Know What Isn't So: The Fallibility of Human Reason in Everyday Life*. New York: The Free Press.

Goetz, Stewart. 2012. *The Purpose of Life: A Theistic Perspective*. London: Continuum.

Goetz, Stewart and Seachris, Joshua. 2020. *What Is This Thing Called the Meaning of Life?* London: Routledge.

Goetz, Stewart, and Taliaferro, Charles. 2008. *Naturalism*. Grand Rapids, MI: William B. Eerdmans Publishing Company.

Hart, David Bentley. 2019. *That All Shall Be Saved: Heaven, Hell, and Universal Salvation*. New Haven, CT: Yale University Press.

Hick, John. 2004. *The Fifth Dimension: An Exploration of the Spiritual Realm*. Oxford: One World.

Hill, Patrick L, and Turiano, Nicholas A. 2014. "Purpose in Life as a Predictor of Mortality Across Adulthood." *Psychological Science* 25: 1482–1486.

Joyce, William. 2012. *The Fantastic Flying Books of Mr. Morris Lessmore*. New York: Moonbot Books.

Kahane, Guy. 2011. "Should We Want God to Exist?" *Philosophy and Phenomenological Research* 82: 674–696.

———. 2013. "Our Cosmic Insignificance." *Noûs* 47: 745–772.

Kass, Jared D. et al. 1991. "Health Outcomes and a New Index of Spiritual Experience." *Journal for the Scientific Study of Religion* 30: 203–211.

Kauppinen, Antti. 2012. "Meaningfulness and Time." *Philosophy and Phenomenological Research* 82: 345–377.

Kershnar, Stephen. 2005. "The Injustice of Hell." *International Journal for Philosophy of Religion* 58: 103–123.

Kitcher, Philip. 2014. *Life after Faith: The Case for Secular Humanism*. New Haven, CT: Yale University Press.

Kvanvig, Jonathan. 1993. *The Problem of Hell*. New York: Oxford University Press.

Landau, Iddo. 1995. "The Paradox of the End." *Philosophy* 70: 555–565.

———. 2017. *Finding Meaning in an Imperfect World*. New York: Oxford University Press.

Levy, Neil. 2021. "Final Thoughts." *Aeon*. (https://aeon.co/essays/why-is-the-deathbed-perspective-considered-so-valuable).

Lewis, C. S. 1947. *Miracles*. New York: Macmillan.

———. 1970. *God in the Dock*. Grand Rapids, MI: Eerdmans.

———. 1986. "On Living in an Atomic Age." In Hooper, Walter, ed. *Present Concerns*. 73–80. San Diego, CA: Harcourt.

———. 1992 [1964]. *Letters to Malcolm: Chiefly on Prayer*. New York: Harcourt.

———. 1996. *The Problem of Pain*. New York: Simon & Schuster.

———. 2001. *Mere Christianity*. New York: HarperSanFrancisco.

———. 2002. *The Last Battle*. New York: HarperCollins.

Lyubomirsky, Sonja, Tkach, Chris, and DiMatteo, Robin M. 2006. "What Are the Differences Between Happiness and Self-Esteem?" *Social Indicators Research* 78: 363–404.

Lutz, Matthew and Lenman, James. 2018. "Moral Naturalism." In Zalta, Edward, ed. *The Stanford Encyclopedia of Philosophy*. (https://plato.stanford.edu/entries/naturalism-moral/).

MacIntyre, Alasdair. 2009. *God, Philosophy, Universities: A Selective History of the Catholic Philosophical Tradition*. Lanham, MD: Rowman & Littlefield Publishers.

Mackie, J. L. 1977. *Ethics: Inventing Right and Wrong*. New York: Penguin.

———. 1982. *The Miracle of Theism: Arguments for and Against the Existence of God*. New York: Oxford University Press.

Makkreel, Rudolf A. 1999. "Dilthey, Wilhelm." in Audi, Robert, ed. *The Cambridge Dictionary of Philosophy*. Cambridge, UK: Cambridge University Press.

Martela, Frank. 2017. "Meaningfulness as Contribution." *Southern Journal of Philosophy* 55: 232–256.

Mavrodes, George I. 1986. "Religion and the Queerness of Morality," in Audi, Robert and Wainwright, William J, eds. *Rationality, Religious Belief, and Moral Commitment*. Ithaca, NY: Cornell University Press.

Mawson, T. J. 2016. *God and the Meanings of Life*. London: Bloomsbury Publishing.

———. 2019. *Monotheism and the Meaning of Life*. Cambridge, UK: Cambridge University Press.

Metz, Thaddeus. 2013. *Meaning in Life: An Analytic Study*. Oxford: Oxford University Press.

———. 2019a. "Recent Work on the Meaning of 'Life's Meaning'." *Human Affairs* 29: 404–414.

———. 2019b. "Accounting for Similarities and Differences in Moral Belief (Atheism)." In Koterski, Joseph and Oppy, Graham, eds. *Theism and Atheism: Opposing Arguments in Philosophy*, 472–477. Farmington Hills, MI: Gale.

———. 2019c. *God, Soul and the Meaning of Life*. Cambridge, UK: Cambridge University Press.

———. 2020. "Meaning in Life in Spite of Death." In Cholbi, Michael and Timmerman, Travis, eds. *Exploring the Philosophy of Death and Dying*, 253–261. London: Routledge.

———. 2021a. "Meaning in Life Through the Good, the True, and the Beautiful." In Oppenheimer, Mark and Werbeloff, Jason, eds. *Conversations about the Meaning of Life*, 38–75. Johannesburg: Obsidian Worlds Publishing.

———. 2021b. "Comparing the Meaningfulness of Finite and Infinite Lives." *Royal Institute of Philosophy Supplement* 90: 105–123.

———. 2022a. "The Concept of Life's Meaning." In Landau, Iddo, ed. *Oxford Handbook on Meaning in Life*, 27–42. Oxford: Oxford University Press.

———. 2022b. "Does the Lack of Cosmic Meaning Make Our Lives Bad?" *Journal of Value Inquiry* 56: 37–50.

Metz, Thaddeus and Molefe, Motsamai. 2021. "Traditional African Religion as a Neglected Form of Monotheism." *The Monist* 104: 393–409.

Mikitish, John and Herman Majkrzak. 2021. *Orthodox Christian Prayers*.

Mill, John Stuart. 1978. *On Liberty*. Indianapolis, IN: Hackett Publishing Company.

Murphy, Mark. 2016. *God and Moral Law: On the Theistic Explanation of Morality*. Oxford: Oxford University Press.

Nagel, Thomas. 1971. "The Absurd." *Philosophy* 68: 716–727.

———. 1986. *The View from Nowhere*. New York: Oxford University Press.

Newsome, Bill. April 29, 2010. "Newsome's Reply to the Question 'How Does Faith Affect Your Life?'" in Test of Faith (YouTube video interview). https://www.youtube.com/watch?v=PMIBfH0qS6Y.

Nietzsche, Friedrich. 1968. *The Will to Power*. Kaufmann, Walter and Hollingdale, R.J., trans. New York: Random House.

———. 1974. *The Gay Science: With a Prelude in Rhymes and an Appendix of Songs*. Kaufmann, Walter, trans. New York: Vintage.

Nozick, Robert. 1974. *Anarchy, State, and Utopia*. New York: Basic Books.

Pascal, Blaise. 1995. *Pensées*. New York: Penguin Books.

Persson, Ingmar and Savulescu, Julian. 2019. "The Meaning of Life, Equality and Eternity." *The Journal of Ethics* 23: 223–238.

Purves, Duncan and Delon, Nicolas. 2018. "Meaning in the Lives of Humans and Other Animals." *Philosophical Studies* 175: 317–338.

Putnam, Hilary. 1975. "The Meaning of 'Meaning.'" In *Mind, Language, and Reality*, 215–271. Cambridge: Cambridge University Press.

Quinn, Philip. 2000. "How Christianity Secures Life's Meanings." In Runzo, Joseph and Martin, Nancy, eds. *The Meaning of Life in the World Religions*, 53–68. Oxford: Oneworld Publications.

Robinson, Marilynne. 2020. *Jack*. New York: Farrar, Straus and Giroux.

Rosenberg, Alex. 2011. *An Atheist's Guide to Reality: Enjoying Life Without Illusions*. New York: W. W. Norton & Company.

———. 2018. *How History Gets Things Wrong: The Neuroscience of Our Addiction to Stories*. Cambridge, MA: The MIT Press.

Ruse, Michael. 1989. "Evolutionary Theory and Christian Ethics." In *The Darwinian Paradigm*. London: Routledge.

Russell, Bertrand. 1957. "A Free Man's Worship." In *Why I Am Not a Christian and Other Essays on Religion and Related Subjects*. New York: Touchstone.

Sartre, Jean-Paul. 1957. *Existentialism and Human Emotions*. Frechtman, Bernard, and Barnes, Hazel E., trans. Secaucus, NJ: Citadel Press.

———. 1973. *Existentialism & Humanism*. Mairet, Philip, trans. London: Methuen.

Schnell, Tatjana. 2021. *The Psychology of Meaning in Life*. London: Routledge.

Schopenhauer, Arthur. 1970. "On the Suffering of the World." In *Essays and Aphorisms*, Hollingdale, R.J., trans. London: Penguin Books.

Seachris, Joshua. 2009. "The Meaning of Life as Narrative: A New Proposal for Interpreting Philosophy's 'Primary' Question." *Philo* 12: 5–23.

———. (ed.) 2013a. *Exploring the Meaning of Life: An Anthology and Guide*. Malden, MA: Wiley-Blackwell.

———. 2013b. "General Introduction." In Seachris, Joshua, ed. *Exploring the Meaning of Life: An Anthology and Guide*, 1–20. Malden, MA: Wiley-Blackwell.

———. 2016. "The Meaning of Life and Narratives: A Framework for Understanding and Answering the Question of Life's Meaning." In Seachris, Joshua and Goetz, Stewart, eds. *God and Meaning*, 13–34. New York: Bloomsbury Academic.

———. 2019. "From the Meaning Triad to Meaning Holism: Unifying Life's Meaning." *Human Affairs* 29: 363–378.

Seachris, Joshua and Goetz, Stewart, eds. 2016. *God and Meaning: New Essays*. New York: Bloomsbury Academic.

Setiya, Kieran. 2017. *Midlife: A Philosophical Guide*. Princeton, NJ: Princeton University Press.

Smith, Christian. 2019. *Atheist Overreach: What Atheism Can't Deliver*. New York: Oxford University Press.

Steger, Michael F. 2012. "Experiencing Meaning in Life: Optimal Functioning at the Nexus of Well-Being, Psychopathology, and Spirituality." In *The Human Quest for Meaning*, Wong, P. T. P., ed. 165–184. New York: Routledge.

Steger, Michael F. and Frazier, Patricia. 2005. "Meaning in Life: One Link in the Chain from Religiousness to Well-Being." *Journal of Counseling Psychology* 52: 574–582.

Strawson, Galen. 2004. "Against Narrativity." *Ratio (new series)* XVII: 428–452.

Stump, Eleonore. 2010. *Wandering in Darkness: Narrative and the Problem of Suffering*. Oxford: Oxford University Press.

Svendsen, Lars. 2005. *A Philosophy of Boredom*. Irons, John, trans. London: Reaktion Books.

Swenson, David. 2000. "The Dignity of Human Life." In Klemke, E. D., ed. *The Meaning of Life*, 2nd edn, 21–30. New York: Oxford University Press. First published in 1949.

Swinburne, Richard. 2016. "How God Makes Life a Lot More Meaningful." In Seachris, Joshua and Goetz, Stewart, eds. *God and Meaning*, 151–163. New York: Bloomsbury Academic.

———. 2019. *Are We Bodies or Souls?* Oxford: Oxford University Press.

Taylor, Charles. 1992. *The Ethics of Authenticity*. Cambridge, MA: Harvard University Press.

Taylor, Richard. 1985. *Ethics, Faith and Reason*. Cambridge, MA: Harvard University Press.

Thomas, Joshua. 2018. "Can Only Human Lives Be Meaningful?" *Philosophical Papers* 47: 265–297.

Tolstoy, Leo. 2006. "A Confession." In Moore, Charles E., ed., *Spiritual Writings*, 46–59. Maryknoll, NY: Orbis Books. First published in 1884.

Trisel, Brooke Alan. 2012. "Intended and Unintended Life." *The Philosophical Forum* 43: 395–403.

Velleman, J. David. 2003. "Narrative Explanation." *The Philosophical Review* 112: 1–25.

Von Balthasar, Hans Urs. 2014. *Dare We Hope "That All Men Be Saved"?* San Francisco: Ignatius Press.

Wainwright, William J. 2005. *Religion and Morality*. Aldershot: Ashgate.

Weinberg, Rivka. January 11, 2015. "Why Life Is Absurd." *The New York Times*. (https://opinionator.blogs.nytimes.com/2015/01/11/why-life-is-absurd/).

———. 2021. "Ultimate Meaning: We Don't Have It, We Can't Get It, and We Should Be Very, Very Sad." *Journal of Controversial Ideas* 1: 1–22.

Weinberg, Stephen. 1994. *Dreams of a Final Theory*. New York: Vintage Books.

Wielenberg, Erik. 2005. *Value and Virtue in a Godless Universe*. Cambridge: Cambridge University Press.

———. 2016. "Metz's Case Against Supernaturalism," *European Journal for Philosophy of Religion* 8: 27–34.

Williams, Clifford. 2020. *Religion and the Meaning of Life: An Existential Approach*. Cambridge, UK: Cambridge University Press.

Wittgenstein, Ludwig. 1979. *Notebooks 1914–1916*. 2nd ed. Anscombe, G. E. M., trans. Chicago: University of Chicago Press.

Wolf, Susan. 2010. *Meaning in Life and Why It Matters*. Princeton, NJ: Princeton University Press.

———. 2015. *The Variety of Values: Essays on Morality, Meaning, and Love*. New York: Oxford University Press.

———. 2016. "Meaningfulness: A Third Dimension of the Good Life." *Foundations of Science* 21: 253–269.

Wolterstorff, Nicholas. 1987. *Lament for a Son*. Grand Rapids, MI: William B. Eerdmans.

Young, Julian. 2014. *The Death of God and the Meaning of Life*, 2nd ed. London: Routledge.

Zagzebski, Linda. 2004. *Divine Motivation Theory*. New York: Cambridge University Press.

Index

absurdity 37–41, 43–4, 51–2, 66, 112, 159, 177; *see also* nihilism; tragic
afterlife 43, 65, 77, 110–4, 121, 123–30, 134–5, 165–6, 170–3, 175, 178, 179, 191–4, 204, 209; *see also* death; eternity; soul
animals 3, 61, 77, 93–4, 102, 106, 154, 222, 223
anti-matter 12, 83–5, 87, 123, 125, 130, 143, 144, 164
anti-meaning *see* anti-matter
Aquinas, St. Thomas 60–1, 153, 174, 189
argumentation xiv, 73, 92–3, 140–1, 186, 194
atheism 6, 13, 31, 36, 41–3, 52–8, 65–6, 77, 149–53, 155, 165–6, 171, 175, 181, 190–11, 203, 220: contrasted with theism 6, 71; definition of 6, 71, 75; optimistic 32, 41; pessimistic 41, 49, 65, 66, 203; *see also* comic; tragic

Baier, Kurt 61–3
Benatar, David 54, 131–4,
Berger, Peter 34, 56, 64–5, 160
boredom 80, 92, 99, 128, 135, 201

Camus, Albert 39–41, 89, 131
causal theory of reference 216–8, 219–20, 222
coherence *see* sense-making
comic 31, 54, 69, 135, 181, 191, 206–7

cosmic meaning 13–14, 17, 19–20, 27, 30, 32–4, 36–42, 53–69, 101–15, 120–9, 131–5, 146, 150, 155, 158–61, 166, 173, 176–7, 180–1, 198, 199–203, 206–9, 219–21; *see also* fabric of the universe; meaning of life; point of view of the universe
Craig, William Lane 113, 116, 124, 126, 146

Darwin, Charles 35, 36, 80
death 4, 34, 38–40, 42–52, 54, 65–8, 110–4, 121–8, 134–5, 165–6, 170–3, 173, 179, 192, 204; *see also* afterlife; eternity; soul
depth *see* desires, deep
desert *see* justice
desires (longings): deep 12, 27, 39–41, 43, 56–7, 65–6, 68, 159–60, 177–80, 203–6; shallow 12, 203
Divine Command Theory 103–7, 108, 110, 111, 143–55, 165, 200, 214, 216, 222–3

Einstein, Albert 35, 80, 85–6, 115–6, 129, 159, 170, 176–7, 200–1
emotions 22, 25–6, 33, 49–50, 72, 78, 94–5, 164, 174–5, 198, 213–4; *see also* happiness
eternity 44, 53, 68, 109–10, 113, 121, 122, 123–30, 134–5, 159,

161, 173, 175–7, 177, 178, 179–80, 180–1, 191–6, 198, 199–203, 205, 206, 209; *see also* afterlife; death; soul
Euthyphro Problem 104, 150n2, 153; *see also* Divine Command Theory
everlasting *see* eternity
existentialism (existential, existentialist) 4–5, 12, 19–20, 32–3, 39, 43–4, 62, 64–5, 72–3, 203
Experience Machine 79, 86, 89, 96–7, 169, 174, 218

fabric (furniture) of the universe (reality) xviii, 13, 27, 35, 55–7, 116, 146, 149–51, 155, 170, 220–1; *see also* cosmic meaning
feelings *see* emotions
fit *see* sense-making
free will 107–10, 115, 120, 126
futility 42–4, 51–2, 111

Gandhi 80, 120–1, 128, 129, 130, 173, 214
God 13, 25, 30, 34–5, 53–68, 71, 103, 146, 165: arguments for existence of 106–7, 153–4, 222–3; arguments for non-existence of 58, 67, 106, 154, 165, 180–1, 222–3; as judge xviii, 110–4, 115, 121, 123–8, 130, 161, 165, 170–3, 175, 179, 188–91; as source of objective value 143–53, 155, 156, 165, 214–23; care by 56–8, 77, 115–7, 158, 161, 170, 177–9, 179, 213; communion with 59, 123–9, 174–5, 175–6, 178, 191–4, 205; creation by 58, 62–3, 77, 103, 115–6, 117, 121, 160–1, 170, 177, 179, 193, 196, 203–4; nature of 6, 55, 103, 146, 149, 165, 198, 222; plan of (purpose for us) 58–64, 76, 77, 102–11, 115–6, 118, 121–4, 130, 145, 151, 152–3, 159–60, 161, 166, 170, 179, 193, 194–6, 208, 216, 219, 222, 223; submission to (worship of) 121, 177–8, 196, 207; *see also* cosmic meaning; Divine Command Theory; fabric of the universe; supernaturalism; theism

happiness (wellbeing) xv, 4, 9, 15, 25–6, 41, 44, 56, 59–64, 78, 84, 85–6, 90, 158, 171, 173–5, 194–6, 204, 207; *see also* meaning in life, contrasted with happiness
Heaven *see* afterlife; eternity; soul
Hell *see* afterlife; eternity; soul
human condition (human predicament) 5, 19, 33, 41, 55–7, 65
hybrid atheism (hybridism) xv–xvi, 24, 99–101, 187, 207

immortality *see* eternity; soul
infinite 40, 53, 55, 61, 113, 126–30, 142, 146–7, 150, 153, 155, 157, 161, 172–3, 176–7, 191–3, 196, 198–9, 201, 204
intelligence theory xvii, 74, 88, 93–101, 116–7, 119–20, 160, 163–5, 211–4, 218, 222, 223–4
intrinsic value *see* value, intrinsic (final)
intuitions xvi–xvii, 25, 88–92, 95, 98, 102, 103, 109, 114, 115, 120, 128–30, 131, 143, 165, 176, 199, 201–2, 221

Jesus 58, 67, 117, 165, 171, 191, 208, 213
justice 25, 34, 39, 41, 44, 54, 57, 65–6, 110–4, 117, 118, 123–7, 159, 161, 165, 166, 169, 170–3, 177, 178, 179, 188–94, 203, 204, 205–6, 222; *see also* morality

knowledge 10, 19–20, 32–3, 78, 80, 81, 95, 96, 98, 102, 201, 208–9, 214, 222, 223–4; *see also* Darwin, Charles; Einstein, Albert; the good, the true, and the beautiful

Lewis, C. S. 52, 61, 67–8, 153, 154, 193
love 24, 25, 38, 39, 41, 44, 54, 57, 65–6, 102, 116, 117, 166, 170, 172, 173, 175, 176, 177, 198, 201, 203, 204, 205–6, 212, 213; *see also* the good, the true, and the beautiful

Mackie, J. L. 147, 150–1, 155
Mandela, Nelson 97, 114, 115, 129
mattering 7, 9, 10–14, 44–5, 51, 54–8, 155, 157, 158–9, 161, 169, 187–8, 196, 207, 208
meaning in life: absence of (meaningless) xvi, 4, 11, 12, 20, 36, 38, 79, 80, 84–5, 89, 90, 115, 130, 144, 161, 212, 214, 215, 218; contrasted with happiness xv, 9, 15, 20, 21, 25–6, 78–82, 85–6, 90–1, 173–5, 188n1, 194–6, 212–3; contrasted with morality xv, 9, 12–13, 14, 21, 23, 24, 79–82, 86–7, 114, 174, 188n1, 212–3; contrasted with the meaning of life xiv–xv, 11, 30, 32, 65, 76, 143, 160; degrees of xiv–xv, 6, 69, 130, 144, 160, 162–5, 176, 181, 209, 211–4; examples of xvi, 4, 10, 11, 12, 14, 24, 44, 59, 65, 78–80, 83, 88–9, 91, 101, 115, 144, 161, 200, 208, 214, 218; sense (definition) of xv, 7, 8–29, 30–1, 73–4, 75–85, 87, 90, 130, 142, 168–9, 176, 186–8, 194–6, 210; theories of xvii, 6, 25, 53–68, 93–101, 143–55, 157–9, 162–6, 170–80, 188–99, 206–9, 211–4, 222, 223–4; worth of xv, 4, 11–12, 23, 85–7, 196; *see also* antimatter; the good, the true, and the beautiful
meaning of life: absence of 32, 36, 65, 76, 155; contrasted with meaning in life xiv–xv, 11, 30, 32, 65, 76, 143, 160;

degrees of xiv–xv, 160; sense (definition) of xiv, 8, 8–29, 30–1, 77, 87, 115; theories of 6, 55–8, 65–8, 115–9, 158, 160–2, 170, 206–7; worth of 53, 64, 67, 116, 121, 161, 162, 170, 177, 203–4; *see also* cosmic meaning
metanarrative *see* worldview
minds 6, 11, 27–9, 53, 142, 148–9, 152, 155–6, 171, 189–90; *see also* personal identity
morality xv, 16, 78–81, 86–7, 91–2, 96, 100, 103–7, 108, 110–4, 120–1, 124, 127, 144–55, 158, 192–3, 196, 212, 219–20; *see also* justice; meaning in life, contrasted with morality
Mother Teresa (St. Theresa of Calcutta) 26, 80, 85–6, 115, 129

Nagel, Thomas xviii, 33, 37, 45, 132
narrative (life story) 46–52, 64, 67, 111, 119, 121, 157, 159, 166
naturalism xvii, 6, 70, 74–5, 93–101, 115–9: arguments for 61–4, 98, 105–6, 113–4, 114–5, 120, 120–1, 125–8, 128–9, 153–4, 172–3, 176–8, 191–4, 199–203, 222–3; definition of 6, 70, 82; objective 99, 164, 187–8, 197, 211–4, 216–23; subjective 21, 99, 155, 156–8, 164–5, 167, 187, 188, 207, 211–2, 213; *see also* intelligence theory; value, objective
nihilism (pessimism) 74, 130–5, 143, 167, 180, 206, 211; *see also* absurdity; tragic

objectivism *see* naturalism, objective; value, objective

Pascal, Blaise 40
personal identity 113–4, 149–50, 153, 171–2, 175, 178, 188–90, 204, 213
pessimism *see* nihilism; tragic
physical *see* naturalism
point of view of humanity (*sub specie humanitatis*) 13–14, 30, 34, 57, 64, 132–4, 180, 201–3, 207, 221
point of view of the universe (*sub specie aeternitatis*) xviii–xix, 13, 30, 33–4, 36–7, 54, 56–7, 131–5, 158, 202–3, 207; *see also* cosmic meaning
problem of evil *see* God, arguments for non-existence of
purpose 7, 9, 14–17, 28, 58–64, 76, 77, 102–10, 118, 121–4, 145, 157, 161, 166, 169, 179, 193, 194–8, 208, 212, 216, 219, 222, 223

rationality 28, 93–8, 103, 109, 116, 149, 153, 163, 218; *see also* intelligence theory
realism (realist) 21, 105, 144, 151, 214, 217–9, 220–1
reference *see* causal theory of reference
repetition 20–1, 80, 97, 128, 135, 163, 174, 212
rightness *see* justice; morality
Russell, Bertrand 45–6, 51, 52

Sartre, Jean-Paul 16, 62–3, 147, 150, 155
scientific method 35–6, 109, 158, 180–1, 217–8
self *see* personal identity
sense-making 7, 10, 17–21, 26–7, 32–4, 39–42, 51, 64–68, 157, 159–60, 169, 188, 188n1, 208
Sisyphus xvi, 89, 98, 169
soul 34, 37, 70–1, 107–14, 121, 123–30, 170–3, 175–6, 178, 179, 188–91; *see also* afterlife; death; eternity

spiritual *see* supernaturalism
sub specie aeternitatis see point of view of the universe
sub specie humanitatis see point of view of humanity
subjectivism *see* naturalism, subjective; value, subjective
supernaturalism 6, 34–5, 53–68, 76–7: arguments for 32–4, 35, 39–41, 42–4, 45–6, 53–4, 57, 63–4, 65–7, 101–14, 115, 120–8, 143–53, 173, 175, 179–80, 196–8; definition of 6, 8, 70–1, 82, 101–2; extreme xvii, 88, 101–15, 120, 131, 142–3, 155–8, 199; moderate xvii–xix, 24–5, 28–9, 31, 53, 58–9, 64, 69, 74, 88, 115, 119, 120–30, 131, 155–6, 158, 167–8, 170, 174, 176, 179, 180, 198, 199, 202; *see also* desires (longings), deep; theism; triad of meaning, theory

the good, the true, and the beautiful 22, 25, 26, 59, 94–6, 102, 111, 167, 176, 179, 193, 208, 213, 218, 222
The Truman Show 63, 116
theism 6, 31, 42, 53–5, 57–9, 66, 71, 101, 121, 124, 125, 132, 146, 149–50, 152, 154, 160, 165, 171, 175, 190, 207; *see also* atheism, contrasted with theism; God
Tolstoy, Leo xiv, 38–9, 131
tragic 31, 36–7, 39–40, 45, 54, 65, 68, 69, 74, 130–2, 159, 164–5, 166, 177, 180–1, 191; *see also* absurdity; nihilism
triad of meaning xvii, 8, 22–3, 27, 29, 68, 142, 156, 159, 174: sense (definition) 6–7, 8–29, 30–1, 156, 168–70, 186–8, 195; theory 25, 54–68, 69, 143–59, 188–99, 207–8; *see also* mattering; purpose; sense-making

value: disvalue 83–5, 87;
  instrumental 3, 83, 164–5,
  196–7; intrinsic (final) 4, 83, 87,
  142, 201, 211, 217; objective
  xvi, 25, 69, 78, 99–100, 102–7,
  143–55, 156–8, 164, 166,
  200–2, 206–7, 211, 214–23;
  subjective 78, 99–100, 102,
  145–6, 151, 155, 156–8, 164,
  214–5, 221; *see also* Divine
  Command Theory; meaning in
  life, worth of

wellbeing *see* happiness
Wolf, Susan xv–xvi, 78, 83, 89,
  99–101
worldview 27, 33–4, 41, 51, 56,
  67, 178, 195, 223–4

For Product Safety Concerns and Information please contact our EU representative GPSR@taylorandfrancis.com
Taylor & Francis Verlag GmbH, Kaufingerstraße 24, 80331 München, Germany

www.ingramcontent.com/pod-product-compliance
Lightning Source LLC
Chambersburg PA
CBHW052015290426
44112CB00014B/2251